balance & harmony

ASIAN FOOD

balance & harmony

ASIAN FOOD

NEIL PERRY

PHOTOGRAPHY: EARL CARTER
STYLING: SUE FAIRLIE-CUNINGHAME

MURDOCH BOOKS

To my beautiful wife Sam,
who brings balance & harmony
to my life.

CONTENTS

Finding Balance and Harmony in the Kitchen

I really love Asian cooking. I suppose what I enjoy most about it are the great flavours, the contrasting tastes and textures, and the way that, with a wok and a bamboo steamer, you can cook just about anything. In fact, you don't even need a wok — you can usually do just as good a job with the other equipment found in Western kitchens. Asian cooking is very achievable at home: you can quite easily prepare a simple meal for the family after a hard day at work, or spend some real time in the kitchen making a few dishes that will have your friends talking for months. Now I think of it, perhaps one of the things I love most about Asian food is that it's often designed for the shared table, and that is how I love to eat. A bowl of rice, a few dishes, some friends and family and, of course, a nice glass of wine... I can't think of a better way to spend an evening or lazy weekend afternoon.

When you cook the dishes in this book it's important to remember that, much of the time, you're dealing with intense flavours. Always remember the most important part of the cooking process: taste, to find balance between those flavours. You will hear me say 'balance, balance, balance' throughout this book and, when I'm not saying 'balance', I'll be talking about harmony. These are the cornerstones of good Asian cooking.

I'm absolutely convinced that my love of Asian cooking has made me a much better cook of Western food. It has taught me so much about the texture of food and, just as crucially, about aroma. When I bring that knowledge to my restaurant cooking, it changes how a dish turns out forever. Now, I'm not necessarily saying that you will be affected in the same way, but I do feel confident that mastering some good basics (considering texture, balance and harmony in a dish) will enhance how you view your Western-style cooking at home.

It all started for me was I was young — very young. I was lucky enough to have a father who was not only a very good cook, but also fascinated by all things Chinese. I have memories from when I was as young as six or seven, of going down to Sydney's then-very-small Chinatown (mainly Dixon and George Street in those days, nothing like the powerhouse that Chinatown Sydney is today). Back in the sixties it was not so crowded and the Chinese restaurants could be counted on two hands. Dad and I would wander through the old food stores and he would pick out exotic ingredients to cook for us that night. I can still remember the smell of dried squid and abalone — a kind of dusty aroma with a pleasing scent of the sea over the top. When we had finished shopping, I would be thrilled if I could see a tin of poached abalone in Dad's grasp; I knew that meant a fabulous steamed soup or stir-fry of one of my favourite ingredients in the world. (To this day I believe the green lip abalone from Tasmania that I serve in all my restaurants is as luxurious and delicious an ingredient as truffles, foie gras, Iberico ham or caviar. I digress though...) We would finish shopping and head to a little Chinese café to eat barbecued pork and roast duck, stir-fried greens and rice — the best part of my day. Dad would often order his favourite dish, especially if there were more than the two of us: a stir-fry of bitter melon and minced pork. I love it now, but I admit that it took about ten years to get there. I used to think they were all mad, crowing after this dish that left a very distinct bitter taste in my mouth. As we left the café for the trip home, Dad would get some takeaway, and we would take little slices of pork, cold, out of the fridge, to chew on all weekend. It was usually the source of some tension in the family if you managed to get the last little jewel as it sat in its rich jellified sauce.

The next great influence in my love of Asian cooking came from two young waiters that Dad and Mum befriended at The Mandarin, our favourite Chinese restaurant in George Street. The Mandarin no longer exists, but I remember going upstairs, past the gun shop, to the tables where Ken and Jenson brought out gorgeous food. We would eat Dad's great love: mud crab with black bean or chilli sauce (this would soon become my great love, too), together with wonderful crisp combination omelettes, steamed fish and silky sweet luscious pork spare ribs. How I loved those pork ribs... I would suck on the bones and marvel at the tenderness and utter balance of flavour. However, even more than the wonderful dishes at The Mandarin, I think the food that Ken and Jenson cooked for us at home were what made me fall in love with Chinese cooking. They were the dishes I wanted to master as I grew older: red braised pork shoulder and master-stock chicken. Essentially just simple home cooking, but to this day, they are two of the foods I could eat every day if given the opportunity. Ken and Jenson went on to become a lawyer and an accountant and opened a great Chinese restaurant, The Shanghai Village, with a shop underneath it. It no longer exists, but I did have some great meals there.

Chinese food was my greatest culinary influence until I reached my thirties. Never having travelled in South-East Asia, I had never experienced a Thai meal that had done anything but leave me cold; I had never experienced that balance of flavour and the amazing aromatic and lively tastes that I had heard about. Enter David Thompson. I went to his first restaurant in Newtown in 1991 and immediately I was converted, no, addicted. This is what I had always expected — balance, harmony, fire, sourness, strength and beauty. The sensation of the chilli burn in my mouth after a great dish was satisfying to the point of bliss. Was this the closest thing to sex with your clothes on? I felt like crying. If this was what Thai cooking could be, I had to find out more. What that first meal did was send me wild, inquisitive and searching for more experiences like it. From that moment David and I have been close friends, and I count him as a brother. Although naughty and mischievous, he is a wonderful cook and generous teacher, instrumental in unlocking in me a love for the great flavours of not just China, but all the countries of South-East Asia.

In 1991 I travelled to Thailand with David and from that trip I knew that I wanted to open a Modern Asian restaurant. By that, I mean a place that respects tradition, and draws from both China and South-East Asia to create a balanced menu of dishes that work together. I had been using Chinese influences in my cooking since 1985, but this was about the desire to create something with personality and purpose. I wanted it to say 'We are eating in an Asian restaurant' — but a restaurant where you could enjoy good wine and wine service as well as having a sense of authenticity in the food.

And so it would be; in 1994, Wockpool was born. After that I started a little Asian bistro, called, for want of a better word, XO (after the chilli sauce that is one of my favourite tastes in the world). This year I will be opening Spice Temple in Sydney — a place that I hope will be a wonderful reflection of all I have learned and loved about Asian food. Many of the dishes in this book will be on the menu.

Much of the food in this book is inspired by Chinese cookery, however the flavours of Thailand, Malaysia, Indonesia, Japan and Korea find their way in as well. Lots of these dishes go well together, but I have structured some menus throughout the second half of the book that will give your meals great balance and harmony at the shared table. Just as importantly, these menus will also give you some balance in the kitchen — it is important to be able to prepare the dishes together, without causing a heart attack for you, the cook, or your family. Always keep in mind that my menu ideas are only suggestions and you should put your favourite dishes together once you get used to putting four or five plates on the table. The dishes in this book are designed to be part of a shared table and as such, I don't specify serves for each recipe. Generally, one dish per person is enough with rice, but at the most I'd suggest one per person, plus one for the table. Remember that, as with cooking Western food, organisation is the key — and always be clear about what you are trying to achieve.

I suggest, particularly if you think you are not a competent Asian cook, that you begin at the front of the book, where I explain the cooking techniques, and practise with the simple dishes in those chapters to learn to stir-fry, steam, braise and deep-fry. When you start cooking these dishes for your family, produce one dish at a time, served with some rice or noodles. As you become more confident, you can make three or four plates for a shared table (some simple ideas are on page 169). Once you've mastered the cooking methods, move on to the recipes in the second part of the book: they may have a few more ingredients or use two or more techniques, but they will be the same techniques you have already practised and you should be able to cook them well. Don't forget: this isn't rocket science. Once you have mastered the simple and straightforward recipes you will be able to sense balance, taste and harmony, understand texture and appreciate a range of flavours that suit your palate.

The same basic kitchen rules apply as with Western cooking. Hygiene and safety are very important. Make sure you clean equipment and surfaces in the kitchen well, wash your hands after handling raw food, and clean chopping boards after cutting meat and before you cut vegetables. Very importantly, store uncooked meats, birds and fish at the bottom of the fridge so they can't drip onto cooked food, or food you may eat raw. Have a good sharp knife or cleaver and respect it, or I promise it will bite you at some stage. The same goes for heat — respect it and always work in a calm and logical way, and you will hopefully not burn yourself.

Have a few important ingredients handy; many can happily live in the cupboard, so get a nice little Asian pantry going. Add a bit of fresh meat, poultry or seafood, some vegetables and herbs, and create wonderful dinners in a flash.

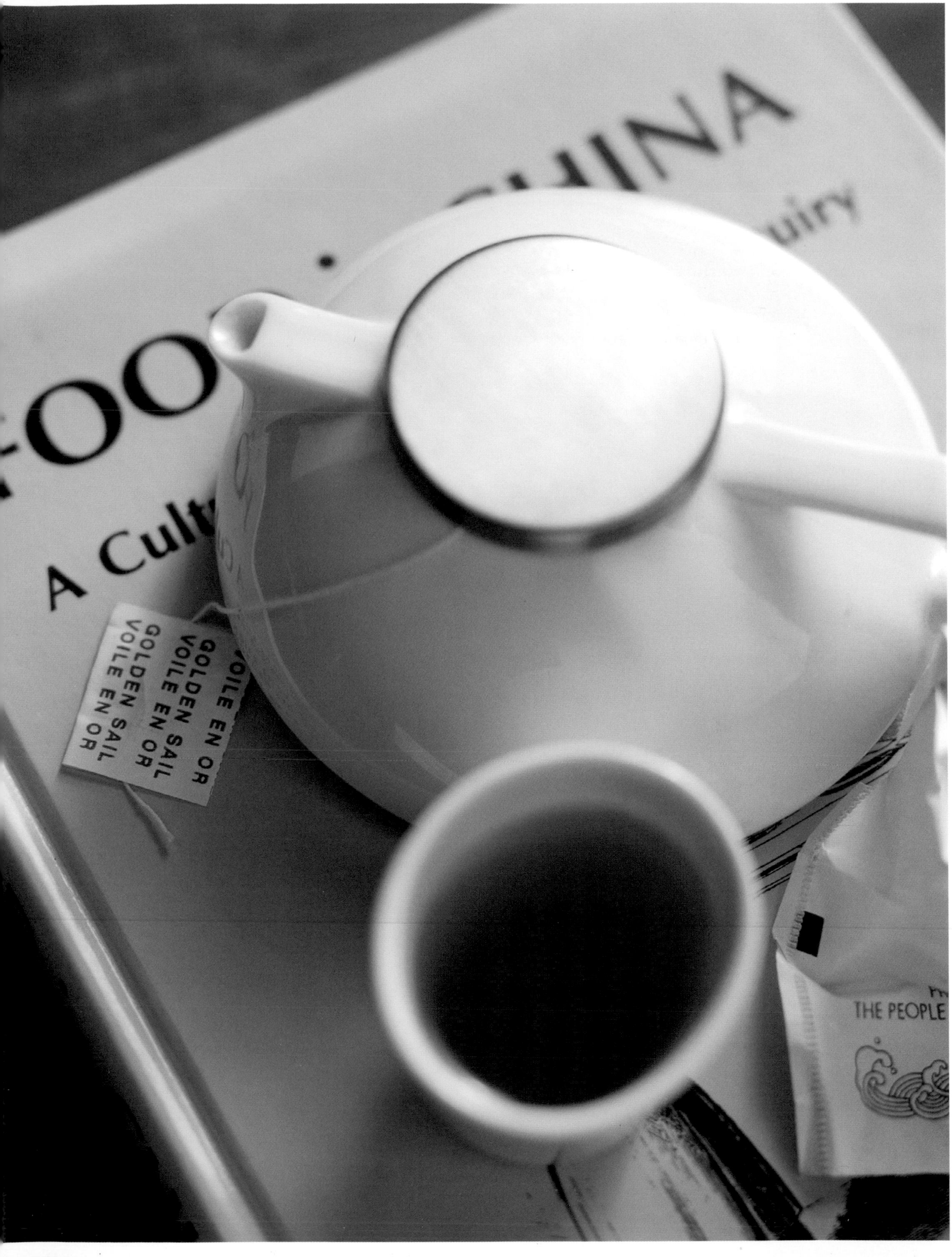
GOLDEN SAIL
VOILE EN OR
GOLDEN SAIL
VOILE EN OR
THE PEOPLE

COOKING EQUIPMENT

WOK

This is the classic Chinese implement, used for stir-frying, deep-frying, steaming, braising and smoking — what an amazing, versatile piece of equipment. Usually made from carbon steel, the thickness (or in fact, thinness) of the steel and its heat-conducting ability mean that the wok heats and cools quickly, enabling the food to respond immediately to temperature variations. The wok is usually deep, meaning that you'll need less oil for frying. The average wok for domestic use is about 33–36 cm (13–14 inches) in diameter.

Steel woks need to be seasoned before their first use. The best way to do this is to wash off the wok's protective coating with hot, soapy water, dry it well, pour in a little oil and heat it until it smokes. Turn off the heat and leave to cool, and then reheat the oil four more times. After the fourth time, allow the wok to cool, and then rub in some oil with paper towel before storing. After each use, wash the wok under hot water and dry it well (over heat is best) before rubbing it gently with oil to prevent rusting. Don't wash with soap again — if you need to then you will have to season your wok again. Over time it will gain a wonderful patina and your food will not stick.

I've never really liked cooking in electric woks, although these days they can get hot enough to stir-fry effectively. The Teflon non-stick coating means that ingredients fall to the bottom easily, making it harder to get a nice crust on the food. What they are good for is steaming; you can place a bamboo steamer in an electric wok on the kitchen bench and it will give you a little more space on the stove. The other thing I like them for is braising — they don't need as much liquid as a pot because of their unique wok shape.

CHINESE CHOPPING BOARD

This is a thick, round, whole piece of wood that is usually very heavy, allowing the cleaver to do its work. A standard chopping board can be used, but the authentic article works much better and looks great in the kitchen. I find myself using it for most of my chopping and cutting needs.

CHINESE CLEAVER

Cleavers come in a variety of sizes. Those with thin blades are more commonly used for chopping and shredding, while the larger, heavier cleavers are for chopping poultry and slicing meat. The broad blade of a cleaver is easy to keep sharp with a sharpening steel or stone. A Chinese chef would use the blade for chopping, slicing and shredding, and the handle for crushing. The flat surface of the blade can also be used for crushing and for scooping ingredients from a board and transferring them. Cleavers are very versatile and, although all the cutting for this book can be done with Western knives, I do recommend learning to cut with a cleaver.

CHINESE STRAINER

With its wire mesh and long bamboo handle, this is an excellent tool to have on hand when deep-frying. It makes it so much easier to remove larger ingredients (chickens are a good example) from the hot oil and allows them to drain before being set down on a cloth or paper towel. I also use it to remove food from boiling water. As a matter of fact, I use it no matter what kind of food I'm cooking.

MANDOLIN

With its extremely sharp blade set into a wooden frame, a Japanese mandolin makes fine slicing and cutting into julienne much easier. Again, it's not essential, but it is something you will use often in the kitchen no matter what you are cutting. Handle with care!

MORTAR AND PESTLE

This is an essential piece of equipment for South-East Asian cooking in general, and for making spice pastes in particular. The weight of the pestle is used to help grind or pound simple ingredients like garlic, salt and pepper against the slightly rough surface of the mortar. Those made of stone seem to be the best for grinding pastes and are readily available in Asian stores. It is the one piece of equipment I would hate to live without.

WOK SPOON

There are two main types of wok spoons: a flat, fish-slice type of implement used for lifting seafood out of woks or steamers; and a shovel-like spoon that allows you to stir the ingredients and keep them moving so that they don't burn in the fierce heat of the wok. I suggest you make the small investment of buying both — they are as cheap as chips and make stir-frying so simple.

Asian Ingredients

BAMBOO SHOOTS

Now available fresh in spring and autumn in Australia, bamboo shoots are truly wonderful—there really is no comparison between fresh and tinned. I find that if you get them fresh and peel them back to the shoot, slice them finely and blanch them three times in boiling salted water, you can rid them completely of the bitter flavour. Their texture and mild straw-like flavour is incomparable to tinned bamboo shoots. However, as it's not always possible to have fresh, tinned are acceptable as they add a nice texture to stir-fries, soups and braises. Just be sure to rinse them very well.

BEAN PASTES AND BEAN SAUCES

Bean paste is a seasoning made from fermented soy beans. Made with salted yellow or black beans, these sauces, which can be bought ready-made, impart body as well as flavour to stir-fries and stews. Korean bean paste has a deep, roast flavour; chilli bean paste is a chunky Chinese paste with chilli flakes through it; and hot bean paste is a smooth emulsion of chilli and soy bean purée. Sweet bean paste, used in a number of dishes in this book, is a purée of spices and soy beans, but no chilli; it's often used in Asian desserts. Hoisin sauce, on the other hand, has a sweet garlic flavour that's deep and mysterious. Generally used in stir-fries and as a dipping sauce for Peking or Sichuan duck, it can also be mixed with sesame oil, sugar and soy sauce to make a great sauce for serving with oysters.

BLACK AND WHITE FUNGI

Both of these fungi are now available fresh and, as far as texture goes, they are far superior to the dried tree mushrooms that have been around for some time. They are silky and crunchy at the same time and are not only used for this interesting texture but also as a good aid to digestion. Again, dried will do in the absence of fresh.

BOK CHOY

Pak choy, choy sum and Shanghai bok choy are all green vegetables available in Chinatown. They make great accompaniments to main courses, and are cooked exactly as you would any other Western vegetable. They have varying degrees of green leaf and white stem and can even be, as in the case of Chinese broccoli, green all the way through. They are usually very refreshing and slightly bitter and always have a pleasing texture and crunchiness (unless overcooked).

CASSIA BARK

This is quite often called 'false cinnamon' or 'Chinese cinnamon'. True cinnamon comes from Sri Lanka and Indonesia, while cassia is the bark of the laurel tree or the Indian bay. It is one of the main ingredients in Chinese red braising.

CHILLIES

The fresh chillies used in this book are mostly the long red variety and the small wild green chillies of Thailand, which are also known as 'bird's eye chillies' or 'heavenly rat droppings'! These chilli varieties have a wonderful immediate heat and a citrus lime flavour. The dried chillies used are the red papery ones sold in large bags in Asian food stores. Just remember that the more you crush chillies for a dressing, and the longer you leave that dressing to stand, the hotter it will become. Unless they say otherwise, the recipes in this book call for fresh chillies.

CHILLI OIL

Chilli oil is made by steeping the crushed flakes of dried red chillies in oil. It is usually red and sharp with heat, and is available from Asian food stores. Chilli oil is great in dressings and to add fire to stir-fries.

COCONUT MILK AND COCONUT CREAM

To prepare fresh coconut milk, chip away at the hard outer coconut shell with a cleaver and break the white flesh into smaller pieces. Grate with a coconut grater (available in Chinatown), add about 500 ml (17 fl oz/2 cups) hot water and steep for 20–30 minutes. Strain through muslin or cheesecloth, squeezing hard to extract all the liquid. This is called the first pressing, and the fat or cream that rises to the top is known as coconut cream. More hot water can be added to obtain second and third pressings, the results of which can be used for poaching or curries.

Tinned coconut milk will never be as good as fresh, but it does make a reasonable substitute. To bring the stronger, more pervasive flavour of tinned coconut milk back into line with the fresh ingredient, dilute it with water. Open the tin (don't shake it beforehand) and scoop the firm top layer into a bowl. Fill the tin back up to the top with water before adding it to the bowl as well. Like dairy cream, coconut cream contains a large percentage of saturated fat. At high temperatures it will split or separate into solids and oil, giving off a heavy coconut perfume.

CORIANDER

Although treated as a herb in Western culture, coriander is used more like a vegetable in many Asian dishes. Copious quantities are used, not as a garnish, but to add flavour and bulk to the dish. It is by far the most used herb in the world and is very aromatic, with a wonderful clean and uplifting flavour that has a slight aniseed quality. When cooking, I toss it into the dish at the end as it has a slightly bitter flavour when overcooked. The root is widely used in Asian cooking for making curry pastes and pastes for stir-fries, and it is always a good flavouring agent for dressings and salad dressings. This member of the parsley family is called cilantro in the United States.

DILL

This strong and powerfully flavoured herb should be used sparingly. Related to coriander, it works very well with seafood. Dill can easily overpower a dish but, if used correctly, it adds a wonderful intensity of flavour to salads and soups.

DRIED SHRIMP AND SCALLOPS

These tiny dried shrimp should always be a nice pink to red colour and quite soft. Do not buy brownish or rock-hard dried shrimp — they have been on the shelf for too long and will have lost their flavour. Before use, the dried shrimp should be soaked in warm water for about 20 minutes and drained well. They are good in stir-fries and are also used to make chilli and sambal pastes. They can also be caramelised and sprinkled over salads — just soak and drain them well, then toss in a wok with a little palm sugar until brown and toffee-like.

Dried scallops, or 'conpoy', can be found in Asian food stores. A fairly exclusive product, I prefer the larger Japanese ones to the smaller Chinese variety — they have a great earthy flavour and are used in XO sauces and Asian soups.

DUCK EGGS

Duck eggs are eaten fresh, salted and preserved. Fresh eggs have a bluish tinge and can be stir-fried or used in omelettes — they have a stronger flavour than hen eggs, but are very delicious. Salted eggs are steamed for 20 minutes and used to garnish all sorts of dishes. They are great stir-fried with minced pork, Thai style. Preserved eggs are covered in a mixture of salt, lime and wood-ash paste and stored for about a month. The whites turn a clear, dark deep–green colour and the yolks are very creamy. Just peel and use them with tofu or in rice porridge. Duck eggs give a welcome texture and taste to many dishes.

ENOKI MUSHROOMS

These have been appearing more and more in Australia lately and their quality continues to rise. These mushrooms grow in little punnets all clumped together and are delicious in salads. They're even better when cooked for a few moments in a soup, or used as a garnish with stir-fries. Reasonably fragile, they only keep for 3–4 days in the fridge, and should ideally be used very fresh.

FERMENTED BLACK BEANS

These little beans are fermented and preserved in salt. While they come in packets that often recommend rinsing before use, I find the flavour more interesting and edgy if they're not rinsed, but added directly to braises and stir-fries.

FERMENTED RED BEAN CURD

This pungent flavouring agent is made from bean curd cubes that have been fermented until they have a very gamey aroma.

FISH SAUCE

This is the juice run-off from salted anchovies or squid. The best sauces come from Thailand and Vietnam and are very highly prized and used for dipping sauces, while the stronger sauces are used for cooking. Three Crab brand is one of the best and Squid brand is a good all-rounder for cooking.

FIVE-SPICE POWDER

Five-spice powder is usually made from a mixture of cloves, cinnamon, star anise, fennel seeds and Sichuan peppercorns.

GALANGAL

This rhizome is a very important seasoning in Thailand, where it is more commonly used in curry pastes and soups than ginger (it is quite often known as 'the lesser ginger'). It is galangal's aromatic quality and uplifting flavour that gives Thai curries much of their charm.

GINGER

It's almost impossible to imagine Chinese cooking without ginger. Ginger, garlic and spring onion come to mind as the main flavours for most dishes and stir-fries in Asian cooking. Ginger is in fact not a root, but a rhizome, meaning that its underground stems grow horizontal to the earth and send shoots down deeper into the ground. Try to buy ginger that has shiny tight skin and is nice and heavy from the juice. Avoid wrinkled ginger that's been sitting around for too long and is dehydrated. Ginger should always be peeled before use.

GROUND ROAST RICE

This is a great textural addition to many dishes. Simply dry-fry (roast in a dry heavy-based frying pan) some jasmine rice over low heat until each grain is opaque but not coloured. When cool, grind it into a coarse powder in either a mortar with a pestle or, for ease, a spice grinder.

HOISIN SAUCE

A great bean sauce, hoisin is made from soy beans and has a sweet garlicky flavour. The texture is usually quite firm and jam-like and it is generally used in stir-fries or as a dipping sauce for Peking or Sichuan duck. My favourite variety of hoisin is from Korea and is seasoned with chilli.

KAFFIR LIMES

Both the skin of the fruit and the leaves of kaffir limes are used extensively in soups and curries in Thailand and much of South-East Asia. The rind has an incredible uplifting flavour and is important to curry pastes. The juice is rarely used as it has an overwhelming scent reminiscent of dishwashing liquid and, for that reason, Thais are known to wash their hair with it. The leaves are used in curries and soups and, when crushed in the hand before adding, give off a wonderful lemon and lime aroma. Be careful not to use too many though as they can impart a bitter flavour. Kaffir lime leaves can be found fresh these days in most Asian food stores and are far superior to the dried or frozen product.

LEMONGRASS

Lemongrass is usually sold in long stalks, but only the white heart — the bottom 10 cm (4 inches) of the inner stalk — is used. For soups and braises, the stalks are often bruised to release the flavour. For pastes, trim off the ends, peel off the first outside leaves and cut into 6 cm (2½ inches) lengths to get the lemongrass ready for pounding or chopping. For salads it might be necessary to remove a few more of the tough coarser outside leaves before slicing.

MIRIN

Mirin is sake (Japanese rice wine) boiled with sugar. It is readily available from Asian and Japanese food stores, but sweet sherry can be used as a substitute.

OYSTER MUSHROOMS

With their delicate flavour and pearl-like colours, these creamy mushrooms need only brief cooking.

OYSTER SAUCE

Ideal in stir-fries and as an all-purpose seasoning, this sauce works well with seafood, meat and vegetables. Look for varieties labelled 'oyster sauce' and not 'oyster-flavoured sauce'.

PALM SUGAR

A staple of South-East Asian cooking, palm sugar has a wonderfully deep flavour reminiscent of golden syrup and there is no substitute for it in curries. Known as jaggery in the United States, it makes a wonderful caramel and works well in desserts.

PANDANUS LEAF

Pandanus leaves are used quite extensively in Thailand and Indonesia in dessert making, as well as in some savoury dishes where meat or fish is wrapped and fried in the leaves. They add colour and a lovely floral dimension to desserts when cooked with things like sticky rice.

PRAWNS

When preparing prawns, remove the dark vein (actually the alimentary tract) to avoid grittiness in the finished dish. The easiest way to do this is to hook it out with a bamboo skewer. To butterfly prawns for quick and even cooking in a stir-fry, simply make a shallow cut along the back of each prawn.

RED SHALLOT

The red shallot is the onion of South-East Asia. Indispensable in curries and salads, red shallots have a mild flavour. They have a shape reminiscent of a garlic bulb, and are very different to the small brown French shallot.

RICE

I serve jasmine rice with all my Asian dishes — even noodles! The best way to cook rice is in an electric rice cooker, so if you cook a lot of Asian food it's a worthwhile investment. Do not salt rice as the sauces are salty enough and the rice, as a vehicle for the sauces, should have a natural, neutral flavour.

RICE VINEGAR

The one we use most is Japanese rice vinegar. This vinegar is generally much softer in acid than European vinegars.

SESAME OIL

Sesame oil is one of the great flavours of China. Nutty and fragrant, a few drops added at the end of cooking gives a nice lift to any dish. It can also be used to make dressings.

SESAME SEED PASTE

Chinese sesame seed paste is made from roasted sesame seeds and is a lot richer and darker than the Middle-Eastern variety, tahini.

SHAOXING

Shaoxing, a Chinese wine made from glutinous rice fermented with water, has a dark straw colour and a unique flavour. Shaoxing is available in Asian food stores and some supermarkets, but dry sherry is a popular and adequate substitute.

SHIITAKE MUSHROOMS

Although delicious, fresh shiitakes aren't a substitute for the dried mushrooms — the texture, quality and intensity of flavour of dried shiitakes is unsurpassed. Dried shiitakes need to be rinsed and reconstituted by soaking in warm water for about 30 minutes. The stalks should always be removed as they remain hard and indigestible. The Chinese wouldn't think of using fresh shiitakes; they much prefer the dried mushroom.

SHRIMP PASTES

There are three types of shrimp paste: belachan from Malaysia; fermented shrimp paste from Thailand; and shrimp paste from China. Belachan is used in Malay and Indonesian dishes and is central to Nyonya cooking. The dark belachan blocks are usually sliced, grilled and crumbled before being added to dishes. Thai shrimp paste is softer and more fragrant and adds a pungent flavour to curries and soups. Chinese shrimp paste is pale and runnier, and is used in dipping sauces, stir-fries and steamed dishes. Do not substitute one for the other as their flavours are very different. To make shrimp paste fragrant, wrap it in foil and grill it for a few moments; to be truly authentic, wrap it in a banana leaf.

SICHUAN PEPPERCORNS

These are not peppercorns at all but little berries from a Chinese shrub. They give your mouth a wonderful sense of numbness and are quite warming. When roasted and ground, they are known as Sichuan pepper. When roasted with sea salt and made into 'Sichuan salt and pepper', they give roasted foods an incredible lift and are great sprinkled on wok-fried crisp dishes. Also known as Chinese pepper, Sichuan pepper is a key ingredient in five-spice powder.

SICHUAN SALT AND PEPPER

Easy to make, either by roasting and grinding salt and Sichuan peppercorns in a mortar with a pestle, or grinding in a spice grinder, Sichuan salt and pepper is always good to have on hand. For a recipe to make your own Sichuan salt and pepper, see page 55.

SOY SAUCES

Soy sauce is the fermented juice of soy beans and is a staple of Chinese and Japanese cooking. Light soy, labelled 'Superior Soy', is used in most cooking and is saltier than dark soy. Dark soy, labelled 'Soy Superior Sauce', is used mostly for braising. It is stronger and maltier, with a thick pouring consistency. Japanese soy is dark in colour with an intense but clean flavour. Mushroom soy sauce is wonderful in steamed dishes and has a fantastic shiitake flavour. Yellow bean soy sauce, a light Thai soy sauce, is a bit more delicate than the Chinese and Japanese varieties and thus is great in stir-fried dishes and salad dressings. Kecap manis is a rich soy sauce used in Indonesia and Malaysia; it is sweetened with palm sugar and flavoured with star anise and garlic.

SPICES

Buy spices whole and roast them briefly in a dry heavy-based frying pan over medium heat to enhance their flavour and make them fragrant. To grind them, use a spice or coffee grinder, or crush them in a mortar with a pestle. Their flavour and fragrance deteriorates over time so it is important to buy them fresh, in small quantities, and use them as soon as you can.

SPRING ONIONS

Also known as scallions, shallots or green onions, spring onions are very common in Chinese cooking. Both the green tops and the white stems are used.

STAR ANISE

This eight-pointed seed pod is one of the most important components of five-spice powder, and is a must for many Chinese braised dishes.

STRAW MUSHROOMS

Commonly used in soups and stir-fries, these small, pale brown mushrooms do not keep well and should be used within a day or two.

TAMARIND AND TAMARIND WATER

The tamarind tree bears fat brown sticky pods from which tart juices are extracted and used as a souring agent in Asian cooking. You will find tamarind pulp plastic-wrapped in bricks in its concentrated form.

To make tamarind water, break off 240 g (8½ oz/1 cup) of pulp, soak it in 375 ml (13 fl oz/1½ cups) hot water for 20 minutes, then push it through a sieve to collect the liquid. Tamarind water is also available in pre-packed liquid form in Asian food stores.

TANGERINE PEEL

This dried peel should be soaked in water before use (unless you need to grind it), and any remaining pith scraped off to remove bitterness. It is available in Asian food stores, but you can also dry strips of fresh peel from tangerines and mandarins in a low oven for a similar result.

THAI (ASIAN) BASIL

This is thought to be the 'original' basil, as Italian basil was imported from South-East Asia and developed into the herb we know today. The two varieties of Thai basil that we use are sweet — more closely related to the Italian basil — and hot basil, which is used for frying, garnishing and adding flavour to different braised and curry dishes in Thailand. Sweet basil is often used as a garnish for soups and stir-fries, and appears with mint and coriander in most salads. It has a wonderful aniseed flavour, yet I find it less pungent than Italian basil. When used in large quantities in soups, it tends to lend a rich, subtle flavour that would be overpowering if the same quantity of Italian basil were used.

TURMERIC

This is another relative of ginger; a rhizome with a wonderful deep orange centre. Once peeled (use gloves to prevent staining your hands) it gives flavour and colour to many curries. It has a wonderful earthiness that reminds me sometimes of truffles and, if possible, should only be used fresh.

VIETNAMESE MINT (RAH RAM)

This herb has a little heat, a very aromatic uplifting quality and a subtle underlying mint flavour. It is used a lot in Vietnam for fresh salads, spring rolls and for making fragrant soups.

VINEGAR

The vinegar I use most is Japanese rice vinegar, as it has a softer taste than most European wine vinegars. Where a more complex flavour is required, I use Chinkiang, a Chinese black vinegar, which has a rich taste reminiscent of balsamic vinegar, although not as sweet. Chinese red vinegar gives a more subtle flavour, and coconut vinegar, made by fermenting coconut in water, is more delicate again.

WATER CHESTNUTS

Fresh water chestnuts are becoming ever more widely available in Australia and once you've eaten a fresh one it's very difficult to go back to the tinned variety. You simply peel off the outer skin, rinse the chestnut under cold water and it's ready to use. If you're keeping them peeled overnight, it's best to keep chestnuts in a little bit of salted water otherwise they will ferment very quickly. Water chestnuts add a wonderful crunchy, starchy flavour and texture to stir-fries, soups and salads.

YELLOW ROCK SUGAR

This crystallised mixture of sugar and honey, essential for red-braised dishes, is available from Asian food stores. Crush the larger crystals in a mortar with a pestle before use.

Basic Techniques and Recipes

For this first chapter, I have chosen recipes that demonstrate some of the basic techniques of Asian cooking. Try them out to see how simple it is to stir-fry, steam and braise. If you are wary of cooking in this style, then I'm confident that making the dishes in this chapter will set you up to master the other recipes in the book. As long as you remember to follow the few instructions at the beginning and to taste for balance, you'll quickly build confidence along the way and soon be set to embark on the marvellous world journey of Asian flavours.

Start by making each of these dishes one at a time for yourself and your family. Once you feel good about it, try putting them together to create a few shared tables. Then, and only then, invite your friends around. I'll talk about which dishes you can cook together to create a great shared table on page 167.

Remember to be organised — it is the key to preparing Asian food and will make anything possible.

Good luck with these basics. They are all very achievable and you will have great fun with them, I promise!

STEAMED RICE

Cooking rice must be the starting point of any Asian cookbook. Focus on this as it will carry the flavours of all the other food you serve with it. As rice is the centre point of most Asian meals, it must be perfectly cooked, no matter whether you're preparing a beautiful banquet or a simple meal.

Never fear — below is a simple and easy method to cook rice in a pot.

However, there is an even easier way, and that is to buy an electric rice cooker. It is a 'never fail' and I count it among my most important pieces of kitchen equipment. If you can, buy one, or at least put it down on your wish list for Christmas or your next birthday. It will keep your rice warm while you make the other dishes for family and friends and, if you follow the simple instructions, your rice will be perfect every time. Always cook extra rice as it can be refrigerated or frozen to make simple but delicious fried rice dishes later. So, let me say it one more time — get a rice cooker and it will all become simple and perfect.

500 g (1 lb 2 oz/2½ cups) Thai jasmine rice

METHOD

Place the rice in a small pot and rinse by running cold water over it to cover, then pouring the water out; do this two or three times.

Run cold water over the rice to cover it (about 750 ml/26 fl oz/3 cups), cover the pot with a lid, place over medium to medium–high heat and bring to the boil. Immediately reduce the heat to low and simmer, covered, for another 10 minutes until the water has completely evaporated.

Turn off the heat and allow the rice to sit, covered, for at least another 5 minutes. Serve hot or at room temperature. Fluff with a fork before serving.

SAUCES, DRESSINGS AND PICKLES

This section is one for you to tackle if you like fresh and vibrant dressings and pickles. By all means, buy any number of ready-made chilli sauces and pastes — there are good brands out there and they will give a decent result. However, if you want an amazing result, try making them yourself, then taste the difference it makes to your food. The recipes are fairly simple and are the building blocks to capturing the flavours of Asia.

I have added Nam Jim and Nuoc Cham dressings in here even though each salad in the book has its own dressing, often a version of one of these two. The reason is that, while they are great to make and dress salads, they also taste great with roast or barbecued fish, meat and poultry; in fact, you can use them as a simple sauce with just about anything.

Again, in each of these recipes, look for balance. If everything in the sauce or dressing adds weight to the outcome, you'll have a great taste; if something is dominant, you won't find balance in the dish and it won't be as pleasant as it should be.

CHILLI SAUCE

This easy sauce has a great rich, caramelised flavour — just purée and cook slowly for a perfect complement to poached meats and poultry.

As the chillies are deseeded, this sauce is not particularly hot. If you do like it hot, just add four or five wild green chillies as well. This sauce can be made in a mortar with a pestle, or in a blender. I use the stick blender I have at home.

500 g (1 lb 2 oz) long red chillies, deseeded and roughly chopped
3 cloves garlic
350 ml (12 fl oz) vegetable oil
2 teaspoons sea salt
1 tablespoon sugar
2½ tablespoons yellow bean soy sauce

METHOD

Pound the chillies and garlic in a mortar with a pestle, or process in a blender until you have a rough paste. Gradually add the oil, and blend until it has a smooth consistency.

Put the chilli purée into a heavy-based pot over low heat with the sea salt and sugar and cook, stirring occasionally. Cook for about 45 minutes, or until the sauce turns bright red and the rawness has been cooked out. Remove from the heat and stir in the soy sauce. Adjust the seasoning to taste.

FRESH CHILLI SAUCE

This is fresh tasting and easy to make — just pound away and you'll have a perfect dipping sauce for many of the following recipes. It's great tossed with some steamed seafood and it also makes a nice fiery dressing. The seeds are in, so make sure you taste this to get a good balance between hot, sweet and sour. By all means, if you like it really killer hot, add some wild green chillies as well.

4 long red chillies
4 cloves garlic
1 tablespoon rice vinegar
2 teaspoons sugar
½ teaspoon salt

METHOD

Pound the chillies and the garlic in a mortar with a pestle until you have a paste. Stir in the vinegar, sugar and the salt, then taste and adjust the seasoning if necessary.

SWEET CHILLI SAUCE

You can simply buy some Thai sweet chilli sauce if you wish, but I really think this is heaps better as a dipping sauce than anything you can buy.

500 ml (17 fl oz/2 cups) vegetable oil
3 cloves garlic, finely sliced
20 g (¾ oz) ginger, peeled and cut into julienne
500 g (1 lb 2 oz) sugar
500 ml (17 fl oz/2 cups) rice vinegar
3 long red chillies, deseeded and cut into julienne

METHOD

Heat the oil in a wok until smoking (180°C/350°F), and deep-fry the garlic, stirring constantly, until it turns light golden brown. Using a slotted spoon, quickly remove the garlic and drain on paper towel, then spread out to dry and let crisp. Repeat the process for the ginger.

In a heavy-based pot, combine the sugar, vinegar and chillies. Bring to the boil over medium heat, stirring until the sugar has dissolved. Reduce the heat and simmer until the sauce has reduced by almost half. Remove the pot from the heat and, using your fingers, crush the garlic and ginger into the sauce.

XO SAUCE

One of the really great things about going to Hong Kong is the XO chilli sauces made by fine-dining Chinese restaurants there. All the chefs are showing off, of course — it is their want to become the king of XO chilli sauce, so it has become a challenge as to who makes the very best. XO chilli sauce is simply the top shelf of sauces, named after XO Cognac. In other words, the house speciality, and the very best the house can offer. I have never once had an XO sauce I thought not worthy of dipping a dumpling into. These sauces may not even be that hot, but what they all have in common is a marvellous blending of the most exotic dried ingredients and seasoning. XO is great with seafood, as a dipping sauce, through stir-fries or dolloped on steamed foods. One of my favourite Hong Kong meals is XO chilli with egg noodles and lobster; I really think the nuttiness of the lobster and the earthiness of the sauce are a magical balance.

4 dried scallops, soaked in warm water for 2 hours and drained

50 g (1¾ oz) dried shrimp, soaked in warm water for 2 hours and drained

200 g (7 oz) long red chillies, deseeded and finely chopped

50 g (1¾ oz) ginger, peeled and finely chopped

50 g (1¾ oz) garlic, finely chopped

2 teaspoons sea salt

2 teaspoons sugar

300 ml (10½ fl oz) vegetable oil

3 spring onions (scallions), finely sliced

METHOD

Put the scallops on a plate and put the plate in a bamboo steamer over a pot or a wok of rapidly boiling water, cover with the lid and steam for 10 minutes. Remove the scallops from the steamer and, while still warm, shred with your fingers, separating all the fibres.

Pound the shrimp until finely ground in a mortar with a pestle, or grind in a spice grinder.

Put all the ingredients, except for the spring onions, in a large heavy-based pot and cook over low heat, stirring occasionally, for about 45 minutes, or until the sauce loses its raw edge and turns deep red. Remove from the heat and let cool, then stir in the spring onions.

CHILLI PASTE

This Thai paste is easy to make and is terrific added to water to make a Tom Yum base, or to coconut milk to make a great sauce for seafood. It also makes a nice salad dressing when thinned with a little coconut milk, and is great added to stir-fried meat, poultry or seafood with some vegetables and herbs. It is quite addictive. The most important part of this recipe is to colour the onions and garlic well; too far and they will be burnt, not enough and the paste will be insipid and not complex in flavour.

Chilli paste is, after green and red curry, the most prolific and flexible ingredient in Thai cooking. I remember eating a stir-fry of king prawns and sator beans (a bit like a cross between a broad bean and an almond in flavour) with chilli paste, down by the river in Bangkok with my old mate David Thompson. I don't think I shall ever forget it. So if you do go to the trouble of making this paste, make sure you use it in all sorts of dishes.

500 ml (17 fl oz/2 cups) peanut oil
320 g (11¼ oz/1½ cups) finely sliced Spanish onion
200 g (7 oz/1¼ cups) finely sliced garlic
60 g (2¼ oz) dried shrimp, pounded
150 g (5½ oz/1 cup) grated palm sugar (jaggery)
125 ml (4 fl oz/½ cup) fish sauce
1½ tablespoons chilli powder
375 ml (13 fl oz/1½ cups) tamarind water (page 32)

METHOD

Heat a wok until smoking. Add the peanut oil and, when hot, add the onion and fry until deep golden. Remove with a slotted spoon (very quickly so as not to let it burn) and drain. Add the garlic and fry until golden, then remove and drain. Next add the dried shrimp and fry until golden, remove and drain. Return the onion, garlic and shrimp to the wok, then add the palm sugar and cook until dark brown and caramelised. Add the fish sauce, chilli powder and tamarind water and boil for 30 seconds. Pour the paste into a blender and process until smooth. Store in a screw-top jar in the refrigerator, where it will keep for several weeks — although it generally doesn't last that long!

CHOPPED SALTED CHILLIES

Easy to make and really great to have hanging around, you can add chopped salted chillies to steamed and stir-fried dishes.

1 kg (2 lb 4 oz) long red chillies
150 g (5½ oz) sea salt

METHOD

Rinse and dry the chillies, trim the stems and roughly chop. Mix the chopped chillies with three-quarters of the sea salt, then put the chilli and salt mixture into a glass jar, sprinkle with the rest of the sea salt and put on the lid.

Store the jar in a cool dark place for at least two weeks before using, and refrigerate after opening. These chillies will easily keep for a few months.

NAM JIM

This famous Thai hot, sour, salty and sweet dressing is beautiful on salads, but great on just about anything — steamed food, stir-fries and seafood. Try opening some mussels or clams, toss with Nam Jim and some fresh herbs, and you will have one of the most spectacular dishes ever. I recommend that you remove the wok from the heat before you fold the sauce through; if you add it while the wok is hot or the other ingredients are boiling, you will destroy the wonderful fresh flavour of the limes.

Make sure you use lime and not lemon juice or it won't have a strong enough sour taste. Other souring agents commonly used are tamarind or coconut vinegar. I always make this dressing just before I want to use it as the freshness is the most wonderful thing about it.

I like the balance of flavour here to be hot, sour, salty then sweet. As with all these dressings, be careful not to make it too sweet.

2 cloves garlic
2 coriander (cilantro) roots, scraped
1 teaspoon sea salt
6 wild green chillies, chopped
2 tablespoons grated palm sugar (jaggery)
2 tablespoons fish sauce
3 tablespoons lime juice
3 red shallots, chopped

METHOD

Pound the garlic, coriander roots and salt in a mortar with a pestle until crushed but not reduced to a paste. Add the chillies and crush lightly (the degree to which you crush the chillies dictates the heat of the sauce, so be careful). Mix in the sugar, fish sauce, lime juice and shallots.

NUOC CHAM

This Vietnamese dressing is great in all the dishes where you could also use Nam Jim; its taste is softer but equally seductive. Again, like all these sauces, taste for balance and find a flavour that suits your palate.

This dressing, as well as being great as a dipping sauce and in stir-fries, also suits something like a barbecued chicken or fish — slice the meat, add some herbs and pour the dressing over. Serve with rice and boiled greens and you have a great Asian lunch for two or three people. Not a bad place to begin if you are starting out in the brave new world of Asian flavours.

2 long red chillies, deseeded and chopped
1 clove garlic
1 tablespoon grated palm sugar (jaggery)
2 tablespoons lime juice
3 tablespoons fish sauce
2 tablespoons rice vinegar

METHOD

Pound the chillies and garlic in a mortar with a pestle to a fine paste. Add the sugar and stir to blend. Slowly stir in the lime juice, fish sauce, rice vinegar and 3 tablespoons water until completely incorporated.

SICHUAN PICKLED CUCUMBER &
BLACK SHIITAKE

This is a classic pickle that is so easy to make. I assure you that once you taste it, you will always have some in the fridge, where, by the way, it should last for at least two weeks. It is the foundation of a few classic Rockpool salads and is great with cold cuts like white-cut chicken, barbecued pork and tea eggs. If you love pickles, you will probably find yourself eating this with roast beef or chicken sandwiches.

7 small Lebanese (short) cucumbers, cut into quarters
   lengthways and deseeded
65 g (2⅓ oz/½ cup) sea salt
250 ml (9 fl oz/1 cup) peanut oil
1 tablespoon Sichuan peppercorns
10 dried small red chillies
100 g (3½ oz) sugar
100 ml (3½ fl oz) rice vinegar
2½ tablespoons light soy sauce
1 large knob of ginger, peeled and cut into very fine
   julienne
20 dried shiitake mushrooms, soaked in warm water for
   30 minutes, stalks removed, finely sliced

METHOD

Put the cucumber in a colander over a bowl, sprinkle with the sea salt and mix well. Leave to stand for 1 hour to draw out any excess moisture and then rinse well under cold running water and drain.

Heat a wok until smoking. Add the peanut oil and, when hot, add the peppercorns and chillies and cook until blackened. Add the sugar, vinegar, soy sauce, ginger, mushrooms and finally, the cucumber. Stir for a minute or two. Pack into a 2 litre (8 cup) sterilised glass jar, allow to cool and then cover and leave for a day or two to mature before using.

PICKLED CABBAGE

This is another classic that is always in the fridge at all my restaurants as well as at home. It's great to eat by itself, amazing with cold cuts and even brilliant on a sandwich with some chicken or beef, as with the last pickle. We also use it to create a great dressing for all sorts of dishes — that recipe is on the following page.

½ savoy cabbage
1 tablespoon sea salt
2 dried long red chillies, deseeded
1 teaspoon whole black peppercorns
500 ml (17 fl oz/2 cups) white vinegar
345 g (12 oz/1½ cups) sugar

METHOD

Cut the cabbage into large chunks, toss with the sea salt and then leave for about 30 minutes.

Roast the chillies and peppercorns in a preheated 200°C (400°F/Gas 6) oven for about 3 minutes, or until the chillies blacken and the peppercorns are fragrant. Pound the spices in a mortar with a pestle until coarsely ground.

Put the vinegar and sugar in a small pot over low heat and stir until the sugar dissolves. Bring to the boil, turn off the heat, then add the ground spices and mix together.

Firmly pack the salted cabbage into a 1 litre (35 fl oz/4 cup) sterilised glass jar (or several smaller jars). Gradually pour in the spice and vinegar mixture, allowing the liquid to find its way to the bottom of the jar before you add more. You should be able to add most, if not all, of the liquid. Seal with a tight-fitting lid and set aside for at least two days before using.

NOTE This pickled cabbage will get better the longer you leave it. The jars can be stored unopened in a cool dark place indefinitely, or in the fridge for several months, once opened.

PICKLED CABBAGE DRESSING

Great as a sauce for just about anything, this dressing has a really complex flavour you're sure to love. Look for balance; this dressing should be hot, sour, sweet and salty, so get it to a level that suits your palate.

115 g (4 oz/½ cup) pickled cabbage (page 53), roughly
    chopped
125 ml (4 fl oz/½ cup) kecap manis
1½ tablespoons Chinkiang vinegar
1½ tablespoons white vinegar
3 tablespoons mushroom soy sauce
3 tablespoons chilli oil
2 teaspoons Sichuan pepper

METHOD

Combine the pickled cabbage, kecap manis, Chinkiang, white vinegar, mushroom soy sauce, chilli oil, Sichuan pepper and 1½ tablespoons water and mix well. Be sure to mix the dressing again just before serving.

VARIATION

You can wok-fry, deep-fry or steam just about anything and dress with this at the end. You also don't even have to add the pickled cabbage to this dressing, although it does taste great with it.

SICHUAN SALT & PEPPER

We use this on several dishes in the book, but you can also try sprinkling it over roast chicken next time you make one; I promise you'll love it. You can also sprinkle it over any roast, barbecued or fried food to really enhance the flavour, or add it to flour to create a delicious crust for fried food. Don't only use Sichuan salt and pepper when cooking Asian food either, but bring it into your Western cooking as well.

100 g (3½ oz/¾ cup) sea salt
35 g (1¼ oz/¼ cup) Sichuan peppercorns

METHOD

Preheat the oven to 180°C (350°F/Gas 4). Roast the sea salt and peppercorns together on a baking tray for 5–6 minutes until fragrant. Let cool, then grind in a spice grinder or pound in a mortar with a pestle to a very fine powder. Pass through a fine sieve, discarding any spice left in the sieve, and store in an airtight container.

NOTE The Sichuan salt and pepper will keep, stored out of direct sunlight, for a couple of months before it starts to lose its flavour.

STOCKS AND SOUPS

Good stock is the basis of many great Chinese soups and most stir-fries. A welcome addition to any steamed dish, you can just pour good stock into a bowl with the meat, poultry or fish and seasoning to make a silky self-saucing dish.

Chinese-style stock is very simple to master. It requires none of the roasting of bones or vegetables and deglazing that a French-style stock does. The reason being that we are looking for a clear, light broth that has the body and essence of the chicken, but is not clouded with the taste of vegetables. The best way to handle stock at home is to make a big batch and freeze it in small containers. We always have lots of this in the freezer at home so it can be pulled out for a soup or a stir-fry. It also makes a great base for risotto and, as Sam, my wife, uses it, for baby food. Simmered with vegetables and puréed it gives baby food more taste and body; our children love it. I now find that at work and at home this is the only chicken stock I use.

Is it worth making my own, I hear you ask. Damn right! There is nothing on the market that will rival the gentle, pure taste of your own stock. Remember to look for balance and not to let the chicken flavour dominate. I use water at home if I don't have any of my own in the fridge or freezer — I think it's a better substitute than the manufactured stocks.

There is a richer stock used in Chinese cooking for some soups and stir-fries, however I think it's too expensive to make for what you'll get out of it for these recipes. It contains a lot of chicken, pork and ham — my advice is not to worry about it.

The easy-to-prepare soups that follow are classic Chinese and simple Thai, and from them you'll be able to make many variations. Generally speaking, in Asia, a soup would be eaten for lunch by itself. At an evening meal it is more than likely to be part of a shared table where it would be served in small bowls and drunk much as we would drink wine during the meal.

CHINESE FRESH CHICKEN STOCK

You can just use chicken bones if you wish, but the stock won't have quite the same body and depth of flavour. I often leave out the ginger and spring onion to make it friendlier for my Western dishes when I pull it out of the fridge for risotto or soup.

1 x 1.6 kg (3 lb 8 oz) free-range or organic chicken
2 slices of peeled ginger
1 spring onion (scallion), cut into 4 cm (1½ inch) lengths

METHOD

Remove the fat from the cavity of the chicken. Rinse the chicken under cold water and pat dry with paper towel. Chop the chicken Chinese-style (see Note, below). Put the chicken, ginger, spring onion and 3 litres (12 cups) water into a pot large enough to fit the chicken snugly, and bring to the boil. Reduce the heat to a low simmer and skim the stock well. Simmer for 30 minutes, skimming continually. Reduce the heat until the surface is barely moving and cook for 2 hours. Remove from the heat, strain through a muslin-lined sieve, discard the solids and strain again.

NOTE To chop chicken or duck Chinese-style, put the bird on a chopping board with its legs facing away from you. Cut the bird in half lengthways with a cleaver. Lay one half in front of you and cut off the leg, then cut off the wing where it joins the breast. Cut the wing lengthways, then cut the leg into six pieces. Slice the breast into six pieces. Repeat with the remaining half.

WONTON SOUP WITH NOODLES

This is a very simple, easy soup to start with as it's just seasoned stock with wontons and noodles. It makes a great lunch, and the stock can come straight out of the freezer — as a matter of fact, so can the wontons. Make some up when you have time and then just remove from the freezer and boil. The noodles are great if fresh, but by all means, have some dried egg noodles in the pantry. They are great for this soup and also form the bulk of a good noodle stir-fry in minutes.

8 pork wontons (page 363)
150 g (5½ oz) fresh egg noodles
½ bunch Chinese broccoli (gai larn), trimmed and cut into
    3 cm (1¼ inch) lengths
1 litre (35 fl oz/4 cups) fresh chicken stock (page 58)
1 small knob of ginger, peeled and cut into julienne
3 tablespoons kecap manis
2 tablespoons yellow bean soy sauce
2 spring onions (scallions), cut into julienne
a pinch of ground white pepper
½ teaspoon sesame oil

METHOD

Blanch the broccoli in a large pot of boiling water, and then remove it with a slotted spoon. Boil the noodles and then the wontons in the same water until just cooked, then transfer the noodles, wontons and broccoli to a serving bowl.

As the noodles and wontons are cooking, put the stock, ginger, kecap manis and soy sauce in a separate pot, bring to the boil and simmer for 3 minutes.

Pour the hot stock over the noodles, wontons and broccoli, sprinkle with the spring onions and pepper, and drizzle with sesame oil to serve.

VARIATION

Once you've mastered this simple soup, you can add things to make it a more grand experience. Try master-stock chicken, braised duck, barbecued pork, prawns, scallops, all the above, or a combination of just a few. If you want to make it amazing, add tinned abalone, sliced and just warmed in the broth, for a truly luxurious soup.

CHICKEN, ASPARAGUS & RICE NOODLE SOUP

A variation on the previous wonton soup with noodles, this version is easy, elegant and perfect for a complete lunch or dinner.

½ roast chicken, skin removed and flesh torn into large
    pieces
6 green asparagus spears, cut on the diagonal into 3 cm
    (1¼ inch) lengths
250 g (9 oz) fresh rice noodle sheets, cut into 2 cm
    (¾ inch) wide strips
1 litre (35 fl oz/4 cups) fresh chicken stock (page 58)
2 tablespoons oyster sauce
2 tablespoons hoisin sauce
1 tablespoon fish sauce
2 slices of peeled ginger, cut into julienne
1 spring onion (scallion), finely sliced
a pinch of freshly ground white pepper
¼ teaspoon sesame oil

METHOD

Bring the chicken stock to the boil in a large pot. Add the oyster sauce, hoisin, fish sauce and ginger, and simmer for 2 minutes. Meanwhile, blanch the asparagus in a large pot of boiling water, then transfer to a serving bowl. Blanch the noodles in the same pot, then drain immediately and add to the asparagus. Drop the chicken into the stock and stir to heat through, then pour over the noodles and asparagus. Sprinkle with the spring onion and pepper and drizzle with sesame oil. Ladle into individual bowls to serve.

HOT & SOUR SOUP

So easy to make, I've placed this soup here as it will open up a world of great flavoured boil-together soups that take no time at all. If you want to go the whole hog, try making your own chilli paste. This is similar to a Tom Yum soup, but if you replace the stock with watered-down coconut milk, it'll be along the lines of a Tom Ka.

Look for balance in this soup — it should be sour, hot, salty and sweet. The sweetness is there to round out the middle palate so that the other flavours can be strong. To make it really sour, just add more lime juice; to make it really hot, add more chilli. This soup is really good for a hangover when loaded with chilli and blisteringly hot — you can adjust the seasoning to suit your tastes.

To keep the taste fresh, make sure you add the lime juice after the soup has stopped boiling.

3 tablespoons chilli paste (page 48)
4 kaffir lime leaves
2 vine-ripened tomatoes, cut into eighths lengthways
2 long red chillies, cut in half lengthways and deseeded
4 wild green chillies, bruised
2 lemongrass stalks, tough outer leaves removed, bruised and cut into 4 cm (1½ inch) lengths
2 slices of galangal, bruised
750 ml (26 fl oz/3 cups) fresh chicken stock (page 58)
6 green king prawns (shrimp), peeled and deveined with tails left intact
1 free-range or organic skinless chicken breast, finely sliced across the grain
10 baby green beans, trimmed
3 tablespoons fish sauce
1 tablespoon grated palm sugar (jaggery)
2 tablespoons tamarind water (page 32)
juice of 1 lime

METHOD

Add the chilli paste, lime leaves, tomatoes, red chillies, wild green chillies, lemongrass and galangal to the stock and bring to the boil. Add the prawns, chicken, green beans, fish sauce and palm sugar, stir and cook for 1 minute. Remove from the heat, add the tamarind water and lime juice, taste and adjust the seasoning if necessary. Spoon into a large bowl to serve.

Salads

Most of the salads I've included in this section are South-East Asian inspired. They're dead easy, bloody delicious and incredibly flexible. And, just as importantly, they are great to have in the middle of your shared table, already prepared and ready to serve as you're plating your other dishes. For example, you could have steamed rice, a salad, something straight off the steamer, a braise or a curry and, at the last minute, a stir-fry — how easy would that be? Remember that the balance of a meal is not only to do with the flavour and texture of the food, but also in your ability to enjoy getting it out of the kitchen.

You can also change the ingredients around to suit your palate; these are a guide, but when you're used to making these dressings, go crazy and have fun with them. And, while these salads are often composed mainly of herbs (which is why they explode with flavour), by all means use lettuce, or a combination of both.

There are a few ingredients you should keep around to add texture and interest to any salad: dried shrimp, fried and raw shallots, fried peanuts, ground roast rice and bean sprouts are just a few examples.

SPICY BEEF SALAD

This Thai classic is so easy to put together. Look for balance with the Nam Jim dressing... if you like it really hot, dial up the other flavours so you get the heat with complexity. Most importantly, keep this very fresh tasting.

200 g (7 oz) beef fillet
1 small Spanish onion, finely sliced
1 small handful of coriander (cilantro) leaves
1 small butter lettuce, leaves separated
a pinch of ground roast rice (page 27)
freshly ground black pepper
1 handful of Thai basil leaves, finely shredded

MARINADE
2 tablespoons oyster sauce
1 tablespoon fish sauce
1 tablespoon grated palm sugar (jaggery)
½ teaspoon sesame oil

DRESSING
1 lemongrass stalk, tough outer leaves removed,
    chopped
1 long red chilli, deseeded and chopped
2 small wild green chillies, chopped
3 cloves garlic, chopped
1 tablespoon caster (superfine) sugar
2 tablespoons fish sauce
juice of 3 limes

METHOD

To make the marinade, mix together the oyster sauce, fish sauce, sugar and sesame oil. Add the beef and refrigerate overnight to marinate. Remove from the fridge 2 hours before cooking.

To make the dressing, pound the lemongrass, chillies, garlic and sugar in a mortar with a pestle to form a fine paste. Mix the fish sauce and lime juice together and taste for balance.

Heat a grill or a barbecue to hot, and cook the beef for about 2 minutes on each side until it forms a good even crust. Remove from the heat and rest in a warm place for 10 minutes. Slice the beef thickly across the grain.

Toss the beef, onion and coriander leaves with some of the dressing. Arrange the lettuce and beef on a serving plate and drizzle with any remaining dressing. Sprinkle with the ground roast rice, give it a good grind of black pepper and top with the shredded Thai basil.

SPICY TOFU SALAD

I love the texture of this pressed tofu with the sour fruitiness the tamarind gives the dressing. It's perfect with a big spoonful of steamed rice.

You can be very precise when cutting the vegetables for this salad, or much more rustic. I like to add some chopped cooked king prawns to this dish — if you want to jazz it up, some white-cut chicken, or a prawn and chicken combination would be great as well.

150 g (5½ oz) marinated pressed tofu, cut into 6 even
    pieces
vegetable oil, for deep-frying
1 small Lebanese (short) cucumber, finely sliced
1 small carrot, cut into julienne
100 g (3½ oz) bean sprouts, trimmed
2 tablespoons peanuts, roasted and crushed

DRESSING
3 long red chillies, deseeded and chopped
4 red shallots, chopped
a pinch of sea salt
2 tablespoons peanuts, roasted
2 tablespoons grated palm sugar (jaggery)
1 tablespoon light soy sauce
1½ tablespoons tamarind water (page 32)

METHOD

To make the dressing, pound the chillies, shallots and sea salt to a paste in a mortar with a pestle. Add the peanuts and continue to pound until smooth. Add the palm sugar, soy sauce, tamarind water and 2 tablespoons water, mix well and check for balance.

Heat the oil in a wok or deep-fryer until just smoking (180°C/350°F). Dry the tofu with paper towel and then deep-fry for 1–2 minutes until golden brown. Drain on paper towel and leave to cool.

Toss together the cucumber, carrot, bean sprouts, peanuts and tofu in a bowl. Add the dressing and toss again before serving.

ROAST CHICKEN SALAD

Again, this salad can be as easy as you want to make it. You can even buy a roast chook from your local shop; just make sure it's free-range and that it doesn't have stuffing — that would be totally bizarre. You could also use master-stock chicken, white-cut chicken or even throw a chicken on the barbecue. I also like to add cucumber and some spring onion to this salad to give it a kick along as well.

½ roast chicken
1 small Spanish onion, halved and finely sliced
1 tomato, finely sliced
½ mignonette lettuce, leaves washed and torn
1½ tablespoons peanuts, roasted and crushed

DRESSING
1 teaspoon chilli powder
2 small wild green chillies, finely sliced
2 tablespoons white vinegar
2 tablespoons tamarind water (page 32)
2 tablespoons lime juice
2 tablespoon caster (superfine) sugar
2 tablespoons fish sauce
½ teaspoon sea salt

METHOD

To make the dressing, mix all of the ingredients together in a small pot and bring to the boil. Remove from the heat and leave to cool.

Remove the chicken from the bones and slice thickly across the grain. Put the chicken, onion and tomato in a bowl, drizzle with the dressing and gently toss together. Put the lettuce on a serving plate and arrange the chicken salad on top. Sprinkle with peanuts to serve.

VARIATION

This is another salad where you can interchange chicken for duck, beef, lamb, quail, or even prawns to create a lively, fresh-tasting dish.

WARM SALAD OF SPICY MINCED CHICKEN

This is a style of larp, or salad, from the north of Thailand, although it's really a stir-fry served on lettuce. The heat from the chillies and the flavour of fresh lime make it irresistible; with a bowl of rice, it's truly a great meal. Think of it as the Thai Sang Choi Bao.

150 g (5½ oz) skinless chicken thigh fillets, finely chopped
2 cloves garlic, chopped
4 small wild green chillies, chopped
2 tablespoons peanut oil
a pinch of sea salt
½ small Spanish onion, halved and finely sliced
50 g (1¾ oz) green beans, trimmed and finely sliced
a pinch of caster (superfine) sugar
1 tablespoon fish sauce
2 tablespoons lime juice
1 small handful of combined mint and coriander (cilantro)
    leaves
½ baby cos (romaine) lettuce, leaves separated and
    washed
1 teaspoon ground roast rice (page 27)

METHOD

Pound the garlic and chillies in a mortar with a pestle to form a fine paste. Heat a wok until just smoking. Add the peanut oil and, when hot, stir-fry the chicken, sea salt, onion and beans for about 1 minute. As soon as the chicken turns white, remove from the heat and add the pounded garlic and chilli, sugar, fish sauce, lime juice and herbs. Stir together, taste and adjust the seasoning if necessary. Put the lettuce leaves on a plate and spoon the chicken mixture over the top. Sprinkle with the ground roast rice to serve.

VARIATION

You can add just about any meat you like to this salad. I love duck — the extra bit of gaminess tastes fantastic with the hot and sour flavours of the dressing.

THAI-STYLE SQUID SALAD

I couldn't resist including this salad as it's another classic. Use spanking fresh squid to move it up to another level.

300 g (10½ oz) squid, cleaned (see below)
3 red shallots, finely sliced
1 kaffir lime leaf, cut into julienne
½ lemongrass stalk, tough outer leaves removed,
    finely sliced
1 small handful of mixed coriander (cilantro), mint and
    Thai basil leaves

DRESSING
4 wild green chillies, finely sliced
1 tablespoon caster (superfine) sugar
juice of 1 lime
2 tablespoons fish sauce

METHOD

To make the dressing, pound the chillies and sugar in a mortar with a pestle to form a paste. Stir in the lime juice and fish sauce and check the seasoning.

To prepare the squid, cut off the tentacles and cut down the centre of the squid so it will open out flat. Score the inside with a crisscross pattern, then slice lengthways into 2 cm (¾ inch) wide strips. Cut the tentacles in half.

Blanch the squid in a large pot of salted water until it just turns opaque, drain and let cool.

Toss the squid, shallots, lime leaf, lemongrass and herbs together in a bowl. Add the dressing, gently toss again and serve.

HOW TO PREPARE SQUID

First, pull out the head, taking the skin off in one go if possible. If your recipe calls for squid rings, leave the squid whole, remove the organs and cartilage and then cut the body into thin rings. Otherwise, cut the squid down the centre, open it out and scrape out all the internal organs and the plastic-looking cartilage. Remove the hard beak, or mouth, from the centre where the tentacles meet, cut the eyes off and discard. (Don't underestimate how delicious the tentacles are barbecued or fried.) Now, starting from the head end and using a sharp knife at a 45-degree angle, score diagonal lines at about 5 mm (¼ inch) intervals over the flesh, cutting halfway through the flesh and going all the way down to the end. Repeat the lines in the opposite direction to form a crisscross pattern. Scoring prevents the squid from curling up completely during cooking.

ROAST DUCK & LYCHEE SALAD

Beautiful and simple, this salad picks up on the richness of the duck and the wonderful sweet perfume of lychees. If you are near a Chinatown, just pick up a roast duck; if not, master-stock, barbecue or roast one yourself. Chicken or quail could happily replace the duck.

½ Chinese roast duck, shredded (page 248)
15 lychees, peeled, halved and seeded
3 spring onions (scallions), cut into julienne
½ knob of ginger, peeled and cut into julienne
1 large handful of coriander (cilantro) leaves
2 cloves garlic, finely sliced and deep-fried until golden
2 tablespoons peanuts, deep-fried until golden
a pinch of sesame seeds, roasted

DRESSING
3 teaspoons hoisin sauce
1¼ teaspoons caster (superfine) sugar
3 teaspoons Chinkiang vinegar
2 tablespoons light soy sauce

METHOD

To make the dressing, mix together the hoisin, sugar, Chinkiang, soy sauce and 1½ tablespoons water.

Put the shredded duck, lychees, spring onion, ginger, coriander, garlic and peanuts in a large bowl, add the dressing, and gently toss together. Pile onto a plate and sprinkle with sesame seeds to serve.

TO ROAST A DUCK

This method of roasting a duck, which I use for both Western and Asian dishes, involves double cooking.

1 x 2 kg (4 lb 8 oz) duck, wing tips and tail removed
a splash of vegetable oil
sea salt

METHOD

Put the duck on the chopping board and remove the fat deposits in the cavity. Cut the neck off and remove the first two wing joints, then season inside and out with salt. Put the duck in a bamboo steamer and steam over boiling water for 45 minutes, making sure not to boil the pot dry. When cool enough to handle, put on a board and remove the legs. Cut the backbone out and cut the two breasts down the middle, leaving the breastbone in place.

Preheat the oven to 220°C (425°F/Gas 7). Rub the duck pieces with the vegetable oil and season with sea salt. Put in a roasting tin, skin-side-down, and cook for 15 minutes, then turn over. Pour out any excess liquid and cook for a further 15–20 minutes. The duck should be cooked through and the skin crisp; remove when done.

TO BARBECUE A DUCK

This is a simple method of preparing duck for the barbecue; you can poach it first or, as in the previous recipe, steam it. I've given you both variations so you can see that they're both very easy.

1 x 2 kg (4 lb 8 oz) duck, wing tips and tail removed
a large pinch of sea salt

METHOD

Poach the duck first in salted water. To do this, put the duck on the chopping board and remove the fat deposits in the cavity. Cut the neck off and remove the first two wing joints. Fill a pot large enough to cover the duck with water and bring to the boil. When the water is boiling, add the sea salt, and then add the duck, breast-side-down. Keep the water simmering and cook for 25 minutes, then turn the duck over and cook for a further 5 minutes. Remove the pot from the heat and allow the duck to cool in the poaching liquid. When cool, remove and pat dry with paper towel. Cut the duck into two legs and two breasts and proceed with the barbecuing. Make sure you place the duck skin-side-down first on the grill, and watch out as the fire flares up when the duck fat drips down.

SPICY PRAWN SALAD

This is one of the simplest seafood salads you will ever make — the combination of lime and chilli is so fresh it will soon be a favourite. It's easy to substitute any seafood you like for the prawns.

500 g (1 lb 2 oz) cooked king prawns (shrimp), peeled and
    deveined with tails left intact
juice of 1 lime
1 tablespoon fish sauce
1 teaspoon caster (superfine) sugar
5 small wild green chillies, finely sliced
1 lemongrass stalk, tough outer leaves removed, finely
    sliced
2 red shallots, finely sliced
1 large handful of mint leaves
1 large handful of coriander (cilantro) leaves
2 kaffir lime leaves, very finely shredded

METHOD

Whisk together the lime juice, fish sauce and sugar. Toss the prawns, chillies, lemongrass, shallots, mint, coriander and lime leaves with the dressing, taste and adjust the seasoning if necessary. Serve immediately.

MARINATED SALMON SALAD

With its crispy charred outside and melting interior, you're sure to love the salmon in this dish as much as I do. Like all the salads in this chapter, this is great as part of a shared table. The texture of ground roast rice on these Thai salads is quite addictive and, if you add lime and chilli, you will be in heaven. This is also a cracker if you deep-fry the fish and break it up and toss together with the salad.

250 g (9 oz) salmon fillet
3 tablespoons fish sauce
a pinch of sea salt
a pinch of caster (superfine) sugar
3 red shallots, finely sliced
2 tablespoons peanuts, roasted and crushed
1 handful of mixed mint and coriander (cilantro) leaves
1 clove garlic, finely sliced and deep-fried until golden
1½ tablespoons salmon roe
a pinch of ground roast rice (page 27)

DRESSING
a pinch of caster (superfine) sugar
a pinch of grated palm sugar (jaggery)
2 tablespoons lime juice
2 tablespoons fish sauce
a pinch of chilli powder

METHOD

Mix together the fish sauce, sea salt and sugar, add the salmon and make sure it's coated well, then refrigerate for about 30 minutes. Transfer the fish to a wire rack positioned over a bowl or tray and refrigerate, uncovered, for several hours, or overnight. This will allow the fish to dry out slightly. Remove the salmon from the fridge about 30 minutes before cooking.

Barbecue the fish over high heat for about 2 minutes on each side, or until the outside is charred but the inside is still rare, and rest for 5 minutes. Coarsely flake the fish.

Mix together the shallots, peanuts, herbs and garlic in a bowl, then gently fold in the fish. For the dressing, whisk together the sugars, lime juice, fish sauce and the chilli powder and drizzle over the salad. Sprinkle with the salmon roe and ground roast rice to serve.

SASHIMI SALAD

If you would like a starter for your shared table, this is probably a good one to try. The only difficult thing about this dish is making sure you have a good relationship with your fishmonger so you can get the best quality fish. If fish is going to be served raw it must be really well handled. Kingfish, trevally, swordfish, mackerel, john dory, snapper and whiting are all magic in this salad; scallops, scampi and squid are also a welcome addition to any raw plate.

300 g (10½ oz) sashimi-grade tuna
1 large handful of small mesclun leaves

DRESSING
1 dried small red chilli
3 tablespoons grated palm sugar (jaggery)
125 ml (4 fl oz/½ cup) rice vinegar
125 ml (4 fl oz/½ cup) Japanese soy sauce
¼ teaspoon mustard powder
½ small Spanish onion, grated
¼ teaspoon freshly ground white pepper
125 ml (4 fl oz/½ cup) vegetable oil

METHOD

To make the dressing, roast the chilli briefly in a hot, dry heavy-based pan until blackened, then grind to a powder. Boil the sugar and 1 tablespoon water in a small pot until the sugar caramelises. Add the chilli and the remaining dressing ingredients to the pot, whisk to incorporate and then leave to cool to room temperature.

With a very sharp knife, cut the tuna into 5 mm (¼ inch) thick slices. Drizzle a little of the dressing over the mesclun and toss lightly. Place the tuna around the outside of a large platter, place the mesclun in the centre and drizzle the remaining dressing over and around the tuna.

Braising and Boiling

Braising is an important part of Chinese cooking. It's particularly ideal for the home cook preparing a shared table — you can make a braise well in advance and simply reheat it when you're ready to serve. That way you'll already have one of your dishes ready, so if you just add a salad, a stir-fry and something steamed, you'll have a great shared table without too much last-minute preparation. I have also added poaching or boiling to this selection of recipes; master-stock and white-cut chicken are important as they can be used as they are, or can form part of the preparation of a stir-fry or deep-fry recipe. I love the notion of multi-cooking that the Chinese do so well.

I find with braising that the same rules apply as with Western cooking: simmer gently for the best result; fierce boiling just dries out your meat.

MASTER-STOCK CHICKEN

This is, in essence, a very simple recipe. You boil all the ingredients in water, add the chicken, poach, and then allow it to cool in the stock with the lid on; this gives the chicken the most succulent flesh and a skin permeated with the flavour of your stock. The reason it's so tender is that you are slow cooking it at the end.

It's called 'master stock' because you keep the stock and use it time and time again, adding more water and flavouring each time. After a while the stock has an incredible intensity of flavour and colour, and your birds will come out a beautiful browny red. Some master stocks in China are rumoured to be centuries old.

At the restaurant we have separate master stocks for chicken, pigeon, duck and pork. We keep them all separately and they are used every day; the mothers are many years old. You can do the same at home by straining the stock into a container and freezing it after every use — you can keep it for years.

A great way to mature a master stock is to buy some bones, in this case chicken bones, and boil them in the stock for 20 minutes. Strain and repeat three or four times, adding more water and seasoning each time. This way the first time you use your stock to cook a chicken, it will lend great colour and flavour — otherwise your first bird might look a bit insipid. You can also use a bit of the stock to moisten the chicken as it makes a great sauce. A variation of this dish is called soy chicken.

1 x 1.6 kg (3 lb 8 oz) free-range or organic chicken
1 spring onion (scallion), white part only, finely sliced in julienne
freshly ground white pepper

MASTER STOCK
500 ml (17 fl oz/2 cups) light soy sauce
250 ml (9 fl oz/1 cup) shaoxing
125 g (4½ oz) yellow rock sugar, crushed
½ bunch spring onions (scallions), dark green ends only
1 large knob of ginger, peeled and sliced
3 cloves garlic, sliced
4 star anise
2 cinnamon sticks
3 pieces dried tangerine peel

METHOD

Remove all visible fat from the chicken and wipe the cavity clean. Bring a large pot of water to the boil, plunge the chicken in for 1 minute, then remove and rinse under cold running water and pat dry with paper towel.

Rinse the pot and add the master stock ingredients and 2.5 litres (10 cups) cold water. Bring to the boil, then reduce the heat and simmer for 30 minutes. Submerge the chicken in the stock and allow it to return to the boil. Reduce the heat to a high simmer and cook, uncovered, for 20 minutes. Turn the chicken over and simmer for a further 3 minutes. Put a lid on the pot, remove from the heat and leave the chicken to cool in the stock. Once the stock has cooled, remove the chicken and drain the stock from the cavity.

Cut the chicken Chinese-style and arrange on a serving plate. Strain the master stock through a fine sieve and discard the aromatics. Simmer 250 ml (9 fl oz/1 cup) of the stock in a small pot to reduce by half. Pour the reduced stock over the chicken, sprinkle with spring onion and give it a good grind of white pepper to serve.

Bring the remaining stock back to the boil in a pot and pour it into an airtight container, cool and then freeze, ready for the next time. Just take the stock out next time around, place it in a pot, top it up with water and more of the seasoning ingredients and simmer... and you're on your way to being a master-stocker.

VARIATIONS

To make the perfect crispy-skin chicken, dry the master-stock chicken of all moisture (otherwise you'll have an exploding chicken when it hits the hot oil) and deep-fry it; serve with lemon or lime wedges and a small bowl of Sichuan salt and pepper (page 55) — squeeze the lemon or lime over the top and sprinkle with the salt and pepper.

You can master stock a 2 kg (4 lb 8 oz) duck by boiling it first, breast-side-down, for 35 minutes, turning it and simmering for a further 5 minutes, then covering and allowing it to cool in the stock. Again, this is great cut and sauced, or dried, floured and deep-fried for the perfect crispy duck.

For a very simple dish, boil 2 kg (4 lb 8 oz) of chicken wings in the stock, for 20 minutes, cover and allow to cool. I promise you a plate of those won't last long.

WHITE-CUT CHICKEN

This process gives you firm chicken with silky skin, succulent from the bird's juices, which turn into jelly after being submerged in iced water. It's perfect for cold cuts, chicken salads, and is great cut Chinese-style and served with spring onion oil or pickled cabbage dressing. Unlike master stock, the cooking medium is not kept. However, I find that the liquid has a nice chicken flavour and can be kept for stock — just strain, reduce by half and freeze; it's great for soups.

1 x 1.6 kg–1.8 kg (3 lb 8 oz–4 lb) free-range or organic
   chicken
250 ml (9 fl oz/1 cup) shaoxing
½ bunch spring onions (scallions), dark green ends only
3 cloves garlic, sliced
1 large knob of ginger, peeled and sliced
lots of ice

GINGER & SPRING ONION OIL
1 large knob of ginger, peeled and finely chopped
4 spring onions (scallions), finely chopped
⅔ teaspoon sea salt
4 tablespoons peanut oil

METHOD

To prepare the chicken, remove the fat from the cavity, rinse in cold water and pat dry with paper towel. In a heavy-based pot large enough to fit the chicken snugly, add the shaoxing, spring onions, garlic, ginger and 3.5 litres (14 cups) water, and bring to the boil. Add the chicken to the pot and return to the boil, then reduce the heat to a high simmer. Put the lid on the pot and simmer for a further 15 minutes. Remove from the heat and leave the chicken to steep for 20 minutes (do not be tempted to lift the lid or the heat will dissipate).

Remove the lid and carefully lift the chicken from the stock. Drain the cavity and submerge the chicken in a large pot of iced water, leaving it to cool for 15 minutes. Thoroughly drain the chicken, put it on a plate and chill it in the refrigerator to completely set the juices.

Meanwhile, to make the ginger and spring onion oil, pound the ginger into a fine paste in a mortar with a pestle. Add the spring onions and salt and continue to pound until combined. Heat the oil until just smoking and pour it over the ginger and spring onion mixture.

Chop the chicken Chinese-style, arrange it on a serving platter and serve with the ginger and spring onion oil.

RED-BRAISED CHICKEN

Red-braising differs from cooking with a master stock because, by the time the ingredients are tender and cooked through, the stock has turned into a sauce that is served with the dish; it is in fact a true braise. It is also called red cooking, the 'red' referring to that deep reddish-brown sheen the soy sauce and yellow rock sugar give the sauce. It's definitely one of my favourite tastes: deep and mysterious, rich, salty and sweet all at the same time. Taste for balance and a nice richness on the tongue; I'm sure it will soon become one of your favourite dishes.

4 chicken legs, cut into 3 cm (1¼ inch) pieces across
   the bone
250 ml (9 fl oz/1 cup) shaoxing
3 cloves garlic, sliced
1 knob of ginger, peeled and sliced
2 spring onions (scallions), cut into 2 cm (¾ inch) lengths
3 tablespoons peanut oil
3 tablespoons dark soy sauce
4 star anise
3 cinnamon sticks
2 pieces dried tangerine peel, soaked in hot water
1 dried small red chilli
3 tablespoons crushed yellow rock sugar

METHOD

Mix together the chicken legs, shaoxing, garlic, ginger and spring onions and marinate for 30 minutes. Drain and pat the chicken dry with paper towel, and set the marinade aside.

Heat a wok until smoking. Add the peanut oil and, when hot, add the chicken and stir-fry for about 5 minutes until nicely brown. Add the reserved marinade and continue cooking for a minute, then add the soy sauce, 750 ml (26 fl oz/3 cups) water, the spices, tangerine peel, chilli and the yellow rock sugar. Cover the wok and simmer gently for about 20 minutes, or until the chicken is tender. Spoon the chicken and all of the aromatics into a bowl. Return the sauce to the heat and boil for about 5 minutes until it thickens, then pour over the chicken to serve.

VARIATIONS

You can cook duck legs in the same way; just add a bit more water and simmer for about 40 minutes, or until tender. Pork belly, cut into 2 cm (¾ inch) cubes, can also be cooked like this — it will take about 1½ hours to become tender.

BRAISED SHIITAKE MUSHROOMS

Dried shiitakes are a great ingredient. They take on a flavour and texture that far outweighs the fresh; a real earthiness that makes them a favourite ingredient in all sorts of dishes. They have a great meaty taste and are perfect as a vegetable for a shared table.

18 dried shiitake mushrooms, soaked in warm water for
    30 minutes (reserve 350 ml/12 fl oz of the soaking
    liquid), stalks removed, cut in half on the diagonal
    through the middle
½ knob of ginger, peeled and chopped
1 clove garlic, chopped
2 teaspoons sugar
1½ tablespoons peanut oil
1½ tablespoons shaoxing
1 tablespoon mushroom soy sauce
1 tablespoon yellow bean soy sauce
1 spring onion (scallion), sliced
a pinch of white pepper
2 teaspoons sesame oil

METHOD

Pound the ginger, garlic and sugar in a mortar with a pestle to form a rough paste. Or use a blender to process the ingredients, adding a little water if necessary.

Heat a wok until just smoking. Add the peanut oil and, when hot, stir-fry the mushrooms until they begin to colour. Add the paste and stir-fry until fragrant, then deglaze the wok with the shaoxing. Add the reserved soaking liquid and both the soy sauces and bring to the boil. Reduce the heat, cover with a lid and simmer for 15 minutes.

Spoon the mushrooms into a bowl and sprinkle with the spring onion and pepper and drizzle with the sesame oil to serve.

RED-BRAISED PORK HOCK WITH SHIITAKE MUSHROOMS

The pork hock is deep-fried to change the texture of the skin after the first braising, but you can also just leave it to cook fully in the sauce. Make sure it's thoroughly dry if you do deep-fry it, or it will spit in the oil. This was one of the first Chinese dishes I cooked when I was a young man and in love with Asian food. It has been on the Rockpool and XO menus for years as the gelatinous texture of the skin with the melting sweet pork flesh is superb.

1 x 400–500 g (about 1 lb) whole fresh pork hock
15 dried shiitake mushrooms, soaked in warm water for
    30 minutes, stalks removed, cut in half on the diagonal
250 ml (9 fl oz/1 cup) shaoxing
1 knob of ginger, peeled and finely sliced
6 cloves garlic, finely sliced
6 spring onions (scallions), trimmed
125 ml (4 fl oz/½ cup) light soy sauce
2 tablespoons dark soy sauce
100 g (3½ oz/½ cup) crushed yellow rock sugar
4 star anise
3 cinnamon sticks
3 pieces dried tangerine peel
peanut oil, for deep-frying
2 tablespoons sesame oil

METHOD

Put the hock into a large pot and cover with 4 litres (16 cups) water. Bring to the boil, then reduce the heat and simmer for 30 minutes, skimming the surface regularly to remove any scum. Add the shaoxing, ginger and garlic and simmer for a further 30 minutes. Add the spring onions, soy sauces, sugar, star anise, cinnamon and tangerine peel, and simmer for 1½–2 hours more, or until the hock is tender. Remove the hock from the stock and leave both the hock and the stock to cool before refrigerating separately overnight.

The next day, skim the fat from the surface of the stock and return the stock to the stove. Bring to the boil and add the mushrooms.

Meanwhile, heat the oil in a wok or deep-fryer until smoking (180°C/350°F), and deep-fry the hock for 10 minutes, or until golden brown. Transfer the hock to the stock and simmer for a further 25 minutes, then remove with a slotted spoon and set aside. Increase the heat and boil the stock until it reduces to 500 ml (17 fl oz/2 cups), then add the sesame oil. Put the whole hock in a serving bowl and pour the stock over the top.

SHANGHAI-STYLE SALTED DUCK

This dish really involves curing the duck in brine, much like a sort of 'duck ham'. I first had this as part of a cold-cut plate in Shanghai and loved it. I use it in the restaurant in salads, sliced over some pickled cabbage and drizzled with chilli oil, or on its own with a chilli or dipping sauce.

A great cold-cut plate to have as a starter for 6–8 people would feature this duck, a master-stock chicken, tea eggs and some pickled cabbage. Just fry some wontons and have a couple of dipping sauces on the side and you're ready to serve.

1 x 2 kg (4 lb 8 oz) duck, wing tips and tail removed
600 g (1 lb 5 oz) salt
6 star anise
2 teaspoons Sichuan peppercorns, roasted
1 tablespoon shaoxing
2 spring onions (scallions), cut into 4 cm (1½ inch)
　　lengths
1 knob of ginger, peeled and sliced
fresh chilli sauce (page 44), to serve
hoisin sauce, to serve

METHOD

Put the salt, star anise, Sichuan peppercorns, shaoxing, spring onions, ginger and 7 litres water in a pot. Bring to the boil and simmer for 40 minutes to make the brine.

Wash the duck inside and out and pat dry with paper towel. Remove the fat from the cavity and pierce the skin all over with a fork. Lower the duck into the brine and simmer for 15 minutes. Remove from the heat and allow the duck to cool in the brine (you may need to put a plate on top of it to ensure it is completely submerged at all times). Transfer the pot to the fridge for 24 hours.

Lift the duck out of the brine, chop Chinese-style and serve cold with chilli sauce and hoisin sauce as accompaniments.

VARIATION

By all means, use duck breasts if you prefer — they're easier, but not quite as authentic. Place them in the boiling brine, cook for 2 minutes, remove from the heat and cover. Leave overnight to cure.

SIMMERED PORK WITH GARLIC DRESSING

Easy to prepare in advance, this is another great starter; just warm, dress and serve. Although garlicky, I'm sure you'll love it. You can also add some finely chopped ginger and wild green chillies to give it a real lift, or use pork hock or shoulder for something a little different.

Make sure that you gently simmer while braising so as not to dry out the meat. This doesn't have to be reheated either — it is cracking as a cold cut.

300 g (10½ oz) pork neck, cut into 2 pieces
1 teaspoon sea salt
1 knob of ginger, peeled and finely sliced
2 spring onions (scallions), cut into 5 cm (2 inch) lengths
1 small handful of coriander (cilantro) leaves, roughly chopped
1 long red chilli, deseeded and finely chopped

DRESSING
8 cloves garlic, finely chopped
2 tablespoons kecap manis
1 tablespoon cold fresh chicken stock (page 58)
2 teaspoons chilli oil
a pinch of sea salt

METHOD

Place the pork in a pot, cover with water and bring to the boil. Drain and rinse the pork, wipe the pot clean and return the pork to the pot. Add the sea salt, ginger and spring onions, cover with fresh water and bring to the boil. Reduce the heat to low and simmer gently for 1½ hours, or until the pork is tender. Drain the pork and leave to cool, then cover and refrigerate overnight.

Finely slice the pork and overlap the slices in a shallow heatproof bowl. Put the bowl in a large bamboo steamer over a pot or a wok of rapidly boiling water, cover with the lid and steam the pork until warm.

Mix the dressing ingredients, pour over the pork and top with coriander and chilli to serve.

VARIATIONS

This dressing is great with chicken; slice white-cut chicken, place in a bowl and steam until just warm, then drizzle with the dressing and add spring onion julienne.

You could also dress this pork with pickled cabbage dressing (page 54); I've used it before and it's absolutely fantastic. Once you have made that dressing, just add it to cold cuts or steamed fish and chicken — it really jazzes up a simple meal.

BRAISED SOY TOFU

This dish could easily sit in the stir-fry section, but I've put it in here as it's saucy and delicious. You can make this ahead of time, pour it into a sand or clay pot and heat it up later on. I've grown to love all sorts of tofu, from fresh to silken to this firmer one, perfect for a cold winter's night, or poured over rice when you feel like something light, tasty and delicious.

300 g (10½ oz) firm tofu, cut into 4 pieces
vegetable oil, for deep-frying
2 spring onions (scallions), cut into 4 cm (1½ inch) lengths
2 dried shiitake mushrooms, soaked in warm water for 30 minutes, stalks removed, cut in half on the diagonal through the middle
½ small carrot, finely sliced on the diagonal
½ pickled bamboo shoot, diced
4 dried black fungi, soaked in warm water for 15 minutes and torn into large pieces
1 tablespoon shaoxing
250 ml (9 fl oz/1 cup) fresh chicken stock (page 58)
2 tablespoons light soy sauce
1 teaspoon sugar

METHOD

Heat the vegetable oil in a wok or deep-fryer until smoking (180°C/350°F), and deep-fry the tofu until golden brown, then drain on paper towel. Carefully pour out the oil and wipe the wok clean.

Add another tablespoon of vegetable oil to the wok and heat until just smoking. Add the spring onions and shiitake mushrooms and stir-fry for 1 minute, then add the carrot, bamboo and black fungi and stir-fry for another minute. Deglaze the wok with the shaoxing, then add the stock, soy sauce and sugar and simmer for 5 minutes. Add the tofu, cover and braise for another 5 minutes, then serve.

VARIATIONS

For a little something extra, stir-fry some chicken or fish and add it to the sauce for the last couple of minutes of cooking time.

SPICY BEEF BRISKET BRAISE

A very simple braise, this relies on slow cooking and the wonderful flavour and kick of chilli bean paste.

400 g (14 oz) beef brisket, cleaned and cut into large
     chunks
4 tablespoons peanut oil
4 cloves garlic, chopped
3 tablespoons chopped ginger
3 tablespoons chilli bean paste
3 vine-ripened tomatoes, roughly diced
2 tablespoons shaoxing
2 tablespoons crushed yellow rock sugar
3 tablespoons yellow bean soy sauce
2 tablespoons oyster sauce
1 litre (35 fl oz/4 cups) fresh chicken stock (page 58)
a few drops of Chinkiang vinegar

METHOD

Place the brisket in a pot of cold water and bring to the boil. Once the scum comes to the top, drain the brisket and wash under cold water, then pat dry with paper towel.

Heat a wok until almost smoking. Add the peanut oil and, when hot, stir-fry the brisket until coloured, then remove from the wok. Add the garlic and ginger to the wok and stir-fry until fragrant. Add the chilli bean paste and, when the oil turns red, add the tomatoes. Add the shaoxing and cook for a further 2 minutes, then add the sugar, soy sauce, oyster sauce and chicken stock. Return the brisket to the wok and bring to the boil, then reduce to a gentle simmer and cook for 2 hours, or until tender. Remove the brisket, return the sauce to a rapid boil and reduce until thickened. Add a few drops of Chinkiang and pour the sauce over the brisket.

SWEET BLACK VINEGAR PORK BELLY

A bit like red braising, this is so delicious and so easy. The balance this time is between sweet and sour, creating a very alluring dish. If 'sweet and sour' makes you think of the red sauce you get in the average Chinese restaurant, this will change your mind forever about how good this dish can really be.

500 g (1 lb 2 oz) boneless pork belly, cut into 3 cm
   (1½ inch) thick pieces across the grain
½ teaspoon sea salt
¼ teaspoon sugar
½ teaspoon shaoxing
2 teaspoons light soy sauce
2½ tablespoons peanut oil
60 g (2¼ oz/⅓ cup) soft brown sugar
4 tablespoons Chinkiang vinegar
finely sliced spring onion (scallion), to serve
roasted sesame seeds, to serve

METHOD

Mix together ¼ teaspoon of the sea salt, the sugar, shaoxing, soy sauce and ½ tablespoon of the peanut oil, add the pork and leave to marinate for at least 2 hours, or overnight. Remove the pork from the marinade and pat dry with paper towel.

Heat a wok until smoking. Add the remaining oil and, when hot, stir-fry the pork in batches for about 4 minutes, turning occasionally, until well coloured on all sides. Return all the pork to the wok and add the brown sugar, vinegar, remaining salt and 375 ml (13 fl oz/1½ cups) water. Bring to the boil and then reduce to a low simmer. Cover and cook for 1–1½ hours, or until the pork is very tender. If the sauce is a little thin, remove the pork from the sauce and return the wok to the heat. Boil until it has a syrupy consistency, then pour over the pork. Sprinkle with the sliced spring onion and sesame seeds.

VARIATIONS

You can also make this dish with spare ribs; there is something nice about chewing the meat off the bone. Try substituting chicken drumsticks or wings for the pork — you just need to cut the cooking time in half.

BRAISED MUD CRAB WITH GLASS NOODLES

This is a great last-minute braise with a wonderful flavour. The noodles soak up the crab juices and you can suck the crab right out of the shell.

1 x 1 kg (2 lb 4 oz) live mud crab
250 g (9 oz) glass noodles
1 small handful of coriander (cilantro) leaves, chopped
2 spring onions (scallions), cut into julienne

SPICE PASTE
4 dried red chillies
1 tablespoon white peppercorns
1 tablespoon coriander seeds
2 coriander (cilantro) roots, scraped and chopped
3 tablespoons finely chopped ginger
5 cloves garlic, finely chopped
1 teaspoon sea salt
1 teaspoon Thai shrimp paste, wrapped in foil and
    roasted until fragrant

STOCK
250 ml (9 fl oz/1 cup) fresh chicken stock (page 58)
100 ml (3½ fl oz) oyster sauce
100 ml (3½ fl oz) light soy sauce
100 ml (3½ fl oz) shaoxing
100 ml (3½ fl oz) Chinkiang vinegar
½ teaspoon sesame oil
115 g (4 oz) sugar

METHOD

Kill the mud crab humanely (see overleaf for instructions), pull off the top shell, discard the grey gills and wash. Pull off the claws, chop the body in half and crack the shell on the claws with the back of a cleaver. Soak the noodles in warm water for 5 minutes, then drain well.

To make the spice paste, place the chillies in a dry heavy-based frying pan and roast until blackened, then grind to a powder. Roast the peppercorns and coriander seeds until fragrant, then crush in a mortar with a pestle. Add the rest of the paste ingredients to the mortar and pound until you form a coarse paste.

Boil the stock ingredients for 1 minute, then add the paste and cook for another minute. Put the noodles and crab in a wok, pour over the broth, bring to the boil and cover. Cook over medium heat for 8 minutes, or until the crab is cooked. Arrange in a bowl and top with the coriander and spring onions.

HOW TO KILL A CRAB

Remove any wrapping (not the string) from your crab and place it in the freezer. This puts the crab to sleep and is the most humane way of dealing with it — it may take up to 2½ hours. When your crab is asleep, cut off the string.

Wear an apron and gloves if you wish. Take the crab and turn it upside down in your sink (juice will come out so it is definitely best to do this in the sink). Pull up the 'V' shaped flap at the back and carefully lift off the whole top shell. Remove the lungs by scraping them off with a spoon, knife or your fingers and, under running water, rinse out the guts and rinse the head. It is very important to remove all the lungs and clean the head thoroughly. Snap off the flap, then chop the crab in half by placing the base of a large chef's knife against the crab and pressing down on the knife with the palm of your hand, cutting firmly through the crab.

When done, clean out any remaining internal organs. Use the same cutting action to cut each half in two, cutting between the claw and the legs. With the back of a meat mallet or a knife steel, crack the claws a couple of times from the nippers down to the elbow and what I call the forearm. Remove any excess cartilage from around the head.

BLACK BEAN CHICKEN STEW

This is one of the easiest dishes ever — by the time the sauce has reduced, the chicken is cooked. You could make this in advance and gently reheat it when you're ready to serve.

450 g (1 lb) free-range or organic chicken thigh fillets,
    skin on, halved
2 tablespoons fermented black beans
1 tablespoon shaoxing
2 teaspoons light soy sauce
4 tablespoons vegetable oil
4 red shallots, finely chopped
1 long red chilli, finely sliced
1 clove garlic, finely chopped
250 ml (9 fl oz/1 cup) fresh chicken stock (page 58)
1 teaspoon oyster sauce
½ teaspoon sugar
1 spring onion (scallion), cut into julienne

METHOD

Soak the black beans in shaoxing for 20 minutes, and marinate the chicken pieces in half of the soy sauce for 20 minutes.

Heat a wok until smoking. Add half of the oil and, when hot, stir-fry the chicken pieces until browned, then remove from the wok.

Heat the remaining oil in the wok until just smoking, then stir-fry the black beans, shallots, chilli and garlic until fragrant. Add the stock, remaining soy sauce, oyster sauce, sugar and chicken pieces, and cook over high heat until the sauce reduces enough to coat the chicken. Spoon into a bowl and sprinkle with the spring onion to serve.

SPICY BEEF SHORT RIBS

These ribs are first roasted to give them colour and render some of the fat, then it's just a matter of making the sauce and braising the beef gently until tender. For such a simple recipe, it has all the great qualities of a well-braised dish: deep flavour and tender melting beef, with an added complexity and deep rich taste from the Korean bean paste. This was a favourite at the bar at XO; you could have ribs, a cold beer and some rice and have a lip-smacking good time.

1 kg (2 lb 4 oz) beef short ribs
3 tablespoons vegetable oil
1 knob of ginger, peeled and finely sliced
10 cloves garlic, finely sliced
a pinch of sea salt
125 ml (4 fl oz/½ cup) shaoxing
5 ripe tomatoes, roughly chopped
115 g (4 oz/½ cup) sugar
1½ tablespoons Korean bean paste
1½ tablespoons oyster sauce
125 ml (4 fl oz/½ cup) mushroom soy sauce
125 ml (4 fl oz/½ cup) tamarind water (page 32)
1 litre (35 fl oz/4 cups) fresh chicken stock (page 58)

METHOD

Preheat the oven to 200°C (400°F/Gas 6). Put the ribs on a baking tray and roast for about 1 hour, or until golden brown.

Heat the wok until smoking. Add the oil and, when hot, add the ginger, garlic and sea salt and stir-fry until fragrant. Deglaze the wok with the shaoxing, then add the tomato and simmer until the tomato breaks down. Stir in the sugar and cook for about 5 minutes, allowing the sugar to caramelise a little. Stir in the bean paste, oyster sauce, soy sauce and tamarind water. Add the ribs to the wok, cover with the chicken stock and stir together. Simmer, covered, for 2 hours, or until the ribs are tender. Remove the lid and skim off any impurities. Remove the ribs, increase the heat and simmer until the sauce reduces and thickens. Pour the sauce over the ribs to serve.

VARIATIONS

You could easily roast four duck legs for 30 minutes, then separate the thigh and drumstick and braise them in the sauce for an hour. Chicken drumsticks would also be good, as would pork spare ribs.

BRAISED DUCK LEGS IN SOY SAUCE

Another versatile dish, this can be served as a cold cut or hot with its broth and some fresh ginger and spring onion julienne. Chicken legs could also be used.

4 duck legs
6 cloves garlic, finely chopped
1 small knob of galangal, roughly chopped
1 teaspoon sea salt
1 teaspoon five-spice powder
1 teaspoon sugar
2 tablespoons dark soy sauce
fresh chilli sauce (page 44), to serve

METHOD

Pound half of the garlic, the galangal, sea salt and five-spice powder in a mortar with a pestle to form a fine paste. Rub the duck legs with the paste and leave to marinate for 2 hours.

Dry-fry the sugar in a hot wok until it melts. Add the remaining garlic, soy sauce and duck legs and toss together, then add 1 litre (35 fl oz/4 cups) water. Cover the wok and simmer for 20 minutes, stirring occasionally to make sure that the duck doesn't stick to the bottom of the wok. Remove from the heat and allow the duck to cool in the stock. Lift the duck out of the stock and chop each leg into three pieces with a heavy cleaver. Serve the chopped duck with fresh chilli sauce, or reheat and serve with some of the cooking broth.

STEAMING

Steaming is a beautiful, gentle way to cook most ingredients, especially seafood. The Chinese technique of steaming is great for keeping food moist and creating light sauces with a very natural taste. It's simple: you just have to have a steamer that is large enough to hold a bowl or plate, and the food is usually steamed in a light broth or with its seasonings.

So first things first: the steamer. You can buy a metal steamer with a base, a lid and as many steamer trays as you like (normally up to two or three layers works well), or you can buy a bamboo steamer and fit it over a pot or a wok filled with boiling water. Another alternative is to place two or three chopsticks in a wok and place a bowl on top of the chopsticks — cover the wok and presto, an instant steamer.

This is one of the times I like to use an electric wok. Have it simmering away with water and place a bamboo steamer on it to free up lots of stove space. I also like to get two bamboo steamers and, with scissors, cut the bottom out of one — this allows me to place a bowl with a lid in the steamer and get enough height to place a steamer lid on top. This works especially well with double-steamed soups and long steamed braises. It is very simple and convenient; the bamboo steamers are cheap and you can go straight from the steamer to the table.

The following dishes are simple steamed dishes that are easy to make, taste great and follow the classic technique. Remember to taste and look for balance as you go. Master them, try some of the variations and soon you'll be able to cruise through any of the steamed dishes in the second section of the book.

Take care when you're steaming; water is a great conductor of heat and you can easily burn yourself. When you lift the lid, let the steam dissipate first before checking if your dish is ready.

SICHUAN-STYLE STEAMED BEEF

This dish is easy but a real show stopper. For extra effect, cook it in a bamboo steamer that you can take straight to the table. I love the texture of the rice-coated beef. Having a steamed dish as part of a shared table will really take the pressure off you in the kitchen as they're generally easy to prepare.

450 g (1 lb) sirloin steak, cut into thin strips
200 g (7 oz/½ cup) ground roast rice (page 27)
1 tablespoon chopped coriander (cilantro) leaves
2 spring onions (scallions), chopped
2 teaspoons sesame oil

MARINADE
1 tablespoon dark soy sauce
1 tablespoon fermented black beans
2 tablespoons shaoxing
1 tablespoon hot bean paste
½ teaspoon Sichuan peppercorns, crushed
1 tablespoon peanut oil

METHOD

To make the marinade, mix together the soy sauce, black beans, shaoxing, bean paste, peppercorns and peanut oil. Add the steak and leave for 30 minutes.

Add the ground roast rice and mix to coat the steak well, then stir in 4 tablespoons water. Put the steak strips, in a single layer, directly onto the slotted base of a large bamboo steamer, cover with the lid and steam for 20 minutes. Sprinkle the coriander and spring onions over the steak and steam for another minute.

Remove from the heat. You can transfer to a plate or serve directly from the bamboo steamer, drizzled with the sesame oil.

STEAMED LEMON CHICKEN

This steamed dish captures the natural flavour of chicken and is, of course, very very easy. The combination of lemon, oyster sauce and a pinch of white pepper is heaven. These light flavours are also great with all manner of seafood, and delightful with pork.

350 g (12 oz) free-range or organic chicken thigh fillets,
    skin on, each cut into 3 pieces
1½ lemons, quartered lengthways
a pinch of freshly ground white pepper
2 spring onions (scallions), cut into julienne

MARINADE
1 tablespoon shaoxing
1½ tablespoons light soy sauce
1½ tablespoons oyster sauce
2 teaspoons sesame oil
1 tablespoon peanut oil
2 teaspoons sea salt
1 tablespoon sugar

METHOD

Place the chicken in a shallow heatproof bowl and squeeze the juice from the lemons over the top, then add the lemon skins to the bowl as well. Add all the marinade ingredients to the bowl, mix thoroughly and leave for 30 minutes.

Cover the bowl tightly with foil and place in a large bamboo steamer over a pot or a wok of rapidly boiling water. Put the lid on and steam the chicken for 25 minutes, removing the lid and foil to turn the chicken once during this time.

Turn off the heat and carefully remove the bowl from the steamer. Remove the foil and sprinkle with the pepper and spring onions to serve.

STEAMED CHICKEN WITH LILY BUDS

What could be easier than this great self-saucing dish? You'll find that these sorts of dishes cook themselves and leave you free to get on and make a stir-fry, so that every novice Asian cook can put together a simple and delicious shared table.

350 g (12 oz) free-range or organic chicken thigh fillets,
   skin on, cut into bite-sized pieces
15 g (½ oz) dried lily buds, soaked in warm water for
   30 minutes
6 dried shiitake mushrooms, soaked in warm water for
   30 minutes, stalks removed, cut in half on the
   diagonal through the middle
a pinch of Sichuan pepper

SEASONING
½ knob of ginger, peeled and finely sliced
2 teaspoons oyster sauce
1 teaspoon soy sauce
1 teaspoon shaoxing
1 teaspoon peanut oil

METHOD

Remove the hard stems from the lily buds and tie each one into a knot.

Mix together the chicken and the seasoning ingredients in a bowl and marinate for 20 minutes. Add the lily buds and mushrooms and mix well. Place in a heatproof bowl and put the bowl in a bamboo steamer. Steam over high heat for about 25 minutes, or until cooked. Remove the bowl from the steamer, spoon the chicken onto a plate, pour any juices over the top and give it a pinch of Sichuan pepper.

VARIATION

This seasoning helps to lift the natural flavour of anything. You could substitute fish fillets for the chicken, or use other seafood and it would be just as beautiful.

STEAMED SIMPLE DUCK

The only difficult thing about this dish is finding a bowl large enough for the duck, and a steamer that will fit the whole lot. Other than that, this is the simplest duck dish I know; the flesh is meltingly tender after long, gentle cooking. Also delicious served at room temperature or even cold, with some chilli dipping sauce, it's a good dish to add to a shared table.

1 x 2 kg (4 lb 8 oz) duck, wing tips and tail removed
2 spring onions (scallions), cut into julienne
1 long red chilli, cut into julienne
fresh chilli sauce (page 44), to serve

SEASONING
1 teaspoon sugar
1 teaspoon sea salt
125 ml (4 fl oz/½ cup) shaoxing
3 slices of peeled ginger
3 spring onions (scallions)
375 ml (13 fl oz/1½ cups) fresh chicken stock (page 58)

METHOD

Remove the fat from the cavity of the duck. Put the duck in a large pot of rapidly boiling water and cook for 5 minutes. Remove, drain and put the duck in a shallow heatproof bowl.

Mix the seasoning ingredients together and pour over the duck. Put the bowl with the duck in a large bamboo steamer over a pot or a wok of boiling water, cover with the lid and steam gently for 3 hours. Carefully lift out the duck and drain. Chop the duck Chinese-style and arrange on a plate.

Skim any fat from the stock and discard the ginger and spring onion. Put a third of the stock in a small pot and bring to the boil, then pour over the duck. Scatter the spring onions and chilli on top of the duck and serve with the chilli sauce.

WHOLE STEAMED SNAPPER WITH GINGER & SPRING ONION

This is simpler than you think; you can buy any whole fish you like and treat it in this manner. The flavours of the fish are naturally enhanced by the seasoning, and the searing of the spring onions with peanut oil gives a great fragrance and adds a delicious complexity of flavour that supports the delicate fish. The scoring on the fish ensures that the thicker body cooks as quickly as the thinner tail section and also makes it much easier to see when the flesh is cooked.

500–600 g (1 lb 2 oz–1 lb 5 oz) whole snapper, scaled and
  gutted
1 Chinese cabbage (wombok) leaf
3 spring onions (scallions), trimmed
1 teaspoon sea salt
125 ml (4 fl oz/½ cup) fresh chicken stock (page 58)
2 tablespoons light soy sauce
1 tablespoon sesame oil
1 tablespoon shaoxing
1 tablespoon sugar
1 large knob of ginger, peeled and cut into julienne
4 spring onions (scallions), cut into julienne
3 tablespoons peanut oil
1 large handful of coriander (cilantro) leaves

METHOD

Pat the fish dry with paper towel. With a sharp knife, make three diagonal cuts in the thickest part of the fish, then do the same in the other direction to make a diamond pattern. Do the same on the other side. Put the cabbage leaf and the whole spring onions in a shallow heatproof bowl that will take the fish comfortably and fit into the steamer. Rub the fish with salt and lay on top of the spring onions. Mix the stock, soy sauce, sesame oil, shaoxing and sugar and pour this over the fish, then top with the ginger. Put the bowl in the steamer over a pot or a wok of rapidly boiling water, cover with the lid and steam for 10–15 minutes (the time will vary depending on the circulation of steam). The fish should be just setting on the bone, exposed by the diagonal cuts. Be careful not to overcook the fish as it will cook a little more when you pour on the oil at the end. Remove the bowl from the steamer and scatter with the spring onion julienne. Heat the peanut oil in a small pot until it is just smoking, then douse the fish with the hot oil — be careful, it will spit! Top with the coriander and serve immediately.

STEAMED KING PRAWNS

Quick and easy — the most important thing about this dish is to get good-quality prawns. You could use chopped lobster or crab for this if you really wanted to spoil your dinner guests.

12 green king prawns (shrimp), peeled and deveined with
　　tails left intact
1 spring onion (scallion), chopped
a pinch of freshly ground white pepper
1 tablespoon chopped coriander (cilantro) leaves

MARINADE
2 tablespoons light soy sauce
2 coriander (cilantro) roots, scraped and chopped
2 red shallots, finely sliced
2 cloves garlic, finely chopped
1 teaspoon finely chopped ginger
2 teaspoons oyster sauce
1 long red chilli, deseeded and finely chopped
1 tablespoon sugar
2 tablespoons peanut oil
1 tablespoon shaoxing

METHOD

Put the prawns in a large shallow heatproof bowl. Mix the marinade ingredients together with 2 tablespoons water and pour over the prawns.

Put the bowl in a large bamboo steamer over a pot or a wok of rapidly boiling water, cover with the lid and steam for about 8 minutes, or until just cooked through. Sprinkle with the spring onion, pepper and coriander to serve.

STEAMED BLUE EYE WITH BLACK BEANS

The flavours of this dish are similar to the steamed snapper with ginger and spring onion, except that the introduction of black beans really kicks the intensity along. When I'm cooking this at home, I often add a few chopped red chillies to really spark things up. I know that a lot of cookbooks advise you to wash the black beans, but I believe it takes away too much of their flavour. Again though, look for balance — if this is too strong for you, just add fewer beans. As an easy steamed dish this fits well with a braise and a stir-fry to create a wonderful shared table.

300 g (10½ oz) blue eye fillet, cut into 2 pieces
2 tablespoons fermented black beans, chopped
2 spring onions (scallions), trimmed and halved
1 tablespoon light soy sauce
1 teaspoon sugar
1 teaspoon sesame oil
2 teaspoons shaoxing
3 tablespoons peanut oil

METHOD

Put the spring onions in a large shallow heatproof bowl and place the fish on top. Combine the black beans, soy sauce, sugar, sesame oil and shaoxing and pour over the fish. Put the bowl in a large bamboo steamer over a pot or a wok of rapidly boiling water, cover with the lid and steam for 7–8 minutes, until the fish is just cooked through. Carefully remove the bowl from the steamer.

Heat the peanut oil in a small pot until just smoking and douse the fish with the hot oil before serving.

VARIATIONS

Prawns and scallops are great with this sauce, but you could use any fish you like. I sometimes cook large Pacific oysters this way as well; they make a great starter for a grand gathering. Of course, if you really want to spoil your guests, split a lobster or chop up a mud crab — that would turn your meal into a royal banquet.

Chicken thighs and pork spare ribs also go well with this sauce. As a matter of fact, it goes well with just about anything!

STEAMED WHOLE MUD CRAB WITH BLACK BEAN & CHILLI DRESSING

I created this sauce back in 1984 at the Blue Water Grill in Bondi. I love it because all you do is steam the crab, toss it with the dressing, some spring onions and coriander, and you have a majestic dish. I love the saltiness of the black beans and I like using the Korean bean paste to give it a deep, rich almost smoky flavour. This sauce is stunning with all sorts of other seafood as well: drizzle it over steamed lobster, scallops, mussels or clams.

1 x 1–1.5 kg (2 lb 4 oz–3 lb 5 oz) live mud crab
90 g (3¼ oz/1 bunch) coriander (cilantro) leaves
2 spring onions (scallions), cut into julienne

BLACK BEAN & CHILLI DRESSING
2½ tablespoons peanut oil
1 large knob of ginger, peeled and cut into julienne
1 Spanish onion, cut into 2 cm (¾ inch) cubes
150 g (5½ oz) fermented black beans, unwashed and lightly crushed
1 red capsicum (pepper), deseeded and cut into 2 cm (¾ inch) squares
4 tablespoons Korean bean paste
500 ml (17 fl oz/2 cups) sake
250 ml (9 fl oz/1 cup) mirin
125 ml (4 fl oz/½ cup) rice vinegar
1½ tablespoons sesame oil

METHOD

To make the black bean and chilli dressing, heat a wok until smoking. Add the peanut oil and, when hot, stir-fry the ginger and onion for a few minutes. Add the black beans, capsicum and bean paste and stir for a minute. Add the sake, mirin, vinegar and sesame oil and simmer for 30 minutes, or until the mixture has reduced by about a third.

Kill the crab humanely, pull off the top shell and clean well (see page 96 for instructions). Pull off the claws, chop the body in half and crack the hard shell on the claws with the back of a cleaver.

Place the crab in a bamboo steamer and steam for 8 minutes. The flesh should be white and firm when done. Remove the crab from the steamer and place in a bowl. Pour on the dressing, sprinkle with the coriander and spring onions and toss to coat the crab.

THREE VEGETABLES STEAMED

This can be prepared, arranged in a nice bowl and then set aside to be finished off just before you're ready to serve.

8 green asparagus spears

6 baby bok choy (pak choy), halved lengthways and rinsed

6 dried shiitake mushrooms, soaked in warm water for 30 minutes, stalks removed, cut in half on the diagonal through the middle

125 ml (4 fl oz/½ cup) fresh chicken stock (page 58)

½ teaspoon sea salt

½ teaspoon sesame oil

METHOD

Blanch the asparagus in boiling salted water for 2 minutes then refresh in iced water. Blanch the bok choy in the same water for 1 minute then refresh in the iced water.

Arrange the asparagus, bok choy and mushrooms in a large shallow heatproof bowl. Put the bowl in a large bamboo steamer over a pot or a wok of rapidly boiling water, cover with the lid and steam for 5 minutes. Remove from the steamer.

Heat the stock and salt in a small pot until boiling, add the sesame oil and pour over the vegetables to serve.

STIR-FRYING

Stir-frying is an important technique to master for Asian cooking. Achievable at home, it's a fast, simple way of creating delicious dishes. The wok is the centre point of stir-frying, but don't worry if you have an electric stove or heat issues; there are ways around this. With a heavy, flat-bottomed pan on the largest element, you should have enough heat to stir-fry successfully.

There are a few different ways to stir-fry and you'll see ingredients added in different orders depending on the book. For instance, some will tell you to add the garlic and ginger to the oil at the start — this flavours the oil for you to then add the meat or seafood. This is the way most commercial kitchens would do it. However, I feel that it is always best to add the aromatics to the oil just before making the sauce, and the reason is simple; the garlic, ginger and perhaps spring onion will quite often burn while the meat or seafood is cooking. This, along with not getting the wok hot enough, is the home cook's biggest problem.

So my simple rules are... protein first, vegetables second, season the oil, make the sauce, add the rest back in and toss together. Be organised: have your food cut and near the wok, heat the wok or pan, and most importantly, don't overload the wok and kill the heat. That's my recipe for being a happy little stir-fryer.

So the golden rules of stir-frying my way are:

1. Have all your preparation ready and your ingredients in the order in which you are going to add them to the wok — that way you won't have to keep checking the recipe.
2. Heat the wok to almost smoking.
3. Add the oil and get it really hot.
4. Add whatever protein you are using, making sure you don't add too much and stop the heat (most recipes are cooked in two batches in this book). When the protein is three-quarters of the way cooked (and this is very important as you'll finish it in the sauce later), remove it to a bowl next to the wok and cook the second batch.
5. Reheat the wok and add the vegetables, again, in batches.
6. Add the aromatics and flavour the oil.
7. Deglaze with shaoxing wine.
8. Add any other sauces and the stock and reduce down.
9. Return all of the ingredients to the wok and fold through.
10. Serve and enjoy!

FILLET OF BEEF WITH GINGER & SPRING ONION

This is probably the simplest stir-fry you can make, so it is a great recipe to perfect. Remember to keep the heat up and not to overcook the beef as you fold it into the sauce at the end; three-quarters cooked on the first fry is plenty.

350 g (12 oz) beef fillet, finely sliced across the grain
250 ml (9 fl oz/1 cup) peanut oil
1 knob of ginger, peeled and finely sliced
3 spring onions (scallions), cut into 4 cm (1½ inch) lengths
1 teaspoon shaoxing
1 tablespoon light soy sauce
1 tablespoon oyster sauce
3 tablespoons fresh chicken stock (page 58)
MARINADE
1 tablespoon light soy sauce
1 teaspoon sugar
1 tablespoon peanut oil

METHOD

To make the marinade, mix together the soy sauce, sugar and peanut oil. Add the beef and leave for 15 minutes, then drain.

Heat a wok until just smoking (180°C/350°F). Add the peanut oil and, when hot, deep-fry the beef in batches until golden, then remove and drain on paper towel. Pour all but 1 tablespoon of oil from the wok, then reheat until just smoking. Add the ginger and spring onions and stir-fry until fragrant, then deglaze the wok with the shaoxing. Return the beef to the wok with the soy sauce, oyster sauce and chicken stock, bring to the boil and toss together.

VARIATION

You can easily substitute chicken, pork or seafood for the beef in this classic stir-fry. By the same token, you can add your favourite vegetables to make it more substantial... bok choy, asparagus, beans, baby corn or spinach would be good by themselves or in combination. Stir-fry the vegetables after the meat, then remove, make the sauce, and return the meat and vegetables to the wok to coat.

STIR-FRIED BEEF WITH ASPARAGUS & MUSHROOMS

This is a classic stir-fry that starts with marinating the beef. Marinating tenderises and adds more flavour to the meat. You could also, if pinched for time, not marinate and just add the sauces at the end. This is also good with other vegetables — beans, snow peas or zucchini — and chicken, pork or seafood. Just follow the rules: meat, vegetable, aromatics, deglaze, sauce, fold through and serve.

This is the simplest beef stir-fry with vegetables in the book, but I know it is one you will come back to time and time again.

350 g (12 oz) beef fillet, cut into 2 cm (¾ inch) slices
2 tablespoons oyster sauce
4 tablespoons light soy sauce
4 tablespoons vegetable oil
6 thick green asparagus spears, cut on the diagonal into
    4 cm (1½ inch) lengths
50 g (1¾ oz) fresh shiitake mushrooms, stalks removed,
    sliced
1 knob of ginger, peeled and cut into julienne
2 cloves garlic, finely chopped
3 spring onions (scallions), cut into 4 cm (1½ inch)
    lengths
3 tablespoons shaoxing
1 teaspoon crushed yellow rock sugar
3 tablespoons fresh chicken stock (page 58)
freshly ground black pepper

METHOD

Mix together half of the oyster sauce, all but 1 tablespoon of the soy sauce and the beef and marinate for 1–2 hours.

Heat a wok until just smoking. Add half the oil and, when hot, stir-fry the beef in batches until well browned and then remove. Add the asparagus to the wok and stir-fry until just tender, then add the mushrooms, stir-fry for 30 seconds more and remove.

Add the rest of the oil to the wok and, when just smoking, add the ginger, garlic and spring onions and stir-fry until fragrant. Deglaze the wok with the shaoxing, then add the sugar, stock, remaining soy and oyster sauces and simmer until the liquid reduces and thickens. Return the beef and vegetables to the wok and cook for another minute to allow the flavours to mingle. Spoon onto a large plate and give it a good grind of black pepper to serve.

BLACK PEPPER BEEF

Simple and delicious, this relies on the freshness of the peppercorns, so buy small amounts regularly and crush them just before you're going to cook with them. I'm very fond of this dish with a bowl of rice and some steamed vegetables as a delicious dinner for two.

350 g (12 oz) beef fillet, thickly sliced across the grain
2 tablespoons vegetable oil
1 small Spanish onion, diced
1 red capsicum (pepper), diced
2 long red chillies, finely chopped
2 garlic cloves, finely chopped
2 teaspoons black peppercorns, crushed
3 tablespoons fresh chicken stock (page 58)
2 teaspoons light soy sauce
1 tablespoon oyster sauce

MARINADE
2 teaspoons shaoxing
1 teaspoon kecap manis
1 teaspoon oyster sauce

METHOD

To make the marinade, mix the shaoxing, kecap manis and oyster sauce. Add the beef and toss until well coated, then leave for 20 minutes.

Heat a wok until just smoking. Add half the oil and, when hot, stir-fry the beef in batches until well browned, then remove. Add the remaining oil to the wok and stir-fry the onion, capsicum, chilli, garlic and pepper until fragrant. Return the beef to the wok with the stock, soy and oyster sauces and stir-fry until the sauce reduces slightly.

VARIATIONS

As with all these dishes, chicken, pork or even lamb could easily be substituted for the beef. Another amazing dish would be to stir-fry some chopped lobster or a mud crab with this pepper sauce; I love seafood with pepper.

STIR-FRIED CHILLI PORK

Here again, marinating adds flavour and helps tenderise the meat even more. With this one I've introduced chilli powder and Sichuan pepper to add a little heat and complexity. You can add any vegetables to make this a meal for two with rice — I really like snake beans or snow peas.

350 g (12 oz) pork fillet, finely sliced across the grain
3 tablespoons peanut oil
6 long red chillies, halved lengthways and deseeded
4 cloves garlic, finely chopped
1 teaspoon chilli powder
½ teaspoon Sichuan pepper
3 tablespoons fresh chicken stock (page 58)
1 tablespoon light soy sauce
2 tablespoons crushed yellow rock sugar

MARINADE
1 tablespoon light soy sauce
2 tablespoons shaoxing
a pinch of sea salt
2 teaspoons sesame oil

METHOD

To make the marinade, mix together the soy sauce, shaoxing, sea salt and sesame oil. Add the pork, toss to coat and leave for 30 minutes.

Heat a wok until just smoking. Add the peanut oil and, when hot, stir-fry the pork and chillies until the pork is well browned, then remove. Reheat the wok and stir-fry the garlic, chilli powder and Sichuan pepper for 30 seconds, then add the stock, soy sauce and sugar and return the pork and chillies to the wok. Cook for another minute for the flavours to mingle. To serve, transfer everything but the sauce to a large plate. Leave the sauce on the heat and allow it to reduce slightly, then pour over the pork before serving.

VARIATION

I like this stir-fry with prawns or slices of fish instead of the pork.

STIR-FRIED PORK FILLET WITH CHILLI & BLACK FUNGI

Very simple and very straightforward, this is a classic stir-fry that will work well with beef, chicken and even some fish pieces. If you can't get fresh black fungi, use dried; just soak them for 30 minutes before use. Or, if both prove difficult to find, use fresh shiitake or oyster mushrooms. The salted chillies add an interesting flavour but, by all means, use hot bean paste.

300 g (10½ oz) pork fillet, sliced into thin strips
100 ml (3½ fl oz) peanut oil
1 large clove garlic, finely sliced
1 tablespoon julienned ginger
1 small Spanish onion, finely sliced
1 small handful of black fungi, torn into pieces
2 tablespoons chopped salted chillies (page 49)
2 tablespoons shaoxing
1 tablespoon light soy sauce
½ teaspoon sugar
1 spring onion (scallion), cut into julienne

METHOD

Heat a wok until just smoking. Add 3 tablespoons of the peanut oil to the wok and, when hot, add the meat in two batches, stir-frying until almost cooked but still pink. Remove the pork and pour off any excess oil.

Reheat the wok until almost smoking and add the remaining 2 tablespoons of peanut oil, then add the garlic, ginger and onion and stir-fry until fragrant. Add the black fungi and salted chillies and continue to stir-fry for a couple of seconds more. Add the shaoxing, soy sauce and the sugar and return the pork to the wok. Stir until heated through, then spoon the pork onto a plate and sprinkle with spring onion. Leave the sauce on the heat and allow it to reduce a little and thicken, then pour over the pork before serving.

STIR-FRIED SNAPPER WITH ASPARAGUS, SNOW PEAS & ENOKI MUSHROOMS

This is a lovely dish, both in colour and texture. Just be sure not to overcook the fish. If enoki mushrooms are hard to find just substitute sliced fresh shiitake mushrooms.

350 g (12 oz) snapper fillet, cut into 2 cm (¾ inch) wide
    strips
6 thick green asparagus spears, cut on the diagonal into
    4 cm (1½ inch) lengths
50 g (1¾ oz) snow peas (mangetout), trimmed
80 g (2¾ oz) enoki mushrooms, trimmed and separated
4 tablespoons peanut oil
½ knob of ginger, peeled and finely chopped
2 cloves garlic, finely chopped
2 spring onions (scallions), finely chopped
1 long red chilli, deseeded and finely chopped
3 tablespoons fresh chicken stock (page 58)
2 tablespoons oyster sauce
2 teaspoons light soy sauce
1 teaspoon sugar

METHOD

Heat a wok until smoking. Add half the peanut oil and, when hot, stir-fry the snapper in two batches until golden and just cooked through, then remove. Wipe the wok clean.

Heat the remaining oil in the wok until just smoking. Stir-fry the ginger, garlic, spring onions and chilli until fragrant, then add the asparagus and snow peas and stir-fry until just tender. Return the snapper to the wok with the chicken stock, oyster sauce, soy sauce and sugar, toss together and bring to the boil. Fold in the enoki mushrooms and spoon onto a large plate to serve.

VARIATION

Any fresh large-flaked fish would be good here, as would prawns or scallops. The dish really highlights the natural flavour of the fish and vegetables.

STIR-FRIED BLUE EYE WITH BEAN SPROUTS & XO SAUCE

This really simple dish relies on the touch of XO at the end to give it a really great flavour. You can make your own XO, which is pretty easy, or there are some reasonable ones you can buy off the shelf. Or you could use Korean bean paste or chilli paste instead; the result would be just as delicious. Just concentrate on not overcooking the fish in its first visit to the wok.

350 g (12 oz) blue eye fillet, cut into bite-sized pieces
2 cloves garlic, finely chopped
1 tablespoon yellow bean soy sauce
¼ teaspoon sesame oil
½ teaspoon sugar
1 teaspoon sea salt
¼ teaspoon freshly ground white pepper
1 tablespoon shaoxing
2 tablespoons vegetable oil
2 spring onions (scallions), cut into 2 cm (¾ inch) lengths
4 tablespoons XO sauce (page 47)
100 g (3½ oz) bean sprouts, trimmed

METHOD

Mix together the garlic, soy sauce, sesame oil, sugar, sea salt, pepper and half the shaoxing in a bowl. Add the blue eye and toss to coat.

Heat a wok until just smoking. Add the vegetable oil and, when hot, add the blue eye and stir-fry until golden and just undercooked, then remove. Deglaze the wok with the remaining shaoxing, then add the spring onions and the XO sauce. Stir-fry for 30 seconds and fold in the bean sprouts to serve.

VARIATION

This stir-fry is great with scallops or prawns.

STIR-FRIED ZUCCHINI

This is a great stir-fry when you're just starting as the zucchini are easy to handle in the wok and much harder to overcook than fish or meat. Make sure you have enough heat to get some colour on the zucchini. You can, of course, not add the dried shrimp, but they do add a nice complexity of flavour that isn't really fishy — I would try it at least once before you change the recipe.

600 g (1 lb 5 oz) zucchini (courgettes), thickly sliced on
    the diagonal
2 tablespoons vegetable oil
2 spring onions (scallions), cut into 4 cm (1½ inch)
    lengths
1 clove garlic, finely sliced
1 tablespoon dried shrimp, soaked in warm water for
    20 minutes
250 ml (9 fl oz/1 cup) fresh chicken stock (page 58)
a pinch of sea salt
2 teaspoons sesame oil

METHOD

Heat a wok until just smoking. Add the vegetable oil and, when hot, add the zucchini and stir-fry until it begins to colour. Then add the spring onions and garlic and stir-fry until fragrant. Add the shrimp, stock and salt, bring to the boil, and then reduce the heat and simmer until the sauce has reduced and thickened slightly. Stir in the sesame oil to serve.

VARIATION

This is a great basic recipe for any vegetable, so if you like beans, bok choy, Chinese broccoli or asparagus, feel free to use them instead of the zucchini; a combination can be great as well.

CLASSIC FRIED RICE

Fried rice is a great thing to make with left-over rice, so make sure you always cook more rice than you need and keep it in the fridge or freezer. This is so simple but utterly delicious. The key is not to use freshly cooked rice — it sticks together easily and soaks up too much of the flavouring. You can add anything you like, or take stuff away, depending on what suits your mood or what you can get your hands on. I use two types of soy here, as the yellow bean adds another layer of complexity, but just use one type if that's easier. I love this as a quick lunch — just a drizzle of chilli sauce and I'm in heaven.

555 g (1 lb 4 oz/3 cups) cooked rice (page 38)
3 tablespoons peanut oil
4 large green king prawns (shrimp), peeled, deveined and
    roughly chopped
2 eggs, lightly beaten
2 cloves garlic, finely chopped
2 teaspoons finely chopped ginger
150 g (5½ oz) Chinese-style barbecue pork (page 202),
    roughly chopped
1 tablespoon light soy sauce
1 tablespoon yellow bean soy sauce
½ teaspoon sea salt
1 teaspoon sugar
2 teaspoons oyster sauce
1 teaspoon sesame oil
3 spring onions (scallions), cut into julienne
a pinch of freshly ground white pepper

METHOD

Heat a wok until just smoking. Add 1 tablespoon of the peanut oil and, when hot, stir-fry the prawns until just cooked, then remove.

Reheat the wok, add the eggs and move them around the wok gently until just set. Turn the egg out onto a plate and roughly chop with your wok spoon.

Wipe the wok clean and reheat with the remaining peanut oil until just smoking. Add the garlic and ginger and stir-fry until fragrant, then add the pork and cook for 1 minute. Add the rice and stir-fry for another minute, then return the prawns to the wok. Add the soy sauces, sea salt, sugar, oyster sauce and sesame oil, and stir-fry until the rice is coated with sauce. Add the egg and spring onions and toss together. Transfer to a serving bowl and sprinkle with ground pepper to serve.

Deep-Frying

This is another cooking method that is well worth mastering. Especially in Chinese dishes, deep-frying is often the last step in the multi-step cooking of things such as chicken, duck and pork. It's also a great trick for dinner parties — the ingredients can be prepared in advance and then just fried crisp and hot when you want to serve. There are two easy ways to deep-fry: the first is to buy a small deep-fryer — there are a lot of good ones on the market and, for how handy they are, they are relatively cheap. The second way is to use a pot or a wok with a thermometer. Thermometers are cheap, easy to use and allow you to always be in the driving seat, as keeping a constant temperature, around 180°C (350°F), is the secret to good deep-frying. I tend to use vegetable or peanut oil for deep-frying, but just make sure that whatever you use, you add enough oil to the wok or pot so that the ingredients can be completely submerged.

After deep-frying, when the oil has cooled down, strain it back into the oil container and re-use. When it is old, pour it back into the container and dispose of it in the rubbish bin. Never tip it down the sink.

I hope it goes without saying, but make sure that all the ingredients you place in the deep-fryer are as dry as they can be. At that temperature, oil and water truly don't mix.

SWEET & SOUR PORK

This is classic sweet and sour pork; the pork is battered and fried until crisp and then folded into the sauce. I suggest you make your own tomato reduction to thicken the sauce (it is quite easy to do), but if you don't have the time or inclination bottled tomato sauce will do.

250 g (9 oz) pork loin, trimmed and finely sliced across
    the grain
30 g (1 oz/¼ cup) cornflour (cornstarch)
1 egg
2 tablespoons vegetable oil
¼ knob of ginger, peeled and finely sliced
½ small Spanish onion, diced
½ red capsicum (pepper), diced
1 spring onion (scallion), cut into 4 cm (1½ inch) lengths
75 g (2⅔ oz/⅓ cup) Chinese mixed pickled vegetables
4 tablespoons rice vinegar
2 tablespoons tomato sauce (ketchup)
4 tablespoons sugar
vegetable oil, for deep-frying

METHOD

Whisk the cornflour, egg and 2 tablespoons water into a smooth batter. Add the pork and stir to coat, then set aside for about 10 minutes.

Heat a wok until just smoking. Add the vegetable oil and, when hot, add the ginger, onion, capsicum and spring onion and stir-fry for 1 minute, then add the pickled vegetables and toss together. Add the rice vinegar, tomato sauce and sugar, bring to the boil while stirring, reduce the heat and simmer until the liquid has reduced by about half, then remove from the wok.

Heat the oil in a wok or deep-fryer until just smoking (180°C/350°F). Deep-fry the pork in batches until golden brown and crispy, then drain on paper towel. Reheat the sauce in the wok, add the pork and toss together.

VARIATION

You could also try slices of chicken, fish or king prawns with this sweet and sour sauce — they work perfectly together.

CRISP-FRIED CHICKEN WITH BLACK VINEGAR GLAZE

This dish uses multiple cooking methods, so get your master stock happening and you can cook the best crispy-skin chicken ever. For tables of six and under, cook a half bird, but if you are serving a table of eight or more, cook the whole chicken. Even though I would cook this whole in the restaurant, I would suggest you still cook it in two halves as it is easier to cut up once out of the fryer. If you are just using one half, keep the other to make a delicious sandwich or use in a salad or stir-fry.

½ master-stock chicken (page 82)
vegetable oil, for deep-frying
1 long red chilli, deseeded and finely chopped
1 long green chilli, deseeded and finely chopped
1 large handful of coriander (cilantro) leaves, finely chopped
2 cloves garlic, finely chopped
1 teaspoon finely chopped ginger

BLACK VINEGAR GLAZE
2 tablespoons sugar
2 tablespoons shaoxing
250 ml (9 fl oz/1 cup) fresh chicken stock (page 58)
1 tablespoon light soy sauce
2 tablespoons oyster sauce
2 tablespoons Chinkiang vinegar

METHOD

To make the glaze, put the sugar and shaoxing in a pot and bring to the boil, then add the chicken stock and simmer until reduced by half. Add the soy sauce, oyster sauce and Chinkiang and return to the boil, then remove from the heat. Taste the sauce for balance and consistency.

Pat the chicken dry with paper towel. Heat the oil in a wok or deep-fryer until just smoking (180°C/350°F), and deep-fry the chicken until crispy and heated through, about 8 minutes. Drain well. Chop the chicken Chinese-style, pour the glaze over the top and sprinkle with chillies, coriander, garlic and ginger.

VARIATION

The ginger and spring onion sauce used on the whole snapper on page 110 is really good with this chicken as well. I also like to cut this Chinese-style and serve it with lemon wedges and Sichuan salt and pepper.

FRIED EGGS WITH SPICY TAMARIND DRESSING

Anyone who owns any of my cookbooks would know that I love egg cookery. In Asian cooking, the egg turns up in some amazingly delicious and usually simple dishes; this is one of my favourites. Try cooking this for lunch with a bowl of rice and I guarantee that it'll be cooked often. The dressing is easy to make as it is a simple Nam Jim. Once you get used to deep-frying eggs, it'll be a breeze. Add some fresh herbs and a little fried red shallot for a counter crunch, or throw a smattering of fried crushed peanuts on the dish as well.

2 large free-range or organic eggs
vegetable oil, for deep-frying
1 small handful of combined mint, coriander (cilantro)
    and Thai basil leaves
1 red shallot, finely sliced
1 red shallot, extra, finely sliced and deep-fried until
    golden

DRESSING
1 long red chilli, deseeded and chopped
3 wild green chillies, chopped
1 clove garlic, chopped
2 coriander (cilantro) roots, scraped and chopped
1½ tablespoons caster (superfine) sugar
1½ tablespoons fish sauce
1½ tablespoons lime juice
1½ tablespoons tamarind water (page 32)

METHOD

To make the dressing, pound the chillies, garlic, coriander root and sugar in a mortar with a pestle to a fine paste. Add the fish sauce, lime juice and tamarind water, then taste to check for balance.

Heat the oil in a wok or deep-fryer until just smoking (180°C/350°F). Carefully crack the eggs into a bowl and then gently pour the whole eggs into the hot oil. Use a large spoon to ladle some of the hot oil over the top of the eggs until they are golden brown all over. Remove from the oil, drain on paper towel and transfer to a serving plate.

Mix the herbs and both the fresh and fried red shallots in a bowl and moisten with some of the dressing. Sprinkle the herb salad over the eggs and then drizzle with the remaining dressing to serve.

CRISPY BLUE EYE MARINATED IN RED BEAN CURD

I love this really interesting flavour. At the restaurant we've used red bean curd to marinate quail, pigeon, chicken and prawns, as well as this blue eye dish. The taste is as close to blue cheese as the Chinese get; in combination with five-spice powder, the flavour is interestingly complex and delicious. It's also easy to make and would fit into your first shared table perfectly to show off your great Asian cooking skills.

350 g (12 oz) blue eye fillet, cut into bite-sized pieces
vegetable oil, for deep-frying
75 g (2½ oz/½ cup) tapioca flour
lemon wedge, to serve

MARINADE
2 tablespoons fermented red bean curd, mashed, plus
     1 tablespoon marinade from the jar
2 tablespoons shaoxing
½ teaspoon five-spice powder
2 cloves garlic, finely chopped

METHOD
To make the marinade, mix together the bean curd, bean curd marinade, shaoxing, five-spice powder and garlic. Add the blue eye and toss until well coated, then leave for 30 minutes.

Heat the oil in a wok or deep-fryer until just smoking (180°C/350°F). Remove the blue eye from the marinade and dust with tapioca flour, shaking off any excess. Deep-fry the fish in batches until golden, then remove from the wok and drain on paper towel. Serve with a wedge of lemon.

LOBSTER WITH XO SAUCE

This lobster is first deep-fried to seal in the flavour, then tossed in a wok with XO — it's one of my favourite dishes; it's incredibly luxurious and believe me when I say that it's achievable at home. Don't be scared of dispatching your lobster; the following page has a detailed explanation that is both easy and humane.

Follow the rules with this one. Spoil yourself first and, once you've practised, cook it for your friends. They'll be happy when you tell them this is on the menu. I enjoy live seafood at a Chinese restaurant in Sussex Street in Sydney's Chinatown. Its name is Golden Century and, lucky for us cooks, it's open until four in the morning. You meet many a tired chef there late at night needing good food after a hectic night's service. This lobster dish is one of my favourites there, along with abalone steamboat.

1 x 700–800 g (1 lb 9 oz–1 lb 12 oz) live lobster
vegetable oil, for deep-frying
½ Spanish onion, cut into wedges
½ red capsicum (pepper), cut into large dice
2 cloves garlic, smashed
½ knob of ginger, peeled and finely sliced
2 teaspoons shaoxing
3 tablespoons XO sauce (page 47)
2 teaspoons light soy sauce
2 teaspoons sugar
100 ml (3½ fl oz) fresh chicken stock (page 58)
½ teaspoon sesame oil
freshly ground white pepper
2 spring onions (scallions), cut into julienne
1 large handful of coriander (cilantro) leaves

METHOD

Kill the lobster humanely (see opposite for instructions), then cut in half lengthways and clean inside. Cut each half crossways into thirds.

Heat the oil in a wok or deep-fryer until just smoking (180°C/350°F), and deep-fry the lobster in batches until golden brown, then remove and drain on paper towel. Discard all but 2 tablespoons of oil.

Add the onion, capsicum, garlic and ginger and stir-fry until fragrant. Deglaze the wok with the shaoxing and add the XO sauce, soy sauce, sugar, chicken stock and sesame oil. Return the lobster to the wok and stir-fry until the sauce thickens enough to coat the lobster. Spoon onto a plate, give a good grind of pepper and top with spring onions and coriander leaves to serve.

HOW TO KILL A LOBSTER

There are two simple ways to dispatch your lobster kindly; if they die without stress the texture will be better.

METHOD

The first method is to put the lobster in the freezer for an hour or two, which puts it to sleep, and is by far the easiest way to do it.

Or put the lobster in a sink filled with fresh water, putting a chopping board over the top as it will thrash about a bit. You are drowning the lobster.

Whichever way you have taken your lobster's life, now put the lobster on a chopping board with its head facing you and its tail away. Carefully place a sharp knife between its eyes. Holding the tail, cut down towards you, right through the shell. Turn the lobster around and, holding it by the head, cut through the tail; you should now have two halves. Pull out the digestive tract that runs down its length.

STIR-FRIED MUD CRAB WITH CURRY POWDER

This is an 'I love my friends' or 'I'm spoiling myself' dish. The egg is the key as it helps the flavours stick to the crab.

My father's great love was mud crab and I have followed in his footsteps. It is, to me, the greatest crab I've ever tasted. The great thing about it is that it's robust enough to handle Asian flavours with aplomb but also happy picked and dressed with lemon and extra virgin olive oil.

1 x 1 kg (2 lb 4 oz) mud crab
vegetable oil, for deep-frying
3 tablespoons curry powder
1 bunch spring onions (scallions), cut into 2 cm (¾ inch)
    lengths
2 tablespoons fish sauce
1 tablespoon sugar
2 eggs, lightly beaten
3 tablespoons coconut milk
1 small handful of coriander (cilantro) leaves
juice of 1 lime

PASTE
2 cloves garlic
a pinch of sea salt
2 long red chillies, deseeded and chopped
½ knob of ginger, peeled and chopped
2 red shallots, chopped

METHOD

To make the paste, pound the garlic, sea salt, chillies, ginger and the shallots in a mortar with a pestle until you have a fine paste. Or use a blender to process the ingredients, adding a little water if necessary.

Kill the crab humanely (see page 96 for instructions), then clean and quarter it.

Heat the oil in a wok or deep-fryer until just smoking (180°C/350°F), and deep-fry the crab in two batches for 3–4 minutes until it turns bright red. Remove from the wok and drain on paper towel. Discard all but 2 tablespoons of oil.

Reheat the wok until smoking, add the paste and stir-fry until fragrant. Add the curry powder and spring onions, stir-fry for 10 seconds, then add the fish sauce and sugar. Stir in the egg and cook until it just begins to set, then add the coconut milk. Return the crab to the wok and toss together, stir through the coriander leaves and squeeze over the lime juice to serve.

PRAWN CUTLETS

This is straightforward, clean food. If you can't get the Japanese panko crumbs, make your own from decent bread or buy good-quality breadcrumbs.

I don't think I've ever known anyone who didn't like crispy food, so be prepared for a plate of these to be demolished quickly.

8 large green king prawns (shrimp), peeled and deveined
    with tails left intact
3 egg whites
2 tablespoons plain (all-purpose) flour
2 teaspoons cornflour (cornstarch)
60 g (2¼ oz/1 cup) Japanese breadcrumbs (panko)
vegetable oil, for deep-frying
fresh chilli sauce (page 44), to serve

SEASONING
½ teaspoon sea salt
1 teaspoon shaoxing
1 teaspoon sesame oil

METHOD

Halve the prawns lengthways and place in a bowl. Mix together the sea salt, shaoxing and sesame oil, and then toss the prawns with this seasoning. Marinate for 5 minutes.

Beat the egg whites to soft peaks and then add the flour and cornflour and beat until the mixture is smooth and stands in stiff peaks. Dip each prawn half in the egg white and flour mixture to coat thickly, then sprinkle evenly with the breadcrumbs.

Heat the oil in a wok or deep-fryer until just smoking (180°C/350°F), and deep-fry the prawns in batches for about 3 minutes, or until they turn deep golden and are cooked through. Drain on paper towel and serve with fresh chilli sauce or sweet chilli sauce.

VARIATIONS

Just about anything you want to crumb works well here. Fish is great, as are slices of pork, chicken and even lamb. Who doesn't like crumbed lamb cutlets with an oriental twist?

You can serve thse cutlets with a spicy mayonnaise, or place lettuce under the prawns and dress with Nuoc Cham.

PRAWN TOAST

This is classic Chinese restaurant fare, and why not? These are delicious morsels — great as a small starter or as pass-around food if you want to add an Asian flavour to your cocktail party. Again, just normal crumbs will do if you can't find the Japanese panko crumbs.

500 g (1 lb 2 oz) green king prawns (shrimp), peeled and
    deveined
2 cloves garlic, finely chopped
½ knob of ginger, peeled and finely chopped
1 teaspoon sugar
½ teaspoon sea salt
1 egg white
1 teaspoon sesame oil
4 spring onions (scallions), finely chopped
5 slices stale white bread, crusts removed
1 egg, lightly beaten
60 g (2¼ oz/1 cup) Japanese breadcrumbs (panko)
vegetable oil, for deep-frying
sweet and sour sauce, to serve

METHOD

Put the prawns, garlic, ginger, sugar, salt, egg white and sesame oil in a food processor and process until smooth. Put the mixture in a bowl and stir in the spring onions.

Spread about 2 tablespoons of the prawn mixture to the edges of each piece of bread and cut each in half diagonally. Brush the tops and sides of each piece with the beaten egg, then press into the breadcrumbs to coat.

Heat the oil in a wok or deep-fryer until smoking (180°C/350°F), and deep-fry the toasts in batches until golden on both sides, about 2 minutes. Remove and drain on paper towel. Serve hot with a sweet and sour dipping sauce.

DEEP-FRIED SQUID WITH GARLIC & PEPPERCORNS

I know I keep saying this but I DO love this dish, and it IS one of my favourites, it really is! I like to serve it with Nam Jim — the lime, chilli and squid are a match made in heaven.

350 g (12 oz) squid, cleaned
1 tablespoon fish sauce
a pinch of sugar
2 coriander (cilantro) roots, scraped and chopped
a pinch of sea salt
½ teaspoon white peppercorns
1 head garlic, cloves separated but unpeeled
vegetable oil, for deep-frying
60 g (2¼ oz/½ cup) plain (all-purpose) flour
freshly ground white pepper, to serve
coriander (cilantro) leaves, to serve
chilli sauce (page 42) or Nam Jim (page 50), to serve

METHOD

To prepare the squid, cut off the tentacles, and cut down the centre of the squid so it will open out flat. Score the inside with a crisscross pattern, then slice lengthways into 2 cm (¾ inch) wide strips.

Marinate the squid strips and tentacles in the fish sauce and sugar for 30 minutes. Meanwhile, pound the coriander roots, salt and peppercorns in a mortar with a pestle, then add the garlic cloves and pound into a coarse paste, removing the garlic's skin and hard base as you go.

Heat the oil in a wok or deep-fryer until smoking (180°C/350°F), and then toss half the squid in the flour until well coated. Shake away any excess. Deep-fry the squid, stirring regularly, until golden. Use a slotted spoon to remove the squid and drain on paper towel. Repeat with the remaining squid.

Scoop out any debris from the oil and then add the garlic mixture — be careful as it will spit. Move the garlic around the hot oil until it is golden, and then remove and drain on paper towel. Put the squid on a serving plate, sprinkle with the crispy garlic, white pepper and coriander leaves and serve with chilli sauce or Nam Jim.

VARIATION

Coat the squid in some Sichuan salt and pepper before deep-frying.

Tea-Smoking

Tea-smoking is usually part of a multi-cooking process; food is also either steamed, fried, roasted, or a combination of all three. I'm a huge fan of the wonderful flavour of tea smoke, and hope that you won't see this technique as difficult. The rules are: marinate, smoke, steam and finish, so everything is ready to the point of heating and serving.

You'll need one of two things to tea-smoke effectively: a powerful extractor fan to dissipate the smoke from your wok; or, as I have, a wok burner on your barbecue so this can be done outside — great from a mess point of view.

I use a wok with a lid and place a rack inside it to hold the food. Another option is to have an aluminium steamer stashed away that you only bring out for smoking. This works particularly well when you need to stack up the layers — just don't get too precious about how it looks!

If you find you enjoy tea-smoking (and I reckon you will because it tastes so good), keep a wok, wok lid and rack just for this job.

TEA-SMOKE MIX

This can be made well in advance and kept in an airtight container for later use. Mix together the following:

200 g (7 oz) Jasmine tea leaves
200 g (7 oz) brown sugar
200 g (7 oz) long-grain rice

TEA- & SPICE-SMOKED DUCK

I've served this classic Sichuan dish at XO. It makes a beautiful shared plate with pancakes and the usual garnishes for Peking duck. It can also be served the traditional way with steamed lotus buns.

2 kg (4 lb 8 oz) duck, wing tips and tail removed
2 knobs of ginger, peeled and sliced
2 spring onions (scallions), cut into 4 cm (1½ inch)
    lengths
150 g (5½ oz) tea-smoke mix (page 147)
1 tablespoon dark soy sauce
1 tablespoon sesame oil
2 tablespoons plain (all-purpose) flour
vegetable oil, for deep-frying

MARINADE
¼ teaspoon ground tangerine peel
2 teaspoons five-spice powder
2 teaspoons Sichuan salt and pepper (page 55)

METHOD

Remove all the fat from the duck cavity. Place the ginger and spring onions inside. To make the marinade, mix together the tangerine peel, five-spive powder and the Sichuan salt and pepper and rub over the duck breasts and legs. Cover and leave to marinate in the fridge overnight.

Place the tea-smoke mix in a piece of foil in the centre of a large wok (big enough to fit the duck). Place a wire rack over the smoking mix and then place the duck on top. Put the wok over medium heat to start the mix smoking, then put the lid on the wok and smoke for 15–20 minutes, until the duck is golden brown.

Remove the duck from the wok and cook in a steamer over boiling water for 1¼ hours. Remove and leave to cool.

Cut the duck in half lengthways and remove the ginger and spring onions from the cavity. Combine the soy sauce and sesame oil and brush over the duck, then sprinkle with the flour and shake off any excess. Heat the oil in a wok or deep-fryer until just smoking (180°C/350°F), and deep-fry the duck for 4 minutes, then leave to rest for 5 minutes before cutting.

TEA-SMOKED QUAIL

Less commitment in effort than the previous duck dish, this quail is no less delicious. We steam the quail first and smoke it later; being smaller, quail seems to keep more of the smoked flavour. You can serve the quail with pickled cucumber and shiitake mushrooms, or pickled cabbage. It also works a treat as part of a cold-cut platter.

2 large quails
1 teaspoon sesame oil
150 g (5½ oz) tea-smoke mix (page 147)
2½ tablespoons peanut oil
Sichuan salt and pepper (page 55), to serve

METHOD

Place a steamer over a pot of boiling water. Put the quails on a plate into the steamer and steam for 8 minutes, then remove and cool. Rub the quails all over with sesame oil.

Cut out a circle of foil about 20 cm (8 inches) in diameter. Scrunch up the sides to make a container about 12 cm (4½ inches) in diameter. Put the tea-smoke mix in the container and place it in the bottom of a wok, then place a rack over the top. Turn up the heat to full and, once the mix starts smoking, add the quails. Cover with the lid and leave over the heat for 5 minutes. Remove the wok from the heat but don't lift the lid. Allow the wok to cool and the smoke to slowly dissipate. Lift the lid after about 20 minutes and remove the quails.

Heat a wok until just smoking. Add the peanut oil and, when hot, stir-fry the quails on all sides until they are crisp and deep mahogany brown. Drain them well on paper towel and sprinkle with Sichuan salt and pepper to serve.

TEA-SMOKED OCEAN TROUT

I love this fish, torn apart, in a salad — try it instead of beef in the spicy beef salad (page 66). It's also delicious with a red-braised sauce; make the sauce and, as it reduces, add the trout to warm through.

1 x 1.8 kg (4 lb) side of ocean trout, skin on
sesame oil
150 g (5½ oz) tea-smoke mix (page 147)

METHOD

To prepare the trout, remove the pin bones from down the centre of the fish with a pair of tweezers.

To smoke the trout, rub the skin side with sesame oil and put on a rack that will fit in your wok (cut the fish in half if it won't fit). Cut out a circle of foil about 20 cm (8 inches) in diameter. Scrunch up the sides to make a container about 12 cm (4½ inches) in diameter. Put the tea-smoke mix in the container and place it in the bottom of a wok, then place the rack over the top. Turn up the heat to full and once the mix starts smoking, add the fish. Cover with the lid and leave over the heat for 3 minutes. Remove the wok from the heat but don't lift the lid. Allow the wok to cool and the smoke to slowly dissipate.

Heat a grill, barbecue or oven to 200°C (400°F/Gas 6). Remove the trout from the wok after 20 minutes and grill on one side for 3 minutes until a crust forms on the fish and the centre is warm, but don't overcook.

Turn the trout over and leave to rest in a warm place before serving.

Curry and Spice Pastes

I've popped this section in to get you used to doing a little pounding and puréeing. Yes, you can simply buy a ready-made paste and cook a curry, or add it to a stir-fry, and that is acceptable. However, if you go to the trouble of making these pastes fresh, you'll be rewarded with amazing flavour and freshness — something you just can't get from the bought varieties. Once you get the hang of this, it won't be long before you're varying the chilli or spice to tailor your curry pastes to your own taste. Remember that tasting for balance when we start using these pastes to make curries is very important.

Making these pastes is as simple as putting all the ingredients in a blender and processing them with a little water. Only add enough water to make the blender work, as you'll have to fry it out later. If you are making a boiled curry, then it doesn't matter how much water you use.

CURRY PASTES

Thai curry pastes are a blend of wonderfully aromatic ingredients and spices. The flavours layer together to create an amazing complex whole that is greater than all its parts. Yes, again, you can buy a prepared paste, but I promise you that nothing will ever approach the flavour of one you make fresh yourself. So, is it really that hard to peel a few ingredients, roast some spices and process them in a blender with a little water? I think not. And when you've made one and tasted the difference, you'll be hooked forever.

Curry pastes are all generally finished with fish sauce and a varying amount of palm sugar, depending on what flavours you are looking for, so always taste for balance as you go. Don't make your pastes too sweet, a major problem most restaurants seem to have in Australia.

The three ways you would usually use a curry paste are: fry it in oil, then add coconut milk; boil it in water, stock or coconut milk; or dry-fry it and use it to flavour a stir-fry. All of the pastes that follow can be used in these three ways.

RED CURRY PASTE

1 teaspoon white peppercorns

2 teaspoons cumin seeds

1 teaspoon coriander seeds

6 star anise

3 cinnamon sticks, broken

1 tablespoon ground paprika

6 dried long red chillies, deseeded, soaked in warm water
    for 30 minutes and chopped

12 cloves garlic, chopped

3 lemongrass stalks, tough outer leaves removed,
    chopped

2 tablespoons chopped galangal

4 coriander (cilantro) roots, scraped and chopped

finely grated zest of 1 kaffir lime

3 tablespoons Thai shrimp paste, wrapped in foil and
    roasted until fragrant

METHOD

Roast the peppercorns, cumin, coriander seeds, star anise and cinnamon
in a dry heavy-based frying pan until very fragrant and darker in colour, but not
burnt. Grind to a powder in a coffee or spice grinder and mix in the paprika.

Pound the chillies, garlic, lemongrass, galangal, coriander root, lime zest
and shrimp paste in a mortar with a pestle until you have a fine paste. Combine
with the dried spices and mix well. Or use a blender to process the ingredients
until smooth, adding a little water or oil if necessary.

RED CURRY OF DUCK & PINEAPPLE

There is something agreeable about the combination of rich red curry, succulent duck and sweet pineapple. It just tastes so good and the texture is perfect — I suppose that's what makes it a classic. You can add some heat to this by cooking the paste with a few squashed wild green chillies; or for a fresh finish, a squeeze of lime is great at the end. You can buy roast duck at Chinatowns around the world or make your own.

1 Chinese roast duck (page 248), boned and cut into 2 cm (¾ inch) chunks
200 g (7 oz) red curry paste (page 155)
250 ml (9 fl oz/1 cup) coconut cream
3 tablespoons vegetable oil
4 kaffir lime leaves
3 tablespoons fish sauce
2 tablespoons grated palm sugar (jaggery)
500 ml (17 fl oz/2 cups) coconut milk
3 long red chillies, halved lengthways and deseeded
160 g (5⅔ oz/1 cup) chopped fresh pineapple
1 handful of sweet Thai basil leaves
1 lime, to squeeze

METHOD

In a heavy-based frying pan over high heat, bring the coconut cream and vegetable oil to the boil, stirring continuously so that it doesn't burn. When the coconut cream 'splits' (the oil separates from the solids), add the curry paste. Crush the lime leaves in your hand, add them to the pan and fry until all the aromas rise from the paste and it is sizzling fiercely. This will take 10–15 minutes (use your nose).

Add the fish sauce and cook for 1 minute. Then add the palm sugar and the coconut milk and bring to the boil. Add the duck and chillies and simmer gently for about 4 minutes until the duck has heated through, then add the pineapple. Stir in the basil with a little squeeze of fresh lime juice before serving.

GREEN CURRY PASTE

5 coriander seeds
5 cumin seeds
5 white peppercorns
6 wild green chillies, chopped
3 long green chillies, deseeded and chopped
2 lemongrass stalks, tough outer leaves removed,
    chopped
2 tablespoons chopped galangal
10 red shallots, chopped
5 cloves garlic, chopped
3 coriander (cilantro) roots, scraped and chopped
1 tablespoon chopped turmeric
finely grated zest of 1 kaffir lime
1 teaspoon Thai shrimp paste, wrapped in foil and
    roasted until fragrant

METHOD

Lightly roast the coriander seeds, cumin seeds and peppercorns in a dry heavy-based pan, then grind to a powder in a coffee or spice grinder. Pound the chillies, lemongrass, galangal, shallots, garlic, coriander roots, turmeric, lime zest and shrimp paste in a mortar with a pestle.

Pass all the ground and pounded ingredients through a mincer twice. Or use a blender to process until smooth, adding a little water or oil if necessary. You can also just keep pounding with the pestle to produce a fine paste.

GREEN CURRY OF BLUE EYE

Again, you can add whatever seafood you like to this curry, or chicken or, my personal favourite, beef fillet. The wild green chillies and fish sauce make it quite salty and hot, which is a nice variation.

350 g (12 oz) blue eye fillet, cut into 2 cm (¾ inch) cubes
130 g (4⅔ oz/½ cup) green curry paste (page 157)
250 ml (9 fl oz/1 cup) coconut cream
3 tablespoons vegetable oil
6 kaffir lime leaves
4 tablespoons fish sauce
1 tablespoon grated palm sugar (jaggery)
500 ml (17 fl oz/2 cups) coconut milk
4 wild green chillies, lightly crushed
3 long red chillies, halved lengthways and deseeded
10 Thai pea eggplants (aubergines)
5 apple eggplants (aubergines), quartered
12 sweet Thai basil leaves

METHOD

In a heavy-based frying pan over high heat, bring the coconut cream and vegetable oil to the boil, stirring continuously so that it doesn't burn. When the coconut cream 'splits' (the oil separates from the solids), add the curry paste. Crush the lime leaves in your hand, add them to the pan and fry until all the aromas rise from the paste and it is sizzling fiercely. This will take 10–15 minutes (use your nose).

Add the fish sauce to the pan and cook for 1 minute. Then add the palm sugar and coconut milk and bring to the boil. Add the blue eye, chillies and eggplants and simmer gently for about 4 minutes, or until the fish is just cooked through and the pea and apple eggplants are still a little crunchy. Stir in the basil just before serving.

CHICKEN CURRY, SOUTHERN THAI-STYLE

I really like dried shrimp in this paste; it gives it extra flavour and a silky texture. I often add 3 tablespoons of fried ground peanuts to this curry as they make the sauce rich and wonderful.

350 g (12 oz) free-range or organic chicken thigh fillets,
   thickly sliced
3 tablespoons vegetable oil
250 ml (9 fl oz/1 cup) coconut milk
4 kaffir lime leaves, crushed
2 tablespoons fish sauce
1 tablespoon sugar
1 handful of Thai basil leaves
juice of 1 lime

CURRY PASTE
3 dried long red chillies, deseeded, soaked in warm water
   for 30 minutes and chopped
6 red shallots, chopped
2 cloves garlic, chopped
1 tablespoon chopped galangal
1 lemongrass stalk, tough outer leaves removed, finely
   chopped
1 coriander (cilantro) root, scraped and chopped
finely grated zest of 1 kaffir lime
a pinch of freshly ground white pepper
1 teaspoon sea salt
1 teaspoon Thai shrimp paste, wrapped in foil and
   roasted until fragrant
2 tablespoons dried shrimp, finely ground

METHOD

To make the curry paste, pound the ingredients in a mortar with a pestle until you have a fine paste. Or use a blender to process the ingredients, adding a little water if necessary.

Heat a wok until just smoking. Add the oil and, when hot, add the paste and stir-fry for about 5 minutes until fragrant. Add the coconut milk and the chicken and simmer gently until the chicken is cooked. Add the lime leaves, fish sauce and sugar and taste for balance. Remove from the heat, sprinkle with the basil and squeeze over the lime juice to serve.

PORK SHOULDER CURRY

This daunting list of ingredients creates a curry with rich flavours.

500 g (1 lb 2 oz) pork shoulder, skin removed
750 ml (26 fl oz/3 cups) coconut milk
2 tablespoons vegetable oil
250 ml (9 fl oz/1 cup) coconut cream
5 kaffir lime leaves
2 tablespoons grated palm sugar (jaggery)
3 tablespoons fish sauce
160 g (5⅔ oz/¼ cup) Thai pea eggplants (aubergines)
5 long red chillies, halved lengthways and deseeded
juice of 2 limes
1 small handful of Thai basil leaves

PASTE
1 teaspoon fennel seeds
1 teaspoon white peppercorns
a pinch of sea salt
8 dried long red chillies, deseeded, soaked in warm water
    for 30 minutes and chopped
2 lemongrass stalks, tough outer leaves removed,
    chopped
1 knob of ginger, peeled and chopped
2 teaspoons Thai shrimp paste, wrapped in foil and
    roasted until fragrant
3 red shallots, chopped
12 cloves garlic, chopped
finely grated zest of 1 kaffir lime

METHOD

Put the pork in a large pot, cover with cold water and bring to the boil. Skim off any scum, add three-quarters of the coconut milk, reduce the heat and simmer, covered, for 2 hours. Remove and cut into bite-sized pieces.

Pound the paste ingredients in a mortar with a pestle to a fine paste. Or process with a blender, adding a little water if necessary.

In a heavy-based pot, heat the oil, coconut cream and lime leaves, stirring until the cream 'splits'. Add the paste and cook over medium heat for 15–20 minutes until fragrant. Add the remaining coconut milk, sugar, fish sauce and eggplants and bring to the boil. Reduce the heat, simmer for 5 minutes, then add the pork and chillies to heat through. Squeeze over the lime juice and sprinkle with basil to serve.

MUSSEL CURRY

I love mussels every which way, and in Mediterranean cooking I use them as both the hero and the support act. They make some of the best sauces to use with seafood. Here they make a cracking curry and all you need for a great dinner is a big bowl of rice. For a real treat, blanch some fresh egg noodles and pour the mussel curry over the top.

300 g (10½ oz) mussels, debearded and scrubbed
3 tablespoons vegetable oil
3 kaffir lime leaves, torn
2 tablespoons grated palm sugar (jaggery)
1 tablespoon fish sauce
1 tablespoon tamarind water (page 32)
1 large handful of mixed Thai basil and coriander
    (cilantro) leaves
juice of 1 lime

PASTE
5 dried long red chillies, deseeded, soaked in warm water
    for 30 minutes and chopped
a large pinch of sea salt
1 tablespoon chopped galangal
3 tablespoons chopped lemongrass
1 teaspoon finely grated kaffir lime zest
1 teaspoon scraped and chopped coriander (cilantro) root
3 red shallots, finely chopped
3 cloves garlic, finely chopped
1 teaspoon shrimp paste

METHOD

To make the paste, pound the ingredients in a mortar with a pestle to form a fine paste. Or use a blender to process the ingredients, adding a little water if necessary.

Heat a wok until almost smoking. Add the vegetable oil and heat until smoking. Reduce the heat a little, add the paste and lime leaves and stir-fry until fragrant. Season with palm sugar, fish sauce and tamarind water, then add the mussels and cover. Shake the wok from time to time — it should take about 5 minutes for the mussels to open. Discard any that remain stubbornly closed.

Add the Thai basil and coriander, remove from the heat and stir through. Add the lime juice, stir through again and check the seasoning before serving.

STIR-FRIED BLUE EYE WITH SNAKE BEANS

Now that you're making curry pastes, this is dead easy. It is, in fact, another way of preparing a curry: a dry-fried curry. You could just use a couple of tablespoons of red curry paste, and instead of blue eye, try any seafood, meat or poultry — so versatile! This is quick to cook, so it makes a great last-minute dish for your shared table.

300 g (10½ oz) blue eye fillet, cut into bite-sized pieces
8 snake beans, cut into 3 cm (1¼ inch) lengths
100 ml (3½ fl oz) vegetable oil
2 tablespoons grated palm sugar (jaggery)
2 tablespoons fish sauce
2 teaspoons dried shrimp, soaked in warm water for
    20 minutes

SPICE PASTE
½ teaspoon white peppercorns
½ teaspoon fennel seeds
½ teaspoon cumin seeds
2 dried long red chillies, deseeded, soaked in warm water
    for 30 minutes and chopped
1 teaspoon sea salt
3 red shallots, chopped
2 cloves garlic, chopped
1 teaspoon finely chopped galangal
1 lemongrass stalk, tough outer leaves removed,
    chopped
6 coriander (cilantro) roots, scraped and chopped
1 teaspoon Thai shrimp paste, wrapped in foil and
    roasted until fragrant

METHOD

To make the spice paste, lightly roast the peppercorns, fennel and cumin seeds in a dry heavy-based pan until very fragrant and dark, then grind to a powder in a coffee or spice grinder. Then pound all the paste ingredients in a mortar with a pestle until you have a fine paste. Or use a blender to process the ingredients, adding a little water if necessary.

Boil the beans until tender, then drain and refresh in iced water. Heat a wok until smoking. Add half the oil and, when hot, stir-fry the blue eye in batches until golden, then remove. Add the remaining oil to the wok and stir-fry the spice paste until fragrant, then add the palm sugar, fish sauce, beans and shrimp and toss together. Return the blue eye to the wok and stir-fry for 1 minute.

SPICY BEEF STEW

This is a sort of half-curry, half-stew or braise. It is easy to make and delicious, and gives you another way to make a curry, by simply boiling the paste in water. What could be easier than that?

500 g (1 lb 2 oz) beef brisket
2 tomatoes, cored and quartered
4 cinnamon sticks
5 kaffir lime leaves
1 teaspoon sea salt
3 tablespoons grated palm sugar (jaggery)
2 tablespoons fish sauce
2 tablespoons tamarind water (page 32)
1 small handful of Thai basil leaves

SPICE PASTE
3 candlenuts, roasted until golden, chopped
6 long red chillies, chopped
3 red shallots, chopped
3 cloves garlic, chopped
1 knob of ginger, peeled and chopped
1 knob of galangal, chopped
2 lemongrass stalks, tough outer leaves removed,
    chopped
1 finger of fresh turmeric, chopped

METHOD

Pound all the spice paste ingredients together in a mortar with a pestle until you have a fine paste. Or process the ingredients with a blender, adding a little water if necessary.

Put the spice paste, brisket, tomatoes, cinnamon, lime leaves and sea salt in a large heavy-based pot. Add enough water to cover the beef by about 2 cm (¾ inch) and bring to the boil over medium heat. Reduce the heat and simmer very gently for about 2 hours, or until the beef is tender. Add the palm sugar, fish sauce and tamarind water, then taste and adjust the seasoning if necessary. Stir through the basil leaves to serve.

NOTE Candlenuts can be toxic if consumed raw, so make sure you roast them well before adding them to the spice paste.

THE SHARED TABLE

When putting together a shared table for family and friends, it's important to remember that the reason they are coming over is to see you. This means you should prepare dishes that are within your realm of possibility and never make something for the first time on the big night.

Also, the key is not to try to cook four stir-fries or too many dishes that need a lot of last minute preparation. As I've said before, balance is not only about taste, but also about balancing your ability to get the meal out of the kitchen with both you and the food in good shape.

Generally, one dish per person is enough with rice, but at the most I would suggest one dish per person, plus one dish for the table. If the numbers increase, don't try to cook eight or ten dishes for that many people, just make the portions larger. I reckon the most you want to prepare is six dishes, otherwise you won't get to enjoy spending time with your guests.

I would suggest that at this stage you don't try to serve starters as you would for a traditional Western dinner — instead, serve all the dishes together, or serve the meal in two halves, then have fruit and tea when you've finished your glass of wine.

Generally speaking, I like to serve a stir-fry, something steamed, a braise or curry, or both, something deep-fried, rice and a salad. Perfect. Then, if I want more dishes I would probably make two braised or steamed dishes. Once one member of your family gets good at helping, they can serve some dishes while you make two quick stir-fries. It's all about being organised and marshalling help when you need it. Most of all, when there are two of you working in the kitchen together, communicate and let your fellow cook know exactly what you want them to do beforehand. There is nothing worse than trying to explain something when you're also trying to cook a dish that requires attention.

So, I would set up the kitchen like this. Have the rice cooker on and the rice warm, and have an electric wok with water in it for the bamboo steamer. Have all the ingredients for the salad in a bowl with the dressing ready on one side. Have a curry or braise just simmering gently on the stove to keep warm. Have your deep-fryer at 180°C (350°F), ready for whatever you want to fry. Have your stir-fry ingredients next to the wok in the order you will add them... and away you go.

With a rice cooker, electric wok and a deep-fryer, all of which are very good value these days, you will have a lot more space on the stove and be in control right from the start.

The other thing to think about is balance. You don't want every dish to be saucy, or all of them dry, too many chicken dishes or everything beef. So try to choose dishes that are complementary.

Here are a few ideas for dishes that go well together and use different techniques to help get your timing right. These six shared table menu ideas will help you get the flavour right and ensure, importantly, that you can get the meal out of the kitchen. Each menu will feed between four and six people. You can add another dish or two if more people are coming, but I would suggest, as I said before, making the portions a little bigger before you try to over-extend yourself. I would also think about adding a curry that can be made in advance and gently warmed to serve.

If you feel that a starter is necessary before the shared table, or you're feeling really confident, arrange a plate of mixed sashimi with dressing, or a large plate of cold cuts with tea eggs and pickles — what a great way to start a meal. Once you've got the hang of putting this much food on the table, you can add a bit of luxury with a mud crab or lobster (either cooked or with one of the sauces I've suggested might go well).

If you want to make a delicious meal for just two of you, select two dishes and have a great time cooking them. Just serve them with rice and don't forget to make extra to keep in the fridge or freezer for your fried rice.

You can drop dishes in and out of my suggestions, or just head straight to the next section and start cooking up a storm if you're feeling confident.

EASY SHARED TABLE MENUS FOR BEGINNERS

169

WINE AND ASIAN FOOD

I eat a lot of Asian food in my life, both at home and in restaurants. I also happen to love wine and have never been of the opinion that Asian food and wine don't mix. Of course they do — I have been involved with the practice for 32 years!

In general, full-flavoured aromatic wines go well with Asian food; you need to remember that you are, for the most part, matching the wine to the experience, as you have a multitude of dishes on the table at any one time.

I'm lucky enough to have two of the best sommeliers in Australia working for me. David Lawler at Rockpool Bar & Grill in Melbourne and Nicole Reimers at Rockpool (fish) in Sydney are both dedicated professionals with not just a great wine knowledge but a great love of sharing their experience. They are both brilliant at what they do, so I thought it might be helpful for them to share their thoughts with you.

DAVID LAWLER

I like to think there is a wine for everyone, and a dish for every wine. I am inclined to place greater importance on making sure the wine matches the guest before contemplating the dish; there are very few immovable rules when it comes to matching wine and food, so you should really drink what you enjoy.

There are, however, some things worth considering; think about matching the body and weight of the wine and dish; lighter, subtle dishes like fragrant salads or delicate shellfish go well with crisp Riesling, Albariño, or dry sherry. Full, rich dishes with powerful flavours like smoked meats, seafood, barbecued pork or roast duck go well with whites of the Rhone Valley, ripe Grüner Veltliner, Shiraz or Tempranillo. Looking to match the weight of the food and wine provides you with many more options.

Consider the importance of texture to a match. If the dish has the delicate crunch of lettuce leaves, or soft-shell crab, it might be appropriate to a wine with racy acidity like Champagne or Semillon; the soft unctuousness of rice noodles might partner well with a fuller softer wine style like Pinot Gris or Gewürztraminer. Robust complex meats like pork belly or roast duck with high contrasts of fat and flesh will be well served by the fine tannins and bright acidity of well-made Pinot Noir or Nebbiolo.

Powerful flavours like chilli, coriander, ginger and soy can all have a profound influence on our perception of wine. When these ingredients are handled with balance and poise, their impact can often be reduced; I suggest you sit back and enjoy the way these elements can interact and play with the flavours of the wine.

There are also many beverages that are worthy matches for those who don't enjoy wine; sherry, ciders, sake and many beer styles are all options for pairing with Asian food.

Much of the cultural aspect of dining throughout Asia places importance on the communal, convivial nature of eating together. While you contemplate which wine will best suit a table full of many dishes and many tastes and textures, some wines are well skilled at matching a number of courses and occasions. For this, it is hard to go past Pinot Gris; lighter styles from Alsace, or fresher styles from New Zealand that can possess savoury qualities, power and weight without oiliness and just a 'kiss' of sugar sweetness. The neutrality and sheer flexibility of these wines makes them a winner with many. For similar reasons Gewürztraminer and various Rosé styles can be equally applicable.

NICOLE REIMERS

Food and wine matching is an interesting subject; it's great when you nail it. I have pondered different combinations and marvelled over perfect matches for as long as I can remember.

One thing I do know for sure is that the way we enjoy ourselves, sensorially speaking, is a collaboration of many individual elements.

- There are certain tried and true guidelines when pairing wine with food.
- Company, atmosphere and involvement in your surroundings are very important seasonings to create the perfect experience.

When it comes to Asian flavours it's great to understand the philosophy of balance. Ultimately we want to achieve harmony when pairing wine with food.

Mentally registering the weight of a dish is important. For example, John Dory sashimi or light aromatic salads warrant a wine of similar lightness and delicacy. Riesling, Spanish whites and other light aromatics work exceptionally well.

Identify the dominant flavours in your dish and look for a wine with a flavour profile that will complement and not compete. Salty fried whitebait? Lemony–limey Aussie Riesling? Absolutely.

If a wine is too heavy for a dish then it will overrule the subtlety of the food. Oaky fruit-driven Chardonnay would totally mask the delicacy of a fresh green papaya salad, for instance.

Unoaked whites and aromatics such as Gewürztraminer, Pinot Gris and Grigio are a wonderful choice and are extremely suitable with a wide range of dishes.

Asian food really asks for clean flavours in wine. Sweetness in wine is a matter of taste and can be a great option with spicy food. Often the sweeter wines are the ones with a lower alcohol content, which helps, as alcohol accentuates chilli and spice.

Sometimes the greater the complexity of the wine, the higher risk it runs of getting muddled up in the cuisine. It may not be the perfect choice to have that Domaine de la Romanée-Conti Montrachet you've always wanted to try with that chilli salt and pepper squid — as much as you might love them both. The different complexities compete and can lose their identities.

For red meat dishes, think about Pinot Noir, Grenache, Tempranillo and Shiraz, providing they are not overly oaked. Their fleshy fruitiness acts as an additional flavour to the dish and their acid tannin can cut through any fat and oiliness.

I remember one of my most memorable experiences was at a late-night dinner party in the hot Australian summer. The highlight of our evening was the tea-smoked quail, a stunning dish. The ultra young Beaujolais (French, vibrant and fruit-driven Gamay) we enjoyed with it, served slightly chilled, was a truly amazing combination. The cherry aromas and red fruit character of the wine acted like a flavour enhancer to the gamey earthiness and complexity of the dish. Pure, clean flavours and total harmony.

Advanced Recipes and Banquet Menus

This chapter contains lots of great recipes that I have cooked in my restaurants and at home. They all work brilliantly both as a simple dinner with a bowl of rice or as part of a beautiful shared table for family and friends. They exemplify the ideals of 'balance and harmony' with all the flavours adding up to a delicious total. I hope you enjoy making them.

Make sure one flavour doesn't dominate your food. Look to balance each dish — not too sweet, not too salty, not too hot or sour. Look for clean flavours that leave a pleasant, long aftertaste — length of flavour is so important in food and wine. You are, in many cases, dealing with bigger flavours than we are used to in Western cooking.

The quality of the finished dish has a direct relationship with the quality of the ingredients going into it, so shop well. Cooking of this kind is about time and detail, patience and care, so enjoy it. If you are lucky enough to be like me and live not too far from a really great Chinatown, spend some time there. Shop, get a bowl of noodles, and spend time looking at the exotic and marvellous ingredients that are foreign to you. Cooking like this is not all about reading a cookbook, it is about living it and loving it. Eat your local version of street food as well as eating in restaurants — the best noodles, stir-fries, curries, laksas and so on will often be at little stalls in the food courts of Chinatown.

If you don't live close to a Chinatown then when you visit a city that has one, spend time there. I can have as much enjoyment visiting markets in Asia and around the world as I do going to a great museum. So, when you have the chance, take your family on food safaris, especially when you are in Asia. To understand the culture, you need to get into the food; it is so important to their way of life.

TOFU AND EGGS

I'm incredibly fond of both tofu and eggs, and in Asian cooking there are many delicious recipes that involve both of them. They are usually simple dishes and, importantly, make a quick meal with great flavour, texture and a good protein base — just as importantly, they are very inexpensive. Tofu and egg dishes are great to make alongside a beef, pork or seafood dish — just add a salad and you have a shared table. They are also ingredients that I have noticed are often sadly forgotten by the home cook.

I tend to use the softest, fresh tofu called 'silken' tofu, but there are also recipes for 'firm' tofu, often just called 'fresh' tofu, and 'pressed' tofu, which is great for salads and Sichuan-style stir-fries. Tofu is made from the milk extracted from soy beans, and you can think of it in terms of cheese. The softer cheeses have a higher moisture content and the firmer have less. It's the same with tofu — the more moisture that is pressed out, the firmer it is.

With eggs, it goes without saying that fresh is best, and use at least free-range, but preferably organic. They give the best results in both taste and texture. Don't forget that the egg is the hero of these dishes, so if a good-quality egg tastes great by itself, when you add flavour and texture it will soar to great heights.

TOFU & PORK SOUP

This is a very simple soup that relies on some of the tofu breaking up and helping to thicken the dish. Feel free to add a couple of chopped chillies at the end to spice it up, or a drop or two of chilli oil if you like it hot — I know I do.

250 g (9 oz) silken tofu, cut into 2 cm (¾ inch) cubes
150 g (5½ oz) pork neck
5 dried shiitake mushrooms, soaked in warm water for
    30 minutes, stalks removed, finely sliced
1.25 litres (44 fl oz/5 cups) fresh chicken stock (page 58)
2 teaspoons grated palm sugar (jaggery)
3 teaspoons oyster sauce
4 cloves garlic, finely chopped
1 knob of ginger, peeled and cut into julienne
1 teaspoon sesame oil
1 tablespoon sea salt
1 tablespoon shaoxing
4 tablespoons yellow bean soy sauce
2 tablespoons Chinese red vinegar
a pinch of Sichuan pepper

METHOD

Put the stock, sugar, oyster sauce and shiitakes into a pot and simmer gently for 30 minutes. Add the pork neck to the soup and simmer gently for a further 20 minutes, skimming the surface of any impurities. Remove the pork and finely slice the meat. Return the pork to the soup, add all the remaining ingredients except the Sichuan pepper, and simmer gently for a further 2 minutes. Sprinkle with the Sichuan pepper to serve.

NYONYA-STYLE TOFU SALAD

I love this dressing and often build salads on these foundations, adding prawns or some boiled pork or barbecued quail. It's also great on just lettuce or, for that matter, anything you want to put it on. The two main ingredients of this chapter come together in this dish. The boiled egg should be firm as it plays an important part in the texture. This salad is also nice with some julienne of carrot thrown in or daikon radish or bean sprouts.

Look for the balance in this dressing — you have hot, sour, salty and sweet all working together here.

150 g (5½ oz) firm tofu, cut into 1 cm (½ inch) cubes
1 free-range or organic egg
1 Lebanese (short) cucumber, peeled, cut in half lengthways, deseeded and finely sliced on the diagonal
½ long red chilli, finely sliced
1 spring onion (scallion), sliced
freshly ground black pepper

DRESSING
1 tablespoon dried shrimp, soaked in warm water for 30 minutes
2 tablespoons kecap manis
½ teaspoon caster (superfine) sugar
1 tablespoon finely grated ginger
2 tablespoons peanut oil
2 tablespoons rice vinegar
1 teaspoon sesame oil
1 teaspoon chilli oil

METHOD

To make the dressing, pound the shrimp in a mortar with a pestle until fine. Mix together the ground shrimp, kecap manis, sugar, ginger, peanut oil, vinegar, sesame oil and chilli oil, along with the tofu and set aside for the flavours to mingle.

Cook the egg in boiling water for 8 minutes. Drain and run under cold water, then peel and quarter lengthways.

Arrange the cucumber slices and egg over a serving plate. Spoon the tofu and the dressing over the top, sprinkle with the chilli and spring onion and give it a good grind of pepper to serve.

SICHUAN SALT & PEPPER SILKEN TOFU

I've been serving this dish in my restaurants for years; it made the perfect start for a meal at XO. I promise you won't believe how something so simple can be so good. It's important to only use silken tofu, as the dish is as much about texture as flavour. Be careful with the tofu as it's very delicate and will break up if you handle it too roughly. To prepare it, remove the lid and invert the tofu onto a board, and from there you can cut it into squares.

300 g (10½ oz) silken tofu
3 teaspoons Sichuan salt and pepper (page 55)
30 g (1 oz/¼ cup) plain (all-purpose) flour
vegetable oil, for deep-frying
1 spring onion (scallion), cut into julienne
1 small handful of coriander (cilantro) leaves
half a lime

METHOD

Mix the Sichuan salt and pepper and the flour and sprinkle onto a tray or plate. Drain the tofu and pat dry with paper towel. Trim the edges and cut evenly into four large blocks, then place on the tray with the flour. Gently press the blocks into the flour, coating all sides, and leave to absorb for a minute. Press into the flour again and shake away any excess.

Heat the oil in a wok or deep-fryer until just smoking (180°C/350°F), and deep-fry the tofu until the crust is pale golden. Drain on paper towel, arrange on a serving plate with the spring onion and coriander and finish with a squeeze of lime.

NOTE   Any remaining flour mix can be passed through a sieve and re-used at a later date.

SILKEN TOFU WITH XO SAUCE

Another simple dish with heaps of flavour, this too relies on the silken texture of the tofu, so don't use any other kind. You could also easily add seafood — perhaps steamed scallops or prawns — to make it a more substantial meal.

300 g (10½ oz) silken tofu
3 tablespoons XO sauce (page 47)
1 tablespoon light soy sauce
2–3 spring onions (scallions), cut into julienne
a pinch of caster (superfine) sugar
2 tablespoons peanut oil

METHOD

Put the tofu in a shallow heatproof bowl and place the bowl in a bamboo steamer over a pot or a wok of rapidly boiling water. Cover the steamer with the lid and steam the tofu for 5 minutes to heat through.

Carefully remove the bowl from the steamer and pour off any excess liquid. Cut the tofu into six pieces, spoon the XO sauce over the tofu, then drizzle with soy sauce and sprinkle with the spring onions and sugar. Heat the peanut oil in a small pot until just smoking, then carefully pour the hot oil over the tofu to serve.

BRAISED TOFU, FAMILY-STYLE, WITH BLACK VINEGAR

Easy and delicious, the interesting flavours of the pickles make it really worth chasing them down. We used to sell loads of this at Wockpool in Sydney. This tofu is firmer than silken and is easier to handle in stir-fries, although this particular dish is really more like making a sauce and heating the tofu through. I love all the complex flavours here... very satisfying.

300 g (10½ oz) firm tofu, sliced into 6 pieces
2 tablespoons vegetable oil
2 braised shiitake mushrooms (page 87), sliced
1 small handful of pickled mustard greens, sliced
1 small handful of pickled salted radish, sliced
½ knob of ginger, peeled and cut into julienne
2 spring onions (scallions), sliced
2 tablespoons shaoxing
1 tablespoon kecap manis
1 tablespoon Chinkiang vinegar
1 tablespoon light soy sauce
1 teaspoon grated palm sugar (jaggery)
250 ml (9 fl oz/1 cup) fresh chicken stock (page 58)
½ Lebanese (short) cucumber, finely sliced
1 teaspoon Sichuan peppercorns, roasted and ground

METHOD

Heat the vegetable oil in a wok until just smoking. Add the mushrooms, mustard greens, radish, ginger and spring onions and stir-fry for 1–2 minutes, or until fragrant, then deglaze the wok with the shaoxing. Add the kecap manis, vinegar, soy sauce, palm sugar and stock. Check for balance, then add the tofu and reduce the heat to very low. Cover with a lid and braise for 4–5 minutes. Carefully transfer to a serving bowl, keeping the tofu intact. Top with the cucumber slices and sprinkle with the Sichuan pepper to serve.

MA PO TOFU

This is a Sichuan classic: grandmother's tofu. For a treat I have a bowl of this with rice for lunch. Another interesting way to make this is to steam the tofu in larger squares and sauce it with the stir-fried pork — it changes the texture of the dish and accentuates the silkiness of the tofu. This is also made with beef; just substitute it for the pork and away you go.

300 g (10½ oz) silken tofu, cut into 2 cm (¾ inch) cubes
2 tablespoons vegetable oil
200 g (7 oz) minced (ground) pork belly
1 clove garlic, finely chopped
2 spring onions (scallions), sliced
2 tablespoons hot bean paste
125 ml (4 fl oz/½ cup) fresh chicken stock (page 58)
1 teaspoon shaoxing
1 teaspoon light soy sauce
½ teaspoon dark soy sauce
2 teaspoons sugar
¼ teaspoon sea salt
a good pinch of Sichuan pepper
½ teaspoon sesame oil

METHOD

Heat a wok until smoking. Add the vegetable oil and, when hot, add the minced pork and stir-fry until browned. Then add the garlic, spring onions and bean paste and stir-fry until fragrant. Add the stock, shaoxing, soy sauces, sugar and salt. Bring to the boil, add the tofu and reduce the heat to a gentle simmer, allowing the liquid to thicken slightly. Add the Sichuan pepper and sesame oil and gently mix together.

CRISPY TOFU & PORK BALLS

These are good to serve with another dish or two that are saucy. They also make perfect cocktail food with a little chilli or sweet soy sauce. The lettuce is important — each tofu and pork ball should be wrapped up with some chilli sauce in a lettuce leaf. It gives a crunchy, simultaneously hot and cooling sensation that really makes the dish.

300 g (10½ oz) firm tofu
100 g (3½ oz) minced (ground) pork belly
30 g (1 oz) piece of ham, finely diced
1 clove garlic, finely chopped
2 teaspoons finely chopped ginger
½ spring onion (scallion), finely sliced
½ teaspoon sea salt
2 teaspoons grated palm sugar (jaggery)
3 teaspoons fish sauce
1 tablespoon plain (all-purpose) flour
vegetable oil, for deep-frying
lettuce, to serve
fresh chilli sauce (page 44), to serve

METHOD

Mash up the tofu with a fork and add the minced pork, ham, garlic, ginger, spring onion, sea salt, palm sugar, fish sauce and flour. Mix together well with your hands. Shape into 3 cm (1¼ inch) balls.

Heat the oil in a wok or deep-fryer until just smoking (180°C/350°F), and deep-fry the balls in batches until golden brown, making sure not to overcrowd the wok. Drain on paper towel and serve on a plate of washed lettuce with the chilli sauce on the side.

OYSTER OMELETTE

This is classic hawker-style fare — if you like oysters, you'll love this omelette. Breathtakingly simple, it relies on getting the oil really hot to give the omelette its crisp texture.

12 freshly shucked oysters
3 free-range or organic eggs
4 cloves garlic, finely chopped
2 spring onions (scallions), finely sliced
1 teaspoon sea salt
1 tablespoon shaoxing
1 tablespoon oyster sauce
4 tablespoons vegetable oil
fresh chilli sauce (page 44), to serve

METHOD

Whisk together the eggs, garlic, spring onions, sea salt, shaoxing and oyster sauce.

Heat the oil in a wok over high heat until just smoking, drop in the egg mixture and gently stir until almost set. Add the oysters and carefully flip the omelette over. Cook until starting to crisp underneath, slide onto a plate, drizzle with chilli sauce and serve.

VARIATION

You can also see mussel omelettes cooked this way in Thai street stalls. The truth is you could add anything to this egg mix to make a delicious omelette for lunch or dinner — try barbecued pork, prawn, shredded chicken, crabmeat, or whatever else you like. As with the scrambled eggs overleaf, the sky is the limit.

PRAWN SCRAMBLED EGGS

This dish is so easy; you cook the prawns, scramble the eggs and add the sauce which, with the perfume of sesame, gives this simple dish a great Asian flavour. I can hear you say 'I don't eat scrambled eggs for dinner', but don't think like that! This is also a perfect lunch with a bowl of rice.

300 g (10½ oz) green king prawns (shrimp), peeled and
    deveined
2 large free-range or organic eggs
3 tablespoons vegetable oil
1 spring onion (scallion), sliced

SAUCE
2 tablespoons light soy sauce
1 teaspoon sugar
a few drops of sesame oil

METHOD

To make the sauce, combine the soy sauce, sugar and sesame oil with 2 tablespoons water in a small pot and bring to the boil, then remove from the heat. Break the eggs into a bowl and lightly break up with a fork.

Heat a wok until almost smoking. Add half the oil and, when hot, stir-fry the prawns in two batches until almost cooked through. Remove the prawns, then wipe the wok clean. Heat the remaining oil and stir-fry the eggs until just beginning to set, then add the prawns and spring onion and gently toss together. Remove from the heat, spoon onto a plate and pour the warm sauce over the eggs to serve.

VARIATION

Of course pretty much anything works here as well. Replace the prawns with scallops, barbecued pork, lobster meat or crabmeat for a real treat.

STIR-FRIED SPANNER CRAB OMELETTE

This was created in 1989 at Rockpool, inspired by all those great Asian omelettes I love. Again, it's really all about getting the oil really, really, really hot. The crisp texture of the outside of the omelette with its centre of melting crab and hot bean sprouts is sublime.

200 g (7 oz) spanner crabmeat, picked through
4 free-range or organic eggs, lightly beaten
1 tablespoon grated palm sugar (jaggery)
1 tablespoon fish sauce
100 g (3½ oz) bean sprouts
50 g (1¾ oz) snow pea (mangetout) sprouts, trimmed
15 g (½ oz) Chinese yellow chives, washed and halved
150 ml (5 fl oz) vegetable oil
4 tablespoons oyster sauce

BROTH
150 ml (5 fl oz) fresh chicken stock (page 58)
3 tablespoons grated palm sugar (jaggery)
2 tablespoons fish sauce
1 teaspoon sesame oil

METHOD

To make the broth, mix together the stock, palm sugar and fish sauce in a pot and bring to the boil. Remove the broth from the heat, add the sesame oil and keep warm.

Dissolve the palm sugar in the fish sauce, then whisk in the eggs. Gently mix together the bean sprouts, snow pea sprouts, chives and crabmeat in a separate bowl.

Heat a wok until just smoking. Add the oil and, when hot, pour in the egg mixture and cook for 3 minutes, moving the egg around the wok until the bottom is golden brown. Spoon the crab mixture into the centre and turn down the heat. Pour off any excess oil and flip the omelette over so that the crab is underneath the egg. Leave for 1 minute, then transfer the omelette to a chopping board, trim the ends and place in a large bowl. Pour in the hot broth and drizzle with oyster sauce to serve.

VARIATION

You can substitute whatever you like for the crab or make this a vegetarian dish if you like by leaving out the crab.

TEA EGGS

The whites are hard, the yolks creamy and these are the most beautiful patterned jewels. By cracking the shells and then cooking the eggs in the soy and tea mix, you get the most amazing crazy patterns. They are great on cold-cut platters or in little composite salads, served with Sichuan pickled cucumbers and pickled cabbage, some barbecued pork or white-cut chicken and chilli sauce.

6 free-range or organic eggs
3 tablespoons Jasmine tea leaves
2 cassia bark sticks
3 star anise
½ teaspoon sea salt
100 ml (3½ fl oz) dark soy sauce

METHOD

Cover the eggs with water in a small pot and bring to the boil. Simmer for 10 minutes, then drain and plunge them into iced water. Tap the eggs gently with the back of a spoon to cover them all over with small cracks. Return the eggs to the pot and cover with fresh water. Add the tea, cassia bark, star anise, salt and soy sauce. Simmer gently for 1 hour, remove from the heat and leave in the mixture until cool. To serve, take the eggs out of the stock and remove the shells.

THAI DEVILLED EGGS

These are pretty simple and make a fun starter for a dinner party. They're a slightly more sophisticated version of 'son-in-law' eggs, which are soft-boiled eggs, fried until crisp, cut in half and drizzled with Nam Jim soured with tamarind.

4 free-range or organic eggs, hard-boiled, peeled and
    halved lengthways
50 g (1¾ oz) minced (ground) pork belly
1 clove garlic, finely chopped
1 coriander (cilantro) root, scraped and finely chopped
2 teaspoons sea salt
vegetable oil, for deep-frying
1 red shallot, finely sliced and deep-fried until golden
½ spring onion (scallion), cut into julienne
1½ tablespoons peanuts, roasted and crushed

FOR CRUMBING
30 g (1 oz/¼ cup) plain (all-purpose) flour
1 egg, lightly beaten
3 tablespoons milk
30 g (1 oz/½ cup) Japanese breadcrumbs (panko)

DRESSING
60 g (2¼ oz/⅓ cup) grated palm sugar (jaggery)
4 tablespoons fish sauce
4 tablespoons tamarind water (page 32)
½ teaspoon chilli powder

METHOD

Remove the egg yolks and put them in a bowl with the pork, garlic, coriander root and sea salt. Work the mixture with your hands until well combined and sticky. Spoon the pork mixture into the egg whites.

Make a crumbing station with a plate of flour, a bowl with combined egg and milk, and another plate with the breadcrumbs. Coat each egg in flour, shaking away any excess, dip in the egg wash and then roll in the breadcrumbs.

To make the dressing, mix together all the ingredients in a small pot. Simmer for about 3 minutes until the dressing reaches a syrupy consistency.

Heat the oil in a wok or deep-fryer until just smoking (180°C/350°F), and deep-fry the eggs in two or three batches until golden brown and cooked through. Remove the eggs with a slotted spoon and drain on paper towel. Pile the eggs onto a plate, pour over the dressing and sprinkle with fried shallots, spring onion and peanuts.

SMOKED TOFU STEAMED WITH BLACK BEANS & CHILLIES

I love the taste of this smoked tofu. It's available in Chinatowns and Asian food stores all around the world. One of my favourite Hunan dishes pairs this, thinly sliced, with thinly sliced pork belly, stir-fried with leek and chilli. Now that is a dish worth travelling for.

250 g (9 oz) smoked tofu
a good pinch of chilli flakes
2 tablespoons julienned ginger
1 tablespoon fermented black beans
3 tablespoons peanut oil
3 tablespoons light soy sauce
1 teaspoon caster (superfine) sugar
1 spring onion (scallion), minced
a few drops of sesame oil
a few drops of chilli oil

METHOD

Cut the tofu into slices about 1 cm (½ inch) thick and place in a heatproof bowl. Sprinkle the chilli flakes, ginger, black beans, oil, soy sauce and the sugar over the top of the tofu. Place the bowl in a steamer and steam over high heat for 15–20 minutes, until the tofu is heated through and the flavours have mingled.

Place the tofu on a plate, stir the sauce well and spoon over the tofu. Sprinkle over the spring onion and drizzle with the sesame oil and chilli oil.

Banquet Menu One

BRAISED SHIITAKE MUSHROOMS ⚘ PAGE 87

BRAISED BITTER MELON ⚘ PAGE 339

CRISP-FRIED CHICKEN WITH BLACK VINEGAR GLAZE ⚘ PAGE 133

STIR-FRIED LAMB WITH BAMBOO SHOOTS ⚘ PAGE 234

HOT & SOUR SOUP ⚘ PAGE 63

RECIPES ARE PICTURED ON FOLLOWING PAGES CLOCKWISE FROM TOP LEFT

PORK

Buy good-quality pork for these dishes — free-range is best, and if you have a chance, try some of the better producers with heritage breeds so you get pork with great texture and flavour. Remember as well that fat is flavour and with slow Chinese red braising the fat is rendered to the point that the meat is incredibly tender. Don't go lean with your pork — it won't taste as good.

I generally use pork fillet or boneless leg for stir-fries. I tend to think that the leg has more flavour and dries out less, unless the pork is twice-cooked. You can also braise pork neck, shoulder, hock and belly and add it, sliced, to any stir-fry or salad with a fiery hot dressing.

CHINESE-STYLE BARBECUE PORK

Interestingly enough, this famous pork is not barbecued, but cooked in an oven, usually the same oven where the ducks are cooked in Chinese restaurants — your oven at home will do a nice job as well. It's delicious.

1 kg (2 lb 4 oz) pork neck, cut lengthways into 4 cm
    (1½ inch) wide strips
260 g (9¼ oz/¾ cup) honey

MARINADE
4 tablespoons fermented red bean curd, mashed
3 tablespoons light soy sauce
3 tablespoons yellow bean soy sauce
100 ml (3½ fl oz) shaoxing
4 tablespoons hoisin sauce
4 tablespoons sugar
3 cloves garlic, finely chopped

METHOD
To make the marinade, whisk the bean curd, soy sauces, shaoxing, hoisin, sugar and the garlic until the sugar has dissolved. Add the pork and toss to coat, then marinate for 2 hours. Preheat the oven to 240°C (475°F/Gas 8).

Fit a wire rack over a roasting tin filled with about 3 cm (1¼ inches) water. Put the pork directly onto the rack and roast in the oven for 30 minutes, or until the pork is well caramelised and quite dark in places.

Melt the honey in a small pot over low heat and brush it all over the pork strips, then leave to cool.

NOTE The pork can be served warm with rice, as a cold cut, or used in stir-fries and soups. One of my favourite ways to start a dinner party, if indeed I'm going to serve something first, is to do a mixed plate of white-cut chicken, barbecue pork, tea eggs, pickled cabbage and serve it all with fried wontons.

THAI-STYLE BARBECUE PORK

Now this is real barbecued pork — a great dish to serve with Nam Jim dipping sauce, and to enjoy with a few other dishes and rice. I often use pork belly for this dish as I love the creamy texture it gets because of the fat content, but shoulder does the trick just as well.

500 g (1 lb 2 oz) pork shoulder, cut into 3 cm
    (1¼ inch) thick slices
1 Lebanese (short) cucumber, sliced on the diagonal
1 tomato, sliced into rounds
2 mignonette lettuce leaves
sweet chilli sauce (page 45), to serve

MARINADE
2 tablespoons light soy sauce
2 teaspoons shaoxing
1 tablespoon sesame oil
4 tablespoons sugar
1 teaspoon sea salt
2 cloves garlic, finely chopped
1 knob of ginger, peeled and finely chopped
2 tablespoons honey

METHOD
Mix together all the marinade ingredients, along with the pork, and leave to marinate overnight.

Heat a grill or a barbecue to hot and grill the pork for about 5 minutes on each side, brushing with the remaining marinade as it cooks. It should be golden on the outside and just cooked through. Remove from the grill and cut each piece into smaller slices. Arrange the cucumber, tomato and lettuce on a plate, then top the salad with pork slices. Serve with the sweet chilli sauce.

PORK SPARE RIBS BRAISED WITH CHILLI & BLACK BEANS

I'm a big fan of ribs anytime; but steamed or deep-fried and then braised like this, with the addition of black beans, they're positively addictive.

1 kg (2 lb 4 oz) pork spare ribs, cut into individual ribs
sea salt
vegetable oil, for deep-frying
1 tablespoon fermented black beans
1 long red chilli, finely sliced
2 cloves garlic, smashed
1 knob of ginger, peeled and finely sliced
3 spring onions (scallions), cut into 4 cm (1½ inch) lengths
2 teaspoons sugar
¼ teaspoon ground white pepper
1 tablespoon dark soy sauce
500–750 ml (17–26 fl oz/2–3 cups) fresh chicken stock (page 58)

METHOD

Season the ribs with the sea salt. Heat the oil in a wok or deep-fryer until just smoking (180°C/350°F), and deep-fry the ribs in batches until golden brown, then drain on paper towel. Discard all but 2 tablespoons of oil from the wok and return the wok to the heat until it just starts smoking. Add the black beans, chilli, garlic, ginger and the spring onions and stir-fry until fragrant, then add the sugar, ½ teaspoon salt, the white pepper and soy sauce and remove from the heat.

Put the ribs and the black bean mixture in a large frying pan with a tight-fitting lid. Add enough chicken stock to reach halfway up the meat, cover and simmer for 45 minutes, turning occasionally, until tender.

PORK SIMMERED IN CARAMEL SAUCE

This is inspired by those wonderful braised caramel dishes from Vietnam. The meltingly soft pork and caramel poured over rice is a fantastic combination. It also works well with chicken thighs instead of pork. A really good grind of black pepper on top is essential to help balance out the flavour.

650 g (1 lb 7 oz) boneless pork belly, skin removed
250 g (9 oz) palm sugar (jaggery), crushed
150 ml (5 fl oz) fish sauce
freshly ground black pepper
half a lime
2 spring onions (scallions), cut into julienne
2 long red chillies, deseeded and cut into julienne
1 small handful of coriander (cilantro) leaves

METHOD

To make the caramel sauce, heat the sugar and a little water in a heavy-based pot, shaking often, until light golden brown and just caramelised. Remove from the heat and add the fish sauce and a little more water. Return to the heat briefly, season with freshly ground pepper and leave it to cool.

Cut the pork belly into eight even pieces. Add the meat to the cooled caramel sauce, mix well and bring to the boil. Reduce the heat to low, cover the pot and simmer for 1 hour, stirring occasionally, until the pork is tender. Season with a squeeze of lime juice. Spoon the pork and some of the caramel into a bowl and sprinkle with some more pepper, the spring onions, chillies and coriander leaves to serve.

STEAMED PORK BELLY WITH PRESERVED SHRIMP PASTE

This is home-style Chinese cooking. I first tasted this in Hong Kong in the early '90s and fell in love with it. I find the flavour quite haunting and, spooned over rice, it's wonderful. The pork belly needs to be sliced to the thickness of bacon, so ask the butcher to cut it on the meat slicer for you.

350 g (12 oz) boneless pork belly, skin removed, halved
    lengthways and very finely sliced
1 knob of ginger, peeled and cut into julienne
2 teaspoons Chinese shrimp paste
1 teaspoon sugar
2 tablespoons shaoxing
1 teaspoon light soy sauce
2 long red chillies, deseeded and cut into julienne

METHOD

Mix together the ginger, shrimp paste, sugar, shaoxing, soy sauce and half the chillies, then add the pork, turning to coat evenly, and leave to marinate for 20 minutes.

Arrange the pork on a large heatproof plate, allowing the slices to overlap slightly. Put the plate in a large bamboo steamer over a pot or a wok of rapidly boiling water, and pour the marinade juices over the pork. Cover the steamer with a lid and steam the pork for 30 minutes. Garnish with the remaining chillies to serve.

STIR-FRIED PORK & EGGPLANT

The pork becomes the dressing for the eggplant in this dish. By the way, this is just as great with only the pork and the sauce over a bowl of rice if you have an aversion to eggplant.

150 g (5½ oz) minced (ground) pork belly
1 eggplant (aubergine), cut into large dice
vegetable oil, for deep-frying
2 spring onions (scallions), sliced
1 knob of ginger, peeled and finely chopped
2 cloves garlic, finely chopped
1 tablespoon hot bean paste
2 teaspoons shaoxing
2 tablespoons light soy sauce
2 teaspoons sugar
4 tablespoons fresh chicken stock (page 58)
2 spring onions (scallions), cut into julienne
a pinch of Sichuan pepper

METHOD

Heat the oil in a wok or deep-fryer until almost smoking (180°C/350°F), and deep-fry the eggplant in batches until golden brown, then drain on paper towel. Carefully pour out the oil and wipe the wok clean.

Heat 3 tablespoons of vegetable oil in the wok, add the minced pork and stir-fry until the meat begins to colour. Add the sliced spring onions, ginger, garlic and hot bean paste and stir-fry until fragrant. Deglaze the wok with the shaoxing, add the soy sauce, sugar and chicken stock, and return the eggplant to the wok and simmer until the sauce thickens slightly. Spoon the eggplant onto a serving plate, top with the julienned spring onions and sprinkle with Sichuan pepper.

TWICE-COOKED PORK WITH LEEK & CAPSICUM

This is a truly delicious Sichuan-inspired dish. The pork belly is twice-cooked, rendering it melt-in-the-mouth tender. It's one of my favourite Sichuan dishes and it can be enhanced by stir-frying some slices of firm tofu with the pork. If you want to try it with the tofu, just add it to the wok when you add the leeks.

400 g (14 oz) piece of boneless pork belly
1 leek, cut into julienne
1 red capsicum (pepper), cut into julienne
vegetable oil, for deep-frying
2 long red chillies, finely sliced
1 clove garlic, finely chopped
1½ teaspoons shaoxing
½ teaspoon dark soy sauce
½ teaspoon light soy sauce
1½ teaspoons hot bean paste
1½ teaspoons sweet bean paste
3 tablespoons fresh chicken stock (page 58)
¼ teaspoon sugar

METHOD

In a medium pot, boil enough water to cover the pork. Add the pork to the boiling water, reduce the heat and cook at a bare simmer for 30 minutes, or until the meat is tender. Drain, let it cool, and then cut it into very fine slices.

Heat the oil in a wok or deep-fryer until just smoking (180°C/350°F), and deep-fry the pork in batches for just long enough to slightly colour the meat, then drain on paper towel. Pour all but 2 tablespoons of oil from the wok.

Reheat the oil in the wok until just smoking. Add the leek, capsicum, chilli and garlic and stir-fry until fragrant. Deglaze the wok with shaoxing, add the soy sauces, bean pastes, stock and sugar, and return the pork to the wok and stir-fry for another 2 minutes.

STIR-FRIED PORK WITH BEANS

This is what I would call a dry curry. Try it — it's simple and delicious. The shrimp paste is important here to add deep flavour and give that real curry taste. If you make this dish once, you'll make it often. Feel free to change the ingredients in the paste, just as long as you remember to taste for balance.

350 g (12 oz) pork loin, skin and excess fat removed, very finely sliced
150 g (5½ oz) green beans, trimmed and halved
2 tablespoons fish sauce
2 tablespoons vegetable oil
1 tablespoon grated palm sugar (jaggery)

PASTE
1 teaspoon sea salt
3 dried long red chillies, deseeded, soaked in warm water for 30 minutes and chopped
1 teaspoon chopped galangal
2 lemongrass stalks, tough outer leaves removed, chopped
2 coriander (cilantro) roots, scraped and chopped
1 teaspoon Thai shrimp paste, wrapped in foil and roasted until fragrant
6 red shallots, chopped
2 cloves garlic, chopped
5 white peppercorns
finely grated zest of 2 kaffir limes
2 tablespoons dried shrimp

METHOD

Mix the pork with 1 teaspoon of the fish sauce and leave to marinate for 10 minutes.

Pound all the paste ingredients in a mortar with a pestle until you have a fine paste. Or process with a blender, adding a little water if necessary.

Heat a wok until just smoking. Add the oil and, when hot, stir-fry the pork in batches until golden, then remove. Put the paste into the wok and stir-fry over medium heat for about 5 minutes, or until fragrant. Add the palm sugar and let it caramelise slightly, then add the remaining fish sauce. Return the pork to the wok with the beans, then stir-fry for another minute before serving.

STIR-FRIED PORK WITH XO SAUCE

We have three different chilli condiments that add complexity and flavour to this dish, but as they're all added at the same time, it makes it very simple. You can make your own XO sauce, or just buy some off the shelf.

The bamboo shoots are added for their texture (make sure you wash them well). You could also add some fresh vegetables for crunch. It's important to remember that these recipes are only a guideline and that you can drive the flavours and textures yourself — just remember to look for balance and to always taste before serving.

300 g (10½ oz) pork fillet, thickly sliced across the grain
3 tablespoons XO sauce (page 47)
a few drops of sesame oil
1½ teaspoons hot bean paste
¼ teaspoon chilli oil
1 tablespoon sugar
1 tablespoon light soy sauce
2 tablespoons vegetable oil
1 clove garlic, finely sliced
3 spring onions (scallions), cut into 4 cm (1½ inch)
    lengths
1 small knob of ginger, peeled and finely sliced
200 g (7 oz) tinned bamboo shoot slices, rinsed and
    drained
1 tablespoon shaoxing

METHOD

Mix together the XO sauce, sesame oil, hot bean paste, chilli oil, sugar and soy sauce in a small bowl.

Heat a wok until just smoking. Add the oil and, when hot, stir-fry the pork in batches until it has browned, then return all the pork to the wok and add the garlic, spring onions, ginger and bamboo shoots and stir-fry until fragrant. Deglaze the wok with the shaoxing, then add the XO sauce mixture and stir-fry until the sauce reduces and thickens slightly.

SPICED PORK SPARE RIBS

These delicious crisp little ribs have quite a different texture to the other rib dishes in this book. The Sichuan salt and pepper coating really kicks these along and they're great with a strong chilli dipping sauce.

1 kg (2 lb 4 oz) pork spare ribs, cut into single ribs
1 teaspoon light soy sauce
½ teaspoon shaoxing
½ teaspoon chilli oil
1 egg, lightly beaten
vegetable oil, for deep-frying
Sichuan salt and pepper (page 55), to serve
fresh chilli sauce (page 44), to serve

DIPPING SAUCE
2 tablespoons caster (superfine) sugar
¼ teaspoon sea salt
2 tablespoons Chinkiang vinegar

METHOD

To make the dipping sauce, combine the caster sugar, sea salt and Chinkiang vinegar with 2 tablespoons water in a small pot and stir over low heat until the sugar dissolves. Set aside to cool.

Mix the soy sauce, shaoxing, chilli oil and egg together with the ribs and toss to coat well, then marinate for about 30 minutes.

Heat the vegetable oil in a wok or deep-fryer until just smoking (180°C/350°F), and deep-fry the ribs in batches until golden brown, then drain on paper towel. Transfer the ribs to a plate, pour the sauce over the top and sprinkle with a little Sichuan salt and pepper. Serve with chilli sauce.

SPICY PORK NOODLES

This is a perfect lunch for two. I'm a big fan of making this dish really hot, with a bit of extra chilli on the side, but if the chilli bean paste is enough for you, just serve it as it is. A julienne of deseeded cucumber is another welcome addition — the dish is then hot and cooling at the same time.

400 g (14 oz) boneless pork belly, skinned and cut into
     bite-sized cubes
320 g (11 oz) fresh hokkien noodles, blanched
3 tablespoons peanut oil
2 small dried chillies
2 cloves garlic
5 slices of peeled ginger
2 tablespoons chilli bean paste
1 tablespoon shaoxing
light soy sauce, to taste
1 teaspoon salt
30 g (1 oz) yellow rock sugar
1 cassia bark stick
600 ml (21 fl oz) fresh chicken stock (page 58)
1 spring onion (scallion), finely sliced on the diagonal
chilli sauce (page 42), to serve

METHOD

Cover the pork with cold water in a pot and bring to the boil. When the scum rises to the top, drain the pork, rinse it under fresh cold water and pat dry with paper towel.

Heat a wok until just smoking. Add the peanut oil to the wok and, when hot, add the dried chillies, garlic and ginger and stir-fry until fragrant. Add the bean paste and stir-fry for a minute more. Add the pork and gently stir-fry for a further 2 minutes. Deglaze the wok with the shaoxing, and add the soy sauce, salt, sugar and cassia bark. Cover with chicken stock. Bring to the boil, then lower to a gentle simmer, simmering uncovered for about 1½ hours, or until tender.

Reheat the noodles in boiling water and drain. Place them in a large bowl and spoon the pork over. If the sauce is not quite thick enough, reduce over high heat for a minute or two, then pour the sauce over the noodles and sprinkle with spring onion. Serve with your favourite chilli sauce.

Banquet Menu Two

GRILLED BEEF WITH SPICY DIP ⚜ page 222

SWEET BLACK VINEGAR PORK BELLY ⚜ page 94

DEEP-FRIED QUAILS ⚜ page 280

STIR-FRIED BLUE EYE WITH SNAKE BEANS ⚜ page 163

RECIPES ARE PICTURED ON FOLLOWING PAGES CLOCKWISE FROM TOP LEFT

BEEF AND LAMB

The key here is to establish a good relationship with your butcher. Good-quality meat will make a huge difference to all your dishes. There is a lot of Wagyu out there in Australia and most of the cuts can be used in these dishes if you like. As a matter of fact, cuts like short ribs from Wagyu, with all that marbling, are really tremendous in the braised dishes.

There are only two recipes in this chapter for lamb, as it's not used all that often in Chinese cooking (mainly in the north of the country). However, we love our lamb in Australia, so in most of the beef recipes you could substitute lamb very successfully. The braised dishes would work well with shank or shoulder, and the stir-fries with thinly sliced lamb loin. Remember that the cheaper braising cuts will have the most flavour, and that double-cooking makes them both tender and delicious.

SPICED BEEF & NOODLE SOUP

This easy delicious soup can be made even hotter by stirring in some freshly chopped wild green chillies before serving.

300 g (10½ oz) beef brisket
2 star anise
1 teaspoon Sichuan peppercorns
1 teaspoon fennel seeds
2 cinnamon sticks, crushed
4 tablespoons peanut oil
2 cloves garlic, finely chopped
4 slices of peeled ginger
1 tablespoon hot bean paste
1 tablespoon shaoxing
2 tablespoons light soy sauce
¼ teaspoon sugar
¼ teaspoon sea salt
150 g (5½ oz) fresh hokkien noodles
¼ Chinese cabbage (wombok), cut into small chunks
1 spring onion (scallion), finely sliced

METHOD

Put the star anise, Sichuan peppercorns, fennel seeds and cinnamon sticks in a small square of muslin and tie together with string. Put this, along with the beef, into a large pot with 3.5 litres (14 cups) water. Bring to the boil, reduce the heat and simmer for 15 minutes, skimming the surface of any impurities, then turn down the heat to a bare simmer and cook for 1½–2 hours, or until the beef is tender.

Lift the beef out of the stock with a slotted spoon and then shred. Strain the stock through a fine sieve lined with muslin, discard the spice bag and reserve the stock.

Heat a wok until just smoking. Add the peanut oil and, when hot, stir-fry the garlic, ginger and hot bean paste until fragrant. Deglaze the wok with the shaoxing, then add the shredded beef, soy sauce, sugar, sea salt and reserved stock. Bring to the boil, then lower the heat and simmer for 10 minutes. Drop the noodles and diced cabbage into the soup and heat through for about 1 minute.

To serve, pour into a large bowl and sprinkle with spring onion.

SPICY BEEF SHANK SOUP

Winter melon is used mainly in soups and braises for its texture and ability to take on the flavours it's cooked with. I also like to steam it, then add it to stir-fries.

500 g (1 lb 2 oz) beef shank in osso buco rounds (this
    may be only 1 or 2 pieces)
3 long red chillies, sliced
1 knob of ginger, peeled and finely sliced
3 tablespoons shaoxing
8 dried shiitake mushrooms, soaked in warm water for
    30 minutes, stalks removed, sliced
1 small winter melon, peeled, deseeded and cut into
    large dice
sea salt
freshly ground white pepper
2 spring onions (scallions), finely sliced
1 small handful of coriander (cilantro) leaves

METHOD

Put the beef shank, chillies, ginger, shaoxing and 2 litres (8 cups) water in a pot and slowly bring to the boil, skimming thoroughly and frequently to remove any scum. Add the shiitakes and winter melon, reduce the heat and simmer slowly for 1–1½ hours, or until the beef is very tender.

Remove the beef from the soup, shred the flesh with your fingers, and remove the marrow from the middle of the bones. Return the beef and the marrow to the soup, taste and season with sea salt and freshly ground white pepper. Ladle into bowls and sprinkle with the spring onions and coriander leaves to serve.

GRILLED BEEF WITH SPICY DIP

This can be made into a beautiful salad by adding sliced Spanish onion, peanuts, fried shallots and some herbs to the sliced meat.

300 g (10½ oz) beef sirloin
1 teaspoon coarsely ground black pepper
1 tablespoon kecap manis
2 tablespoons peanut oil
lettuce or Chinese cabbage leaf, to serve

DIPPING SAUCE
1 tablespoon chilli powder
3 tablespoons fish sauce
3 tablespoons lime juice
1 tablespoon caster (superfine) sugar
1 red shallot, finely sliced
1 teaspoon finely chopped coriander (cilantro) leaves

METHOD

To make the dipping sauce, mix together the chilli powder, fish sauce, lime juice, caster sugar, shallot and coriander leaves.

Mix together the beef, pepper, kecap manis and peanut oil and leave to marinate for about 30 minutes.

Heat a barbecue or a grill to hot and cook the beef for 2 minutes on each side, allowing a good crust to form, then rest for 10 minutes. The beef should be medium-rare. Slice across the grain into thin slices, fan out on the lettuce or cabbage leaf if you like and serve with the dipping sauce.

FIVE-SPICE BEEF SHIN

This is really easy and delicious. You can make it in advance and reheat it when you're ready to serve, but it's also great cold with some pickled cabbage and fried wontons.

800 g (1 lb 12 oz) beef shin on the bone
200 g (7 oz) soft brown sugar
125 ml (4 fl oz/½ cup) shaoxing
4 cloves garlic, finely sliced
1 large knob of ginger, peeled and finely sliced
2 cinnamon sticks
1 star anise
½ teaspoon Sichuan peppercorns
2 tablespoons sea salt
250 ml (9 fl oz/1 cup) light soy sauce
1 large handful of coriander (cilantro) leaves

METHOD

Put the brown sugar, shaoxing, garlic, ginger, cinnamon, star anise, Sichuan peppercorns and sea salt along with 2 litres (8 cups) water in a large pot. Cover and bring to the boil over high heat. Add the soy sauce and return to the boil. Lower the heat, add the beef and simmer, covered, for about 4 hours, or until very tender. Remove from the heat and allow the beef to cool to room temperature in the liquid.

Shred the meat off the bone and put in a serving bowl. Strain the stock through a fine sieve and discard the solids. Reheat about 500 ml (17 fl oz/2 cups) of the stock and pour over the beef. Sprinkle with coriander leaves to serve.

NOTE Freeze or refrigerate left-over stock for use as a soup base.

SICHUAN SPICY BEEF POT

I first ate this in Sichuan restaurants and loved the breathtaking simplicity and hot, nutty flavour the chilli bean paste brings. The hot numbing sensation of the chillies and peppercorns is pretty special too.

I first cooked this dish from Fuchsia Dunlop's *Sichuan Cookery* — it's a truly great book and, like anything from her, very insightful. By the way, this spicy broth with some fish, prawns or squid waved through at the end would be delightful as well.

400 g (14 oz) tender lean beef, cut into slices 3–4 cm
    (1½ inches) thick
185 ml (6 fl oz/¾ cup) peanut oil
10 dried long red chillies, halved lengthways and
    deseeded
2 teaspoons Sichuan pepper
2 celery sticks, cut into 4 cm (1½ inch) julienne
1 small leek, cut in half lengthways, then cut into 4 cm
    (1½ inch) julienne
2 spring onions (scallions), cut into 2 cm (¾ inch) lengths
sea salt
90 g (3¼ oz/1 cup) bean sprouts, trimmed
3 tablespoons chilli bean paste
750 ml (26 fl oz/3 cups) fresh chicken stock (page 58)
2 teaspoons dark soy sauce

METHOD

Heat a wok until it just starts smoking. Add 3 tablespoons of peanut oil and stir-fry the chillies and Sichuan pepper over medium heat until fragrant and the chillies are just beginning to brown — don't blacken them. Immediately remove from the wok and allow to cool, then chop finely.

Reheat the wok, add 3 tablespoons of peanut oil and stir-fry the celery, leek and spring onion for 2 minutes, adding some sea salt to taste. Tip the vegetables straight into a serving bowl and sprinkle the bean sprouts on top.

Heat another 3 tablespoons of peanut oil in the wok. Add the chilli bean paste and stir-fry for 30 seconds until the oil is fragrant. Add the stock and the dark soy sauce and, when boiling, fold in the beef slices. Wait for the sauce to return to the boil and stir. Simmer for a minute and pour over the vegetables.

Wipe the wok and return to the heat. Heat until almost smoking and add the rest of the peanut oil. Add the chopped chillies and stir quickly, pour over the beef and send your sizzling beef to the table.

STIR-FRIED BEEF FILLET WITH LEEK &
SPANISH ONION

The addition of black vinegar to this simple stir-fry starts a little sweet and sour thing happening, adding real interest to the dish.

350 g (12 oz) beef fillet, thickly sliced across the grain
3 tablespoons vegetable oil
1 small leek, cut into julienne
1 small Spanish onion, halved and finely sliced
1 small knob of ginger, peeled and finely sliced
2 spring onions (scallions), cut into 2 cm (¾ inch) lengths
125 ml (4 fl oz/½ cup) fresh chicken stock (page 58)
1 tablespoon light soy sauce
2 teaspoons oyster sauce
1½ teaspoons sugar
1 tablespoon Chinkiang vinegar

MARINADE
1 tablespoon light soy sauce
1 teaspoon shaoxing
a pinch of sea salt

METHOD

To make the marinade, mix together the soy sauce, shaoxing and sea salt. Add the beef and leave for 30 minutes.

Heat a wok until just smoking. Add the vegetable oil and, when hot, stir-fry the beef in batches until well browned. Remove the beef from the wok. Stir-fry the leek and onion until they soften, then add the ginger and spring onions and stir-fry until fragrant. Return the beef to the wok, add the stock, soy sauce, oyster sauce, sugar and vinegar and cook over high heat until the sauce has almost completely evaporated.

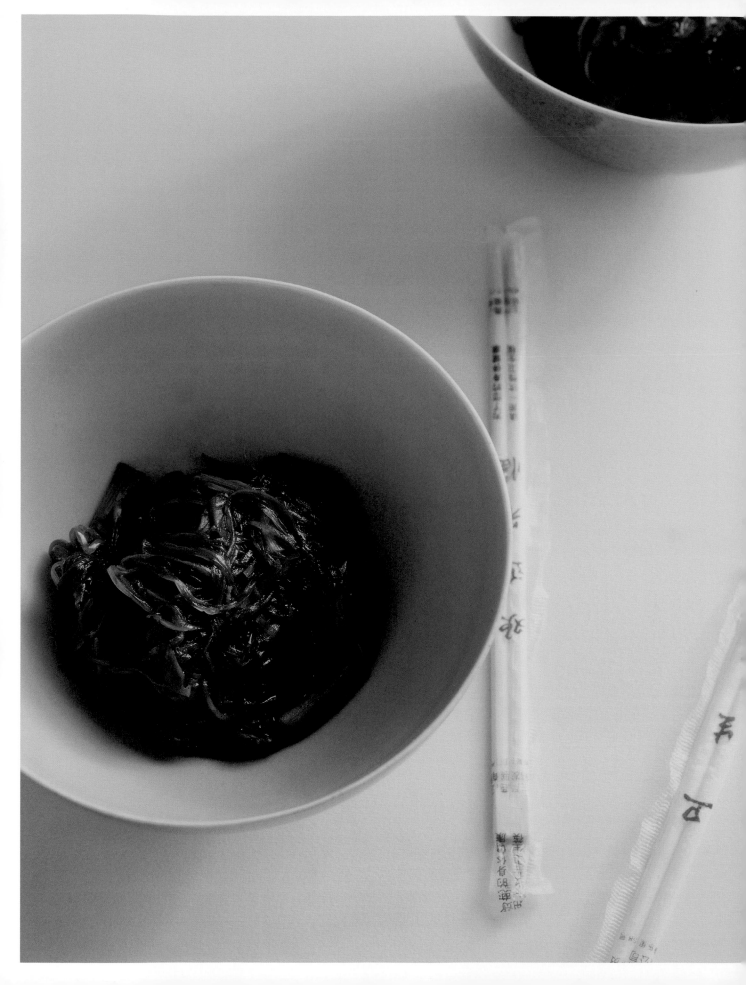

STIR-FRIED BEEF WITH SPRING ONIONS

The marinating here gives flavour to the meat, and the subtle flavour of spring onion works beautifully with the taste and texture of the beef. You can use this recipe as a base and add snow peas or beans, or any other vegetable you like. I love this with a few drops of chilli oil.

350 g (12 oz) beef fillet, thickly sliced across the grain
3 tablespoons peanut oil
1 bunch spring onions (scallions), cut into julienne
2 tablespoons light soy sauce
2 tablespoons sugar
1 teaspoon sesame oil
a pinch of freshly ground white pepper
chilli oil, to serve

MARINADE
2 cloves garlic, finely chopped
2 tablespoons light soy sauce
1 tablespoon shaoxing
2 teaspoons sugar

METHOD

To make the marinade, mix together the garlic, soy sauce, shaoxing and sugar, add the beef, leave for 1 hour, then drain.

Heat a wok until just smoking. Add the peanut oil and, when hot, stir-fry the beef in batches until well browned, then remove from the wok.

Add the spring onions to the wok and stir-fry for 1 minute, then add the soy sauce, sugar, sesame oil, pepper and the beef. Toss to coat the meat with the sauce and then use a slotted spoon to transfer the meat to a serving plate. Increase the heat under the wok and simmer the sauce until it reduces and thickens. Pour over the beef and serve with chilli oil.

STIR-FRIED BEEF FILLET WITH OYSTER SAUCE

It's not hard to see why this is one of the classics — it's simple and delicious. This has pickled ginger in it for a lift, but if you don't have any on hand, no matter. The same goes for the rock sugar — it adds a little more complexity, but if you don't have any handy, white sugar will do the trick. Like many of the other stir-fries, this is a good base for other meat or seafood, and you can add some vegetables for texture and flavour.

350 g (12 oz) beef fillet, thickly sliced across the grain
3 tablespoons peanut oil
1 red capsicum (pepper), diced
2 spring onions (scallions), cut into 4 cm (1½ inch)
    lengths
2 cloves garlic, finely chopped
1 small knob of ginger, peeled and cut into julienne
10 slices of pickled ginger

SAUCE
1 tablespoon light soy sauce
1 teaspoon dark soy sauce
4 tablespoons oyster sauce
2 tablespoons crushed yellow rock sugar
3 tablespoons fresh chicken stock (page 58)

METHOD

Heat a wok until just smoking. Add the peanut oil and, when hot, add the beef and stir-fry until browned, then add the capsicum and spring onions and stir-fry for 30 seconds. Add the garlic and ginger and stir-fry until fragrant, then add the sauce ingredients and stir-fry for another minute.

With a slotted spoon, transfer everything except the sauce to a large platter. Reduce the sauce until it thickens slightly and pour over the beef and vegetables. Top with pickled ginger to serve.

STIR-FRIED STEAK WITH GREEN & RED CAPSICUM

It's important to cut the beef fairly thin for this stir-fry, as sirloin isn't as naturally tender as beef fillet, but it does have a great flavour. The marinating will also help tenderise the beef.

300 g (10½ oz) beef sirloin, cut into thin slices
3 tablespoons vegetable oil
1 small onion, finely sliced
1 clove garlic, finely chopped
½ red capsicum (pepper), cut into large dice
½ green capsicum (pepper), cut into large dice
1 tablespoon shaoxing
1 tablespoon kecap manis
1 teaspoon Chinkiang vinegar
½ teaspoon sugar
freshly ground white pepper

MARINADE
½ egg white
1 tablespoon light soy sauce
1 tablespoon vegetable oil

METHOD

To make the marinade, mix the egg white, soy sauce and vegetable oil, add the beef, and leave for 30 minutes.

Heat a wok until just smoking. Add the vegetable oil and, when hot, stir-fry the beef until well browned. Remove from the wok and drain on paper towel. Add the onion, garlic and capsicum to the wok and stir-fry until fragrant. Deglaze the wok with the shaoxing and add the kecap manis, vinegar and sugar. Bring the sauce to the boil, return the beef to the wok and continue to stir-fry until the sauce has thickened and the beef is medium-rare. Sprinkle with white pepper to serve.

STIR-FRIED BEEF WITH SICHUAN PEPPERCORNS & SWEET BEAN SAUCE

I really love the numbing effect of the Sichuan peppercorns and the touch of heat the chilli oil gives this stir-fry. By all means, dial up the heat by adding more chilli oil.

350 g (12 oz) beef fillet, finely sliced across the grain,
    cut into thin strips
2 teaspoons Sichuan peppercorns
4 tablespoons peanut oil
1 teaspoon finely chopped ginger
1 clove garlic, finely chopped
2 teaspoons shaoxing
1 celery stalk, cut into julienne
2 spring onions (scallions), cut into julienne
1 small handful of coriander (cilantro) leaves

SWEET BEAN SAUCE
1½ tablespoons sweet bean paste
1 tablespoon Chinkiang vinegar
1 tablespoon caster (superfine) sugar
¼ teaspoon chilli oil
a pinch of sea salt

METHOD

To make the sweet bean sauce, mix together the sweet bean paste, Chinkiang vinegar, caster sugar, chilli oil and sea salt.

Heat a wok until just smoking. Add half the oil and, when hot, stir-fry the beef in batches until well browned, then remove and wipe the wok clean.

Heat the remaining oil in the wok until just smoking and stir-fry the ginger and garlic until fragrant. Deglaze the wok with the shaoxing, return the beef to the wok with the sweet bean sauce and toss well to ensure the beef is evenly coated. Add the Sichuan peppercorns, celery and spring onions and toss to heat through. Spoon onto a plate and sprinkle with coriander leaves to serve.

THAI-STYLE BEEF WITH CHILLIES & SNOW PEAS

This is, in essence, a dry-fried curry. You'll love the fresh flavours the paste brings to the dish, but be careful not to burn it. You could add a teaspoon of shrimp paste to the spice paste to really add to its depth of flavour.

350 g (12 oz) beef fillet, thickly sliced across the grain
100 g (3½ oz) snow peas (mangetout), trimmed
3 tablespoons vegetable oil
3 tablespoons grated palm sugar (jaggery)
2 tablespoons fish sauce
50 g (1¾ oz) fresh black fungi, torn
1 tablespoon chopped coriander (cilantro) leaves
juice of half a lime

SPICE PASTE
2 dried long red chillies, deseeded, soaked in warm water
    for 30 minutes and chopped
3 red shallots, chopped
2 cloves garlic, chopped
1 tablespoon chopped galangal
2 lemongrass stalks, tough outer leaves removed,
    chopped
6 coriander (cilantro) roots, scraped and chopped
½ teaspoon coriander seeds, roasted and crushed
6 white peppercorns, roasted and crushed
1 teaspoon sea salt

METHOD

Pound the spice paste ingredients in a mortar with a pestle until you have a fine paste. Or process in a blender, adding a little water if necessary.

Heat a wok until just smoking. Add the vegetable oil and, when hot, stir-fry the beef in batches until well browned, then remove from the wok. Add the paste to the wok and stir-fry until fragrant, then add the palm sugar and fish sauce. Return the beef to the wok with the snow peas and black fungi and stir-fry for a minute or so to integrate the flavours. Stir through the coriander and season with the lime juice to serve.

STIR-FRIED LAMB WITH BAMBOO SHOOTS

A very simple stir-fry, this is also delicious if you substitute beef or chicken for the lamb. You can use other vegetables instead of bamboo shoots, sliced asparagus for example. If you are using bamboo shoots, remember that they need to be rinsed well.

350 g (12 oz) lamb loin, finely sliced across the grain
150 g (5½ oz) tinned bamboo shoots, rinsed, drained and
   finely shredded
250 ml (9 fl oz/1 cup) peanut oil
1 tablespoon finely chopped ginger
1 clove garlic, finely chopped
2 teaspoons shaoxing
1 tablespoon light soy sauce
1 teaspoon dark soy sauce
1 teaspoon sea salt
1 teaspoon rice vinegar
4 tablespoons fresh chicken stock (page 58)

MARINADE
1 tablespoon light soy sauce
1 teaspoon sugar
2 teaspoons shaoxing
½ teaspoon sesame oil
½ teaspoon freshly ground white pepper

METHOD

To make the marinade, mix together the soy sauce, sugar, shaoxing, sesame oil and white pepper, add the lamb, and leave for 15 minutes.

Heat a wok until just smoking. Add 185 ml (6 fl oz/¾ cup) of the peanut oil and, when hot, add the lamb and stir-fry for 30 seconds, then remove and drain. Next add the bamboo shoots and stir-fry for 30 seconds, then remove and drain. Discard the oil.

Reheat the wok with the remaining oil until just smoking. Add the ginger and garlic and stir-fry until fragrant. Deglaze the wok with the shaoxing and add the soy sauces, sea salt, vinegar and stock. Simmer the liquid to reduce by about half, then return the lamb and bamboo shoots to the wok and toss together.

STIR-FRIED LAMB WITH CUMIN

I have a favourite Sichuan restaurant north of Sydney and tend to stick to the few classic dishes they do really well. Sam and I often have their twice-cooked pork with chilli, a wonderful combination of poached and stir-fried pork belly with tofu and chilli — it's definitely worth the trip over the Harbour Bridge. The other dish we order is this one: the cumin lamb. I particularly love it with their steamed buns. We mop up the chilli oil and eat the buns with pieces of lamb. You can add cumin powder to the dish instead of the seeds, but I love the crunch and intense flavour burst of the whole seeds.

350 g (12 oz) lamb loin, finely sliced across the grain
peanut oil, for stir-frying
1 teaspoon finely chopped garlic
1 tablespoon finely chopped ginger
2 long red chillies, deseeded and sliced
1 teaspoon chilli flakes
2 teaspoons roasted cumin seeds
1 teaspoon light soy sauce
1 spring onion (scallion), finely sliced
10 drops of chilli oil
1 teaspoon sesame oil

MARINADE
1 tablespoon shaoxing
¼ teaspoon salt
1 teaspoon light soy sauce
1 teaspoon dark soy sauce

METHOD

To make the marinade, mix together the shaoxing, salt, soy sauces and the lamb and leave for an hour.

Heat a wok until just smoking. Add the peanut oil and, when hot, stir-fry the lamb in batches until coloured, stirring so it won't stick. Remove the lamb and place in a bowl.

Add another 3 tablespoons of peanut oil to the wok and reheat until almost smoking. Add the garlic, ginger, fresh chilli, chilli flakes and cumin seeds and stir-fry until fragrant. Return the lamb to the wok, stir and season with the soy sauce, then heat through. Add the spring onion, chilli oil and sesame oil and remove from the heat. Spoon the lamb onto a plate to serve.

Banquet Menu Three

WHOLE STEAMED SNAPPER WITH GINGER
& SPRING ONION ⚹ PAGE 110

CHICKEN CURRY, SOUTHERN THAI-STYLE ⚹ PAGE 159

STIR-FRIED BEEF WITH ASPARAGUS & MUSHROOMS ⚹ PAGE 119

RECIPES ARE PICTURED ON FOLLOWING PAGES CLOCKWISE FROM TOP LEFT

POULTRY

The most important thing with poultry is, whenever possible, to buy free-range or organic as the taste difference between them and their battery-raised cousins is vast. The same rule applies to ducks, pigeons and quail.

Many of my recipes call for chicken leg or duck with the bones in. I know that it can be a bit of a hassle to eat, but the flavour and texture is worth the effort; chicken cooks much moister on the bone. To me, it's the real way of eating.

To be completely honest, I don't really like chicken breast, except when roasted to perfection or, at a pinch, well poached. But give me a leg or a wing and I'll chew on it all day. There is something very authentic about taking some chicken leg in your mouth, chewing it around and gently spitting the bone out.

CHICKEN, LILY BUD, CHESTNUT & SHIITAKE NOODLE SOUP

These double-boiled soups are wonderful — they're no work at all and they highlight the natural taste of the ingredients. It's important to blanch the chicken legs first or you'll end up with bits floating in your broth.

4 chicken drumsticks
10 dried lily buds, soaked in warm water for 30 minutes
10 dried chestnuts, soaked in warm water for 30 minutes
6 dried shiitake mushrooms, soaked in warm water for
    30 minutes and stalks removed
4 tomatoes, peeled and quartered lengthways
1 litre (35 fl oz/4 cups) fresh chicken stock (page 58)
2 tablespoons shaoxing
2 tablespoons oyster sauce
1 teaspoon sea salt
200 g (7 oz) fresh egg noodles, blanched
1 spring onion (scallion), finely sliced
1 small handful of coriander (cilantro) leaves

METHOD

Blanch the chicken drumsticks in boiling water, then rinse them to remove any impurities.

Put the drumsticks, tomatoes, lily buds, chestnuts, shiitake mushrooms, chicken stock, shaoxing, oyster sauce and sea salt into a large heatproof bowl. Cover the bowl tightly with foil and put in a bamboo steamer over a pot or wok of rapidly boiling water. Cover and steam for 50 minutes. Remove the chicken from the bowl and set aside to cool slightly. Remove the skin, then shred the meat from the bones. Stir the chicken meat, noodles, spring onion and coriander through the soup and ladle into bowls to serve.

SHREDDED CABBAGE & CHICKEN SALAD

I make this at home all the time. While I'll often just use a roast chock, it's also great with duck or a combination of prawns and chicken. I find the easiest way to shred the cabbage is to use a Japanese mandolin, a piece of equipment I find indispensable, but do watch your fingers.

½ master-stock chicken, shredded (page 82)
125 g (4½ oz/2 cups) finely shredded Chinese cabbage
1 small carrot, cut into julienne
1 small handful of mint leaves, finely shredded
freshly ground black pepper, to serve

DRESSING
2 long red chillies, deseeded and finely chopped
2 small wild green chillies, finely chopped
3 cloves garlic, finely chopped
2 tablespoons caster (superfine) sugar
1 tablespoon rice vinegar
juice of 3 limes
3 tablespoons fish sauce
3 tablespoons vegetable oil
1 small Spanish onion, finely sliced
freshly ground black pepper

METHOD
To make the dressing, mix together all the ingredients and leave for 30 minutes for the flavours to mingle.

Mix together the chicken, cabbage, carrot and mint, pour the dressing over and toss together. Transfer the salad to a beautiful bowl and give it a good grind of black pepper to serve.

SPICY BARBECUED CHICKEN WINGS

This marinade works well with any meat you like to barbecue. I particularly love lamb cutlets done this way — there's something so nice about chewing on a chicken or a lamb bone.

1 kg (2 lb 4 oz) free-range or organic chicken wings,
    wing tips removed
1 knob of ginger, peeled and roughly chopped
3 cloves garlic
1 tablespoon kecap manis
1 tablespoon light soy sauce
1 tablespoon shaoxing
1 tablespoon honey
1 teaspoon five-spice powder
1 teaspoon chilli powder
2 tablespoons vegetable oil
½ teaspoon sesame seeds, roasted
sweet chilli sauce (page 45), to serve

METHOD

Pound the ginger and garlic in a mortar with a pestle to form a paste. Transfer the paste to a bowl and stir in the kecap manis, soy sauce, shaoxing, honey, five-spice and chilli powder. Add the chicken wings and toss until well coated, then set aside for at least 2 hours.

Remove the wings from the marinade, brush with oil and barbecue over medium–high heat until golden and crispy. Sprinkle with sesame seeds and serve with sweet chilli sauce.

GARLIC & CHILLI BRAISED CHICKEN

This simple classic braise sees the chicken deep-fried first to add colour and texture, then gently braised for tenderness as it makes its own sauce. You can use chicken thighs, boneless if you wish, but I much prefer to suck the chicken off the bone, as it has heaps more flavour that way and stays moist. Don't use chicken breasts — they dry out too much.

4 free-range or organic chicken legs, chopped into
    bite-sized pieces
peanut oil, for deep-frying
4 small dried chillies
10 cloves garlic, peeled and cut in half
2 tablespoons sliced ginger
2 cassia bark sticks
2 tablespoons chilli bean paste
750 ml (26 fl oz/3 cups) fresh chicken stock (page 58)
2 tablespoons shaoxing
1 tablespoon light soy sauce
sea salt
1 spring onion (scallion), finely sliced

METHOD

Heat a wok until smoking. Add 1.5 litres (52 fl oz/6 cups) peanut oil and, when hot, deep-fry the chicken pieces in batches until light golden brown. Drain the oil, strain and reserve for future use.

Reheat the wok over medium heat and add 3 tablespoons of peanut oil. Add the chillies and cook until they start to colour. Add the garlic, ginger and cassia and cook until fragrant. Add the chilli bean paste and continue to fry until well incorporated.

Add the fried chicken, the stock, shaoxing, soy sauce and salt to taste. Bring to the boil, reduce the heat and simmer gently, uncovered, for about 20 minutes, stirring from time to time. By the time the chicken has cooked, the sauce may not have reduced enough. If that is the case, remove the chicken, return the wok to high heat and reduce for a minute or two more until it has thickened. Pour the sauce over the chicken and sprinkle with spring onion.

BARBECUED CHICKEN WITH TAMARIND

This is a lovely sweet and sour combination. You can buy ready-made tamarind water these days, but I think it's better if you make your own by soaking tamarind pulp in hot water — it tends to be thicker and more fruit flavoured.

1.6 kg (3 lb 8 oz) free-range or organic chicken, cut into
    8 pieces
2 tablespoons vegetable oil
1 large handful of mixed herbs such as coriander
    (cilantro), mint and Thai basil
2 long red chillies, deseeded and cut into julienne
2 spring onions (scallions), cut into julienne

MARINADE
2 tablespoons coriander seeds, roasted and ground
125 ml (4 fl oz/½ cup) tamarind water (page 32)
3 tablespoons grated palm sugar (jaggery)
1½ tablespoons light soy sauce
2 tablespoons oyster sauce
2 teaspoons sea salt
1 teaspoon freshly ground white pepper

METHOD

To make the marinade, mix together the coriander seeds, tamarind water, palm sugar, soy sauce, oyster sauce, sea salt and white pepper, add the chicken pieces and refrigerate for several hours or overnight. Drain the chicken and reserve the marinade.

To cook the chicken, heat the barbecue to hot. Brush the grill with vegetable oil and place the chicken skin-side-down. Cook for 5 minutes before turning, and then cook for another 5 minutes, or until just cooked through. Remove the chicken and leave to rest in a warm place for 10 minutes.

Meanwhile, put the reserved marinade in a wok and simmer over high heat until it reduces and thickens slightly. Arrange the chicken, skin-side-up, on a serving plate, then pour the marinade over the top. Mix the herbs, chillies and spring onions together and scatter over the chicken to serve.

CHINESE ROAST DUCK

This is a classic and it's really not as difficult as it sounds — just a few steps and away you go. You need to loosen the skin from the meat, blow the duck up with a bike pump, glaze the skin, dry the duck, fill the cavity with hot broth so it steams from within and roast — what could be easier!

There's a reason it's one of the most loved duck dishes in the world — it tastes bloody fantastic. You can take the skin and meat off the bone to serve with mandarin pancakes, hoisin, cucumber batons and spring onions; Peking duck in other words.

1 x 2 kg (4 lb 8 oz) duck, wing tips and tail removed
1 teaspoon Sichuan salt and pepper (page 55)
3 star anise
2 cinnamon sticks
185 ml (6 fl oz/¾ cup) fresh chicken stock (page 58)
3 tablespoons light soy sauce
50 g (1¾ oz/¼ cup) crushed yellow rock sugar
1 tablespoon sesame oil

MALTOSE MIXTURE
185 ml (6 fl oz/¾ cup) maltose
125 ml (4 fl oz/½ cup) light soy sauce
3 tablespoons rice vinegar

METHOD

Remove the fat from the cavity of the duck. Put the bird breast-side-up on a chopping board, with the legs facing you. Massage the skin on the breasts and legs for about 5 minutes (this helps loosen the connecting tissue between the skin and the meat). Make a small slit in the skin. Carefully work a chopstick under the skin and down the breast and over the legs to loosen the skin without tearing it. Once the skin is loose, rub the meat of the duck (under the skin) with Sichuan salt and pepper and position the star anise and cinnamon sticks in between the meat and the skin.

Secure the rear cavity of the duck with a bamboo or metal skewer, as if you were sewing cloth together. Tie a double piece of string firmly around the top of the neck, above the slit, leaving one end long. Tie off the neck below the slit using a slip knot, and insert a drinking straw or the tube of a bicycle pump into the slit. Inflate the cavity you have made between the skin and the body of the duck and, when fully inflated, tighten the second string around the neck to make it airtight.

To make the maltose mixture, put the maltose, soy sauce, rice vinegar and 5 litres (20 cups) water into a large pot, bring to the boil and cook for 5 minutes. Holding onto the top string, submerge the duck for 20 seconds, breast-side-down, in the boiling maltose. Then, holding it above the maltose, baste the duck with the mixture for about 5 minutes until the skin tightens. Take care not to let the glaze become too dark or the duck will burn in the oven before it cooks. Drain the excess maltose from the duck and hang it to dry over a bowl in front of a fan for 3 hours. The skin should now feel like parchment.

Preheat the oven to 220°C (425°F/Gas 7) and put a roasting tin full of water on the bottom of the oven. Now bring the stock, soy sauce, sugar and sesame oil to the boil in a large pot. Remove the skewer slightly from the rear of the duck, insert a funnel and carefully pour the boiling liquid into the cavity, securing the skewer tightly once again when this is done. Put the duck into the oven directly on the rack and in the tin of water, with its legs pointing towards the door. Roast for between 45 minutes and 1 hour. When cooked (the juices will run clear), remove from the oven and rest for 10 minutes. Then remove the skewer, drain out the juice, strain and reserve.

To serve, chop the duck Chinese-style and pour the reserved juice over the top.

STEAMED FRIED CHICKEN

This can seem messy, but deep-frying the chicken changes the skin texture and is an important part of the dish. It's great at room temperature, so make it a few hours before your guests arrive and just pop it on the table.

1 x 1.1 kg (2 lb 7 oz) free-range or organic chicken
1 teaspoon sea salt
2 teaspoons five-spice powder
vegetable oil, for deep-frying
2 teaspoons finely chopped ginger
3 spring onions (scallions), finely chopped
1 tablespoon dark soy sauce
1 tablespoon shaoxing
1 tablespoon peanut oil
½ teaspoon sea salt, extra
1 small handful of coriander (cilantro) leaves

SPICY DIPPING SAUCE
2 long red chillies, deseeded and chopped
2 cloves garlic, chopped
4 coriander (cilantro) roots, scraped and chopped
1 small knob of ginger, peeled and chopped
a pinch of sea salt
2 tablespoons peanut oil

METHOD

Rinse the chicken inside and out and pat dry with paper towel. Rub the salt and five-spice powder into the skin and leave for 20 minutes. Heat the oil in a wok or deep-fryer until just smoking (180°C/350°F), and deep-fry the whole chicken for 8 minutes, until the skin turns golden. Remove and leave to cool.

Put the bird on a chopping board and cut out the backbone, then push down to flatten slightly and put on a deep, round plate.

Mix together the ginger, spring onions, soy sauce, shaoxing, peanut oil and extra sea salt and pour over the chicken, rubbing into the skin. Put in a steamer over a pot or a wok of rapidly boiling water, cover and steam for 20 minutes, or until cooked through.

For the spicy dipping sauce, pound the chillies, garlic, coriander roots, ginger and sea salt in a mortar with a pestle to form a paste. Heat the oil until just smoking and carefully pour the hot oil over the sauce, then mix together. To serve, shred the chicken meat into large pieces. Put on a plate, skin-side-up, pour the juices over, sprinkle with coriander and serve with the dipping sauce.

Banquet Menu Four

PICKLED CABBAGE ⚜ page 53

CHINESE-STYLE BARBECUE PORK ⚜ page 202

TEA EGGS ⚜ page 193

SICHUAN PICKLED CUCUMBER & BLACK SHIITAKE ⚜ page 52

MASTER-STOCK CHICKEN ⚜ page 82

RECIPES ARE PICTURED ON FOLLOWING PAGES CLOCKWISE FROM TOP LEFT

BRAISED CHICKEN, TOFU & GLASS NOODLE HOT POT

This dish is best cooked in a clay pot; you can use a standard pot, but the clay pots are so pretty and look great taken straight to the table. They're cheap to buy in Chinatown — just soak them overnight to make sure they don't crack when you heat them.

350 g (12 oz) free-range or organic chicken thigh fillets,
    cut into bite-sized pieces
100 g (3½ oz) fried tofu, soaked in warm water for
    5 minutes and gently squeezed dry
100 g (3½ oz) glass noodles
1 tablespoon vegetable oil
2 spring onions (scallions), cut into 5 cm (2 inch) lengths
3 slices of peeled ginger
4 tablespoons light soy sauce
1 tablespoon shaoxing
1 teaspoon crushed yellow rock sugar
2 spring onions (scallions), extra, finely chopped

METHOD

Soak the noodles in warm water for about 5 minutes until tender. Drain, chop into 3 cm (1¼ inch) lengths and toss with a splash of vegetable oil.

Heat the vegetable oil in a large clay pot, add the spring onion lengths and ginger and stir-fry until fragrant, then add the chicken pieces and move them around the pot until they become opaque. Add the soy sauce, shaoxing and rock sugar and stir to coat the chicken, then add 1 litre (35 fl oz/4 cups) water. Bring to the boil, reduce the heat and simmer gently for 15 minutes, skimming the surface occasionally to remove any scum. Add the tofu and simmer for a further 5 minutes. Stir through the noodles and extra spring onions to serve.

SPICY BRAISED DUCK & YAM CURRY

This is an easy boiled curry and, although there are quite a few ingredients, it's simple as well as delicious. You can use a chopped whole duck if you like, but I think the legs are best as they remain moist.

4 duck legs, halved
300 g (10½ oz) yam, diced
4 tablespoons vegetable oil
5 kaffir lime leaves
2 lemongrass stalks, tough outer leaves removed, bruised
    and cut into 4 cm (1½ inch) lengths
1½ tablespoons grated palm sugar (jaggery)
1½ tablespoons fish sauce
juice of 1 lime

SPICE PASTE
2 teaspoons black peppercorns
8 candlenuts, roasted until golden, chopped
4 long green chillies, deseeded and chopped
2 long red chillies, deseeded and chopped
4 small wild green chillies, chopped
4 red shallots, chopped
1 knob of galangal, chopped
½ knob of ginger, peeled and chopped
2 fingers of fresh turmeric, chopped
1 teaspoon sea salt

METHOD

Pound the spice paste ingredients in a mortar with a pestle to a fine paste. Or use a blender to process the ingredients, adding a little water if necessary.

Heat a wok until just smoking. Add the oil and, when hot, add the spice paste and stir-fry for about 5 minutes, or until the rawness has been cooked out and the paste becomes fragrant. Add 1 litre (35 fl oz/4 cups) water and bring to the boil. Add the duck pieces, lime leaves and lemongrass and cover and simmer gently for 1 hour. Remove the lid and simmer for a further 30 minutes, or until the duck is tender and the sauce has reduced and thickened slightly.

Meanwhile, steam the yams over a pot or a wok of boiling water for 15–20 minutes, or until tender. Stir the yams into the curry, then season with palm sugar, fish sauce and lime juice to serve.

NOTE Candlenuts can be toxic if consumed raw, so make sure you roast them thoroughly before adding them to the spice paste.

STIR-FRIED CHICKEN WITH CASHEWS

This is the simplest version of this delicious dish — the texture and taste of chicken and cashews is delightful. You can also stir-fry a couple of large dried chillies, deseeded and roughly chopped, and add a pinch of Sichuan pepper at the end.

350 g (12 oz) free-range or organic chicken thigh
   fillets, skin on, diced
1 tablespoon vegetable oil
1 small knob of ginger, peeled and finely sliced
4 celery stalks, sliced on the diagonal
3 tablespoons fresh chicken stock (page 58)
40 g (1½ oz/¼ cup) cashews, roasted

MARINADE
1½ teaspoons shaoxing
1 teaspoon vegetable oil
1½ teaspoons light soy sauce
1 teaspoon finely chopped ginger
1 teaspoon sea salt
1 teaspoon sugar

METHOD

To make the marinade, mix together the shaoxing, oil, soy sauce, ginger, sea salt and sugar, add the chicken, and leave to marinate for 20 minutes.

Heat a wok until just smoking. Add the vegetable oil and, when hot, add the ginger and stir-fry for 10 seconds, or until fragrant, then add the chicken mixture, spreading it evenly around the wok. Cook undisturbed for 1 minute, allowing the chicken to start browning, then stir-fry until the chicken is lightly browned all over. Add the celery and stir-fry for 1 minute, then swirl in the stock and continue frying until the chicken is just cooked through and the sauce has thickened slightly. Transfer to a plate and sprinkle with cashews to serve.

KUNG PAO CHICKEN

This is one of the first Sichuan dishes people learn to cook — you've probably had it many times in Chinese restaurants.

350 g (12 oz) free-range or organic chicken thigh
    fillets, skin on, diced
3 tablespoons vegetable oil
2 dried long red chillies, halved lengthways
8 cloves garlic, finely chopped
1 small knob of ginger, peeled and finely chopped
2 red capsicums (peppers), diced
1 tablespoon shaoxing
2 teaspoons light soy sauce
2 teaspoons Chinkiang vinegar
2 tablespoons fresh chicken stock (page 58)
1 teaspoon sea salt
120 g (4½ oz/¾ cup) peanuts, roasted
4 spring onions (scallions), finely chopped

MARINADE
2 teaspoons light soy sauce
1 teaspoon shaoxing
½ teaspoon sugar

METHOD

To make the marinade, mix together the soy sauce, shaoxing and sugar with the chicken, and leave to marinate for 20 minutes.

Heat a wok until just smoking. Add half the oil and, when hot, stir-fry the chillies until they blacken. Add the chicken and cook undisturbed for 1 minute, allowing the chicken to start browning, then stir-fry for 1 minute, or until the chicken is brown on all sides but not completely cooked through. Remove.

Heat the remaining oil in the wok and stir-fry the garlic and ginger until fragrant. Add the capsicums and stir-fry for 30 seconds, then deglaze the wok with shaoxing. Return the chicken and chillies to the wok with the soy sauce, Chinkiang, stock and sea salt and stir-fry until the chicken is cooked through. Add the peanuts and spring onions and stir-fry for 30 seconds, or until the spring onions are bright green. Transfer to a serving plate and discard the chillies before serving.

STIR-FRIED CHICKEN WITH HOT BEAN PASTE

You'll love this easy little stir-fry with some steamed rice; it's a quickie after a hard day at the office. The addition of the hot bean paste really adds to the complexity of flavour in this stir-fry.

350 g (12 oz) free-range or organic chicken thigh fillets,
    skin on, cut into bite-sized pieces
2 tablespoons hot bean paste
2 tablespoons vegetable oil
1 long red chilli, finely chopped
1 teaspoon finely chopped ginger
1 tablespoon shaoxing
120 g (4¼ oz) snow peas (mangetout), trimmed
1 tablespoon yellow bean soy sauce
½ teaspoon sea salt
1 teaspoon sugar
125 ml (4 fl oz/½ cup) fresh chicken stock (page 58)
1 spring onion (scallion), finely chopped

METHOD

Heat a wok until it is just smoking. Add the oil and, when hot, stir-fry the chicken in batches until the meat begins to brown. Add the chilli, ginger and hot bean paste and stir-fry until fragrant. Deglaze the wok with shaoxing and then add the snow peas, soy sauce, sea salt and sugar. Add the stock and simmer for 2–3 minutes, or until the sauce has reduced and the chicken is tender. Stir in the spring onion to serve.

CHICKEN WITH SNOW PEAS & SICHUAN PEPPER

This dish has a wonderful hot and sour thing going on. Watch those blackened chillies; one little bit can leave you with a very hot mouth and the hiccups.

350 g (12 oz) free-range or organic chicken thigh fillets,
    skin on, cut into bite-sized pieces
100 g (3½ oz) snow peas (mangetout), trimmed
¼ teaspoon Sichuan pepper
1 tablespoon vegetable oil
8 dried small red chillies
2 spring onions (scallions), cut into 2 cm (¾ inch) lengths
1 small knob of ginger, peeled and finely sliced
1 clove garlic, finely sliced
2 tablespoons shaoxing
1 teaspoon sea salt
¼ teaspoon freshly ground white pepper
1 tablespoon yellow bean soy sauce
1 tablespoon Chinkiang vinegar
2 teaspoons sesame oil
1 teaspoon sugar
1 teaspoon chilli oil

METHOD

Heat a wok until just smoking. Add the vegetable oil and, when hot, add the chillies and chicken, spreading them evenly around the wok. Leave undisturbed for about 1 minute, allowing the chicken to brown. Then start to stir-fry the chicken until it has browned all over and the chillies have blackened. Add the snow peas to the wok and stir-fry for a further 30 seconds, then remove the chicken, chillies and snow peas from the wok.

Add the spring onions, ginger, garlic and Sichuan pepper to the wok and stir-fry for 15 seconds, then deglaze with the shaoxing. Return the chicken, chillies and snow peas to the wok, along with the salt, white pepper, soy sauce, vinegar, sesame oil, sugar and chilli oil. Stir-fry for a further 30 seconds and then discard the chillies to serve.

STIR-FRIED ROAST DUCK WITH BEAN SPROUTS

I adore the richness of the duck and the texture of the bean sprouts in this dish. It's a classic quick stir-fry, so you can substitute slices of lamb, pork, beef, chicken or fish for the duck — hell, anything works well here.

½ Chinese roast duck (page 248), skin and flesh
   shredded, bones discarded
200 g (7 oz) bean sprouts, trimmed
3 tablespoons peanut oil
¼ knob of ginger, peeled and finely sliced
2 cloves garlic, roughly chopped
1 red capsicum (pepper), cut into julienne
2 spring onions (scallions), cut into julienne
1 tablespoon shaoxing
2 tablespoons light mushroom soy sauce
2 tablespoons plum sauce
2 teaspoons sugar
100 ml (3½ fl oz) fresh chicken stock (page 58)

METHOD

Heat a wok until smoking. Add the oil and, when hot, add the ginger, garlic, capsicum, spring onions and duck and stir-fry for 1 minute. Deglaze the wok with the shaoxing, then add the soy sauce, plum sauce, sugar and chicken stock. Bring to the boil, add the bean sprouts and stir-fry for 30 seconds to heat through. Spoon onto a large plate to serve.

Banquet Menu Five

STIR-FRIED BEEF WITH SICHUAN PEPPERCORNS
& SWEET BEAN SAUCE ⚘ PAGE 232

RED CURRY OF DUCK & PINEAPPLE ⚘ PAGE 156

BRAISED TOFU, FAMILY STYLE, WITH BLACK VINEGAR ⚘ PAGE 185

RECIPES ARE PICTURED ON FOLLOWING PAGES CLOCKWISE FROM TOP LEFT

LEMON CHICKEN

In the first chapter there was a recipe for a steamed lemon chicken. This, on the other hand, is more like the classic lemon chicken you'd see in Chinese restaurants. The chicken is battered, fried and then sauced. You could substitute slices of fresh fish, like blue eye or snapper, for a lovely light dish.

300 g (10½ oz) free-range or organic chicken thigh fillets,
    skin on, trimmed, cut into 1 cm (½ inch) slices
1 egg, lightly beaten
¼ teaspoon sea salt
2 tablespoons cornflour (cornstarch)
vegetable oil, for deep-frying
2 lemons
3 tablespoons sugar
3 tablespoons white vinegar
a pinch of Sichuan pepper
2 spring onions (scallions), finely sliced

METHOD

Put the chicken, egg and sea salt in a bowl, toss together and leave for 20 minutes.

Remove the chicken from the egg, allowing the excess to drip away, and toss in the cornflour until evenly coated. Heat the oil in a wok or deep-fryer until just smoking (180°C/350°F), and deep-fry the chicken pieces until golden brown and cooked through, then drain on paper towel.

Finely grate the zest from half a lemon, then juice the whole lemon. Peel and fillet the other lemon. Put the sugar, vinegar, 3 tablespoons water, lemon fillets, zest and juice in a small pot. Stir over low heat until the sugar dissolves, then bring to the boil and remove from the heat. Pour the sauce over the chicken and sprinkle with Sichuan pepper and spring onions to serve.

TANGERINE PEEL CHICKEN

This Sichuan-inspired dish has a lovely fragrance and taste from the tangerine peel. You can buy the dried peel in Chinese food stores, but it's really nice to make your own by eating the fruit and then drying the peel yourself — it tastes better and is certainly more fragrant. This will also work with mandarins and oranges; use whichever one you have available.

500 g (1 lb 2 oz) free-range or organic chicken breast
    fillets, skin on, cut into bite-sized pieces
3 pieces dried tangerine peel, crumbled
vegetable oil, for deep-frying
3 dried long red chillies, chopped
2 teaspoons shaoxing
2½ teaspoons sugar
1 teaspoon dark soy sauce
3 teaspoons light soy sauce
3 teaspoons Chinkiang vinegar
a few drops of sesame oil

MARINADE
1 knob of ginger, peeled and finely chopped
2 spring onions (scallions), finely chopped
1 teaspoon sea salt
1 teaspoon dark soy sauce
1 teaspoon shaoxing

METHOD

To make the marinade, mix together the ginger, spring onions, sea salt, soy sauce and shaoxing. Add the chicken and toss together. Leave for 15 minutes, then drain.

Heat the oil in a wok or deep-fryer until just smoking (180°C/350°F), and deep-fry the chicken in batches until golden, then drain on paper towel. Pour the oil from the wok and wipe clean.

Reheat the wok with 1 tablespoon of vegetable oil and stir-fry the chillies and tangerine peel until they darken. Add the chicken pieces and toss together, then deglaze the wok with the shaoxing. Stir in the sugar, soy sauces, vinegar and sesame oil and stir-fry until the sauce thickens and coats the chicken.

DOUBLE-BOILED PIGEONS WITH SHIITAKE MUSHROOMS

My favourite pigeon dish is when the bird has been master-stocked and wok-fried until the skin is crisp; this comes a close second. Try to get plump Number 4 or 5 size birds and get rid of the cutlery — this is definitely a dish to eat with your fingers.

2 x 500 g (1 lb 2 oz) baby pigeons (squabs)
6 dried shiitake mushrooms, soaked in warm water for
    30 minutes, stalks removed, cut in half on the
    diagonal through the middle
1.5 litres (52 fl oz/6 cups) fresh chicken stock (page 58)
½ knob of ginger, peeled and finely sliced
4 thin slices of prosciutto
1 teaspoon sea salt
2 tablespoons light mushroom soy sauce
1 tablespoon shaoxing
2 spring onions (scallions), cut into julienne
freshly ground white pepper

METHOD

Blanch the pigeons in boiling water for 1 minute. Cool slightly, then wipe with paper towel to remove any membrane that may be stuck to the skin. Put the pigeons in a clay pot and place the pot in a large bamboo steamer.

Heat the chicken stock in a small pot and pour over the pigeons, then add the ginger and prosciutto slices. Cover the clay pot and cover the steamer with the lid, then steam over a pot or a wok of rapidly boiling water for 1¼ hours. Carefully remove the lid from the steamer and the cover from the pot. Add the mushrooms, sea salt, soy sauce and shaoxing to the pot, then re-cover and steam for another 30 minutes.

Remove the pigeons from the pot and chop them Chinese-style. Arrange the pigeons in a deep plate, sprinkle with the spring onions and pour over some of the broth. Give it a good grind of white pepper to serve.

CRISPY-PRESSED DUCK WITH MANDARIN SAUCE

This dish was on the menu at Rockpool for the first 10 years and I still cook it at home. It's a classic multi-cooking method that's used by the Chinese to create great flavour and texture. The marinating imparts flavour, the steaming is done to remove the bones and create a parcel of duck that the pressing tenderises. The coating that gets steamed onto the duck creates a super crispy crust when fried. There you have it in just a few steps — one of the best duck dishes ever. The Chinese certainly know a thing or two about cooking duck.

1 x 2 kg (4 lb 8 oz) duck
2 egg whites
4 tablespoons cornflour (cornstarch)
2 tablespoons rice flour
3 tablespoons grated palm sugar (jaggery)
zest from 2 mandarins, cut into very fine julienne
1 large knob of ginger, peeled and cut into julienne
2½ tablespoons fish sauce
2½ tablespoons mandarin juice
2 mandarins, filleted
vegetable oil, for deep-frying

MARINADE
1½ tablespoons light soy sauce
3 tablespoons shaoxing
2 spring onions (scallions), white part only, finely sliced
2 pieces dried tangerine peel
1 knob of ginger, peeled and finely chopped
1 star anise, crushed
1 tablespoon crushed yellow rock sugar

METHOD

Put the duck on a chopping board and remove the fat from the cavity. Use a heavy cleaver to chop off the wing tips at the first joint, to chop off the neck, and to split the duck in half lengthways.

Put all the marinade ingredients in a small pot and simmer for 2 minutes, then leave to cool. Rub the cooled marinade all over the duck and marinate for at least 3 hours, or preferably overnight.

Put the duck into a large bamboo steamer over a pot or a wok of rapidly boiling water, cover with the lid and steam the duck for 1 hour. Remove from the heat and allow to cool slightly.

While the duck is still warm, gently remove the bones, being careful not to break the skin. Use a small knife to ease out the wing and leg bone. You should now have two rectangles of duck. Place them, skin-side-up, on a board and fold any excess skin underneath the flesh. Wrap them loosely in plastic wrap, allowing some slack so they can spread. Put them into a container, side by side, put another container that fits inside the first on top and place a 5 kg (11 lb) weight on top of that, then refrigerate overnight.

Remove the ducks from the container and plastic wrap. You should now have two solid pieces of duck with flat, smooth sides. Whisk the egg whites until they start to thicken, but before soft peaks form. Sift the flours together. Dip the skin side of each piece of duck into the egg white, making sure the skin is evenly covered, then dust with the combined flours, blowing off any excess.

Put the duck on a plate, crust-side-up, then put the plate into a large bamboo steamer over a pot or a wok of rapidly boiling water, cover with the lid and steam for 25 minutes. The crust should be dry to the touch — if it's undercooked the crust will detach from the duck during the frying process, so make sure that it's cooked through.

Meanwhile, to make the sauce, put the palm sugar and 3 tablespoons water in a pot and bring to the boil. Add the zest and ginger and simmer until the palm sugar turns a dark caramel colour. Add the fish sauce and mandarin juice and stir, then add the mandarin fillets and keep warm.

Heat the oil in a wok until just smoking (180°C/350°F), and deep-fry the ducks for about 6 minutes, or until the crust is crispy and the duck is warmed through. Remove and drain on paper towel.

Cut the ducks into 2 cm (¾ inch) wide slices and arrange on a serving plate. Spoon the mandarin sauce over the ducks and serve immediately.

STEAMED CHICKEN WITH BLACK BEANS & CHOPPED SALTED CHILLIES

This easy self-saucing dish has plenty of fire from the chopped salted chillies. You could also just use fresh chillies and the dish would still be great, but the chopped salted ones add another level of complexity. This simple Sichuan-style steaming really suits fish as well — try a blue eye trevalla or bar cod.

3 free-range or organic chicken legs, chopped through
   the bone into bite-sized pieces
2 tablespoons chopped salted chillies (page 49)
1 tablespoon fermented black beans
1 teaspoon finely chopped ginger
1 clove garlic, finely chopped
1 tablespoon shaoxing
½ teaspoon sea salt
1 tablespoon light soy sauce
2 teaspoons sugar
125 ml (4 fl oz/½ cup) fresh chicken stock (page 58)
1 spring onion (scallion), cut into julienne

METHOD

Blanch the chicken for 1 minute in boiling water, then remove, rinse and dry well. This is important to stop the sauce getting protein scum in it.

Mix together the chicken, ginger, garlic, shaoxing, chillies, black beans, sea salt, soy sauce, sugar and chicken stock in a heatproof bowl that fits into your steamer.

Place the bowl in a large steamer over a pot or a wok of boiling water, place the lid on the steamer and cook over high heat for 30 minutes, or until the chicken is cooked through.

Spoon the chicken and sauce into a large serving bowl or serve straight from the steamer. Sprinkle with spring onion to finish.

CHICKEN & PICKLED GINGER IN HONEY SAUCE

This is delicious with the pickled ginger. You can use the ginger that the Japanese use on sushi if you like — it has a compelling sweetness that's perfect for this recipe.

If you don't like bones as much as I do (I find they give the meat more flavour), buy chicken thigh fillets and cut each into four pieces.

4 free-range or organic chicken legs, chopped through
    the bone into bite-sized pieces
125 g (4½ oz) pickled ginger, finely sliced
peanut oil, for deep-frying
1 red capsicum (pepper), cut into large dice
1 green capsicum (pepper), cut into large dice
1 teaspoon shaoxing
2 tablespoons honey
1 tablespoon dark soy sauce
1 teaspoon sea salt
250 ml (9 fl oz/1 cup) fresh chicken stock (page 58)

MARINADE
1 tablespoon light soy sauce
1 teaspoon dark soy sauce
1 teaspoon shaoxing
½ teaspoon salt

METHOD

To make the marinade, mix together the soy sauces, shaoxing and salt, add the chicken pieces, and leave for 30 minutes.

Heat the oil in a wok or deep-fryer until just smoking (180°C/350°F), and deep-fry the chicken pieces in batches until lightly browned, then remove and drain on paper towel. Pour all but 2 tablespoons of oil from the wok.

Reheat the wok until just smoking. Add the ginger and capsicum and stir-fry for 30 seconds until fragrant, then deglaze the wok with the shaoxing. Add the chicken to the wok along with the honey, dark soy sauce, sea salt and chicken stock. Cover and simmer over medium heat for 3 minutes, or until the chicken is cooked through.

MANDARIN PANCAKES

200 g (7 oz) plain (all-purpose) flour, plus extra for
    dusting
100 ml (3½ fl oz) boiling water
vegetable oil, to knead
sesame oil

METHOD

Mix the flour and boiling water together in a bowl. Add 3 tablespoons cold water and continue to mix until you form a dough. Cover the dough with plastic wrap and leave to rest for 30 minutes. Then knead the dough on a lightly oiled surface for 10 minutes until smooth and silky.

Set half the dough aside and cover with plastic wrap. Roll the remaining dough into a sausage and cut into 16 even pieces. Use your fingers to flatten each piece into a 5 cm (2 inch) diameter circle. Brush half the pancakes with a little sesame oil, and then top each with one of the remaining pancakes so you have eight double pancakes. Repeat this process with the dough you have set aside. You should now have 16 double pancakes. Cover the pancakes with a damp cloth to stop them drying out.

Dust each double pancake with a little flour and roll out to form a circle about 13 cm (5 inches) in diameter. You can make perfectly round pancakes by trimming with a 12 cm (4½ inch) round cookie cutter if you like.

Heat a small heavy-based pan over medium heat and dry-fry the double pancakes for about 20 seconds, or until faint brown spots begin to appear. The heat of the pan is crucial here — too hot and the pancakes will brown too quickly and won't cook through; too cold and the pancakes will cook for too long and will dry out. This stage will probably involve some trial and error, but with perseverance you will get the temperature just right. Flip the pancakes over and continue to cook until they begin to puff up, then remove from the pan and 'clap' the pancakes between your hands — this will force the air out of the centre and allow you to separate them. Gently peel the pancakes apart, place on a plate and cover with a damp cloth. The pancakes can be frozen at this point if you wish.

When ready to eat, wrap the pancakes in a thin tea towel on a plate. Put the plate in a bamboo steamer over a pot or a wok of rapidly boiling water, cover with the lid and steam the pancakes for 4–5 minutes, or until all the pancakes are piping hot. If they aren't hot enough they will be unpalatable. Serve with the crispy Sichuan duck (page 276).

NOTE This recipe will make 32 pancakes.

CRISPY SICHUAN DUCK WITH MANDARIN PANCAKES

I am a freak for this crispy duck; it rates up there with smoked duck. I alternate these two in my modern Asian restaurants and people can't get enough of them. The duck is first marinated and steamed for a long time to tenderise it and render the fat. Then it's fried until crisp, and the meat is shredded off the bone and eaten in pancakes with traditional garnish. You can also just fry the duck, chop it up and serve with the mandarin sauce from page 270. Substitute blood oranges for the mandarin and the sauce will be out of this world.

1 x 2 kg (4 lb 8 oz) duck
1 tablespoon sea salt
1 teaspoon five-spice powder
1 large knob of ginger, peeled and cut into four slices
2 spring onions (scallions), cut into 4 cm (1½ inch) lengths
2 tablespoons light soy sauce
plain (all-purpose) flour, for dusting
vegetable oil, for deep-frying

TO SERVE
½ quantity of mandarin pancakes (page 274)
16 small spring onions (scallions), trimmed, white parts with a bit of green left
2 Lebanese (short) cucumbers, deseeded and cut into batons
125 ml (4 fl oz/½ cup) hoisin sauce
2 tablespoons sesame oil

METHOD

Rinse the duck inside and out, pat dry with paper towel, and remove any fat from the cavity. Place the duck on a board and cut off the wing tips at the first joint. Use the palms of your hands to push down firmly on the breast bone so you snap the bones inside and flatten the duck slightly.

Pound the sea salt and five-spice powder in a mortar with a pestle until fine. Rub the salt mixture over the duck, then cover and refrigerate overnight.

Push the ginger and spring onions into the cavity of the duck. Put the duck in a shallow bowl and place in a bamboo steamer over a pot or a wok of rapidly boiling water. Put the lid on the steamer and steam the duck for 3 hours. This steaming process will render the fat from the duck and prepare the skin so it crisps up nicely when you fry it. Check the water level in the pot several times during steaming and top up with boiling water from the kettle as necessary. Remove the duck from the steamer, drain any liquid, remove the ginger and spring onion from the cavity and leave the duck to cool.

Brush the duck all over with soy sauce and then lightly dust it with flour, blowing off any excess. Heat the oil in a wok or deep-fryer until almost smoking (180°C/350°F), and deep-fry the duck for about 12 minutes, turning occasionally, until the skin is golden and crispy all over. Remove from the oil and drain on paper towel.

To serve, shred the warm duck meat and crispy skin with a fork and arrange on a serving plate. Put the spring onions and cucumbers on a separate plate. Mix the hoisin sauce with the sesame oil and put in a small serving bowl. Steam the pancakes until they are hot, and fold them into quarters. Allow people to prepare their own pancakes at the table.

CHICKEN CURRY

This really simple delicious dish relies on the aromatics in the paste for a lovely fresh flavour.

6 free-range or organic chicken thigh fillets, halved
125 ml (4 fl oz/½ cup) coconut cream
3 teaspoons sea salt
3 tablespoons vegetable oil
375 ml (13 fl oz/1½ cups) coconut milk
juice of 1 lemon
¼ teaspoon freshly ground white pepper
5 red shallots, finely sliced and deep-fried until golden

PASTE

10 long red chillies, deseeded and chopped
10 dried long red chillies, deseeded, soaked in warm
    water for 30 minutes and chopped
2 lemongrass stalks, tough outer leaves removed,
    chopped
3 red shallots, chopped
3 cloves garlic, chopped

METHOD

For the paste, pound the chillies, lemongrass, shallots and garlic in a mortar with a pestle until you have a fine paste. Or use a blender to process the ingredients, adding a little water if necessary.

Mix the chicken pieces with the coconut cream and salt. Heat the oil in a heavy-based pot and stir-fry the paste for 10 minutes, or until fragrant. Add the chicken and stir-fry for a further 5 minutes, or until the coconut cream 'splits'. Stir in the coconut milk and allow to simmer, stirring occasionally, for about 25 minutes, or until the curry has thickened slightly and a layer of oil has risen to the surface. Season the curry with lemon juice and freshly ground pepper. Sprinkle with fried shallots to serve.

RED CURRY OF CHICKEN

What an easy way to start making curries — you could even just buy a roast chook, cut the meat off the bone and warm it in the curry. Or stir-fry whatever meat, poultry or seafood you feel like and add the curry sauce. Make sure you taste as you go and that you find a nice balance; if you like it a little saltier, add some more fish sauce; if you want it hotter, fry the paste with about four crushed wild green chillies. I like to squeeze a lime over the curry at the end as it gives it a very fresh lift.

½ master-stock chicken (page 82), boned and cut into
  2 cm (¾ inch) chunks
200 g (7 oz) red curry paste (page 155)
625 ml (21½ fl oz/2½ cups) coconut milk
100 g (3½ oz) grated palm sugar (jaggery)
4 tablespoons fish sauce
125 ml (4 fl oz/½ cup) fresh chicken stock (page 58)
2 tomatoes, quartered
4 kaffir lime leaves
1 handful of sweet Thai basil leaves

METHOD

Pour the coconut milk, curry paste, sugar and fish sauce into a pot and boil for 2 minutes. Add the chicken meat, stock, tomatoes and lime leaves and simmer gently for about 4 minutes to completely heat the chicken. Add the basil leaves immediately before serving.

DEEP-FRIED QUAILS

These quails make a great starter. I love picking up the pieces with my fingers and chewing on the bones.

4 quails
1 teaspoon Sichuan salt and pepper (page 55)
1 teaspoon sugar
1 tablespoon light soy sauce
1 tablespoon shaoxing
vegetable oil, for deep-frying
30 g (1 oz/¼ cup) plain (all-purpose) flour
1 spring onion (scallion), finely chopped
1 tablespoon finely chopped coriander (cilantro) leaves
1 long red chilli, finely chopped
1 clove garlic, finely chopped
chilli sauce (page 42), to serve

METHOD

Quarter the quails, remove the backbones and wing tips, clean the insides and pat dry with paper towel. Mix the Sichuan salt and pepper, sugar, soy sauce and shaoxing until the sugar dissolves, then add the quail pieces, toss together and marinate overnight.

Heat the oil in a wok or deep-fryer until just smoking (180°C/350°F). Coat each quail piece in flour, shaking away any excess, and deep-fry in batches until golden brown. Remove from the wok and drain on paper towel.

Arrange the quails on a plate and sprinkle with the combined spring onion, coriander, chilli and garlic. Serve with chilli sauce on the side.

Banquet Menu Six

STIR-FRIED OYSTERS WITH BLACK BEANS ⚜ PAGE 314

TEA- & SPICE-SMOKED DUCK ⚜ PAGE 148

COLD SPINACH & SESAME SALAD ⚜ PAGE 338

PORK SIMMERED IN CARAMEL SAUCE ⚜ PAGE 205

RECIPES ARE PICTURED ON FOLLOWING PAGES CLOCKWISE FROM TOP LEFT

Seafood

When buying fish it's important to select the most vibrant, handsome-looking specimen you can find. It's easier to tell if the catch is fresh by looking at the whole fish: the eyes should be clear and shiny and it will smell of the sea — a sweet fresh smell, not a fishy one. The gills should be bright red, not brown or grey, and the texture firm. Run your finger along the flesh, from the back of the head to just past the fin (the shoulder of the fish); even if the fish is a soft-fleshed fish it should spring back to shape. The scales should be shiny and tight, not loose and falling off. Shellfish should be either live, or look bright and vibrant if dead. Seafood such as oysters, mussels and clams (vongole) should be heavy and full of salt water. Squid and octopus should be vibrantly coloured and shiny. When buying seafood, either take a coolbox with an ice brick to carry it home or make the trip quickly. Lastly, don't buy too far in advance; you don't want to keep seafood in the refrigerator for more than two days.

PRAWN, WONTON & VEGETABLE SOUP

With plenty of flavour from the shrimp paste and dried shrimp, this simple Thai-inspired soup has a nice kick to it. You can swap ingredients in and out to create different textures and flavours. Serve this in small bowls as a starter, or in a large bowl in the centre of a shared table. Have a ladle in the soup and some small bowls on hand — this is how it is served in Thailand; you simply drink the soup while eating the rest of the meal.

6 green king prawns (shrimp), peeled and deveined with tails left intact
6 pork wontons, blanched (page 363)
750 ml (26 fl oz/3 cups) fresh chicken stock (page 58)
1 tablespoon fish sauce
2 teaspoons sugar
1 bunch of English spinach, trimmed and blanched
250 g (9 oz) pumpkin (winter squash), cooked until tender and cut into bite-sized pieces
4 fresh shiitake mushrooms, stalks removed, cut in half on the diagonal through the middle
a pinch of freshly ground white pepper

PASTE
4 red shallots, finely sliced
4 slices of peeled ginger
1 tablespoon Thai shrimp paste
2 tablespoons dried shrimp, pounded
3 small wild green chillies

METHOD

To make the paste, pound the shallots, ginger, Thai shrimp paste, dried shrimp and green chillies in a mortar with a pestle until you have a fine paste. Or use a blender to process the ingredients, adding a little water if necessary.

In a small pot, heat the stock until boiling. Add the paste, fish sauce and sugar and simmer for 2 minutes, then add the prawns, wontons and vegetables and cook until heated through.

ABALONE, CHICKEN, HAM & MUSHROOM SOUP

These soups are called double-boiled even though they're steamed. My father used to make versions of this when I was younger — he loved tinned abalone and I must say that I love it too. Make sure that, if you're using tinned bamboo shoots to add some texture, you rinse them very well.

420 g (15 oz) tinned baby abalone, drained and halved
600 g (1 lb 5 oz) chicken thigh fillets, chopped into
    bite-sized pieces, blanched
80 g (2¾ oz) prosciutto slices
3 dried shiitake mushrooms, soaked in warm water for
    30 minutes, stalks removed, sliced
6 dried scallops, soaked in warm water for 30 minutes
1.5 litres (52 fl oz/6 cups) fresh chicken stock (page 58)
2 teaspoons shaoxing
1 teaspoon sea salt
¼ Chinese cabbage, shredded and blanched
12 snow peas (mangetout), trimmed and blanched
150 g (5½ oz) tinned bamboo shoots, rinsed and trimmed
300 g (10½ oz) block fresh tofu, cut into bite-sized pieces
freshly ground white pepper

METHOD

Put the scallops in a bamboo steamer over a pot or a wok of boiling water, cover with the lid and steam for 10 minutes. While still warm, shred the scallops into strands with your fingers.

Put the stock, shaoxing and sea salt in a pot and bring to the boil. Put the abalone, chicken, prosciutto, shiitakes, scallops, cabbage, snow peas, bamboo shoots and tofu in a large heatproof bowl and pour the stock over the top. Cover the bowl with a sheet of baking paper and a tight-fitting lid or several layers of foil tied in place with string. Put the bowl in a large bamboo steamer over a pot or a wok of boiling water, cover with the lid and steam gently for 40 minutes.

Remove the bowl from the steamer, uncover and sprinkle with white pepper to serve.

SPICY GRILLED WHOLE OCEAN PERCH

This dish can be made with any whole fish or fish fillet; snapper is particularly good. There are a few ingredients, but once you get them together, the preparation is simple. It's nice to get the barbecue going for this dish as well.

1 x 500–600 g (1 lb 2 oz–1 lb 5 oz) whole ocean perch
1 tablespoon vegetable oil
125 ml (4 fl oz/½ cup) coconut milk
1 lemongrass stalk, tough outer leaves removed, bruised
    and cut into 2 cm (¾ inch) lengths
juice of 1 lime
1 small handful of coriander (cilantro) leaves

SPICE PASTE
6 long red chillies, deseeded and finely sliced
3 red shallots
2 cloves garlic
4 coriander (cilantro) roots, scraped and chopped
1 finger of fresh turmeric, chopped
1 tablespoon garam masala
1 teaspoon sea salt
1 teaspoon sugar
finely grated zest of 2 limes

METHOD

Pound all the spice paste ingredients in a mortar with a pestle until you have a fine paste. Or use a blender to process the ingredients, adding a little water if necessary.

Make a few deep cuts in the thickest part of the fish. Turn over and repeat on the other side. Rub half the spice paste all over the fish and leave to marinate for 30 minutes.

Heat the vegetable oil in a wok until almost smoking. Add the remaining spice paste and stir-fry for about 5 minutes until fragrant. Add the coconut milk and lemongrass and simmer for a few minutes. Taste and adjust the seasoning with the lime juice. Remove from the heat and keep warm.

Heat a barbecue or grill until hot and cook the fish for about 5 minutes on each side, or until just cooked through. Put the fish on a serving plate, spoon the sauce over and sprinkle with coriander leaves to serve.

KOREAN-STYLE OCTOPUS SALAD

I love this salad. As a matter of fact, I love many Korean dishes — the taste of hot bean paste is wonderful.

Make sure that you cook the octopus over high heat as you want the tentacles to be crispy. I use this same dressing for squid, prawns and barbecued chicken and I'm sure you'll end up loving it as much as I do.

400 g (14 oz) baby octopus, cleaned
1 celery heart (pale inner stems and leaves), finely sliced
2 spring onions (scallions), cut into julienne
1 small carrot, cut into julienne
1 small cucumber, deseeded and cut into julienne
¼ daikon radish, cut into julienne
¼ Chinese cabbage, finely shredded
sea salt
1 tablespoon vegetable oil
2 teaspoons roasted sesame seeds

DRESSING
1 tablespoon finely chopped ginger
1 tablespoon finely chopped garlic
2 tablespoons hot bean paste
freshly ground black pepper
1 teaspoon chilli powder
2 teaspoons sesame oil
2 tablespoons caster (superfine) sugar
2 teaspoons sea salt

METHOD

Put the celery, spring onions, carrot, cucumber, radish and cabbage in a bowl and sprinkle generously with sea salt. Toss together and leave for 10 minutes, then rinse under cold water and squeeze dry.

Mix the dressing ingredients in a bowl with 1 tablespoon water and allow the flavour to develop.

Toss the octopus with the oil and season with a little sea salt, then barbecue over high heat until just cooked through. Set aside to cool slightly, and halve if large. To serve, mix together the vegetables, warm octopus and dressing and sprinkle with sesame seeds to serve.

SEAFOOD & CHINESE CELERY SALAD

This classic little Thai salad can be put together with any seafood you like. I love the celery in it as it works both texturally and taste-wise. Chinese celery is much milder than normal celery and you should make sure you use the leaves. I chop the celery on the diagonal, as it makes it all a bit prettier on the plate.

12 large black mussels
24 clams (vongole)
6 freshly shucked oysters
140 g (5 oz/1 cup) chopped Chinese celery
juice of 1 lime
1 lemongrass stalk, tough outer leaves removed,
    very finely sliced
3 red shallots, finely sliced
1 small handful of combined mint and coriander (cilantro)
    leaves
3 red shallots, finely sliced and deep-fried until golden

DRESSING
½ long red chilli, deseeded and finely chopped
a pinch of sea salt
2 teaspoons caster (superfine) sugar
juice of 2 limes
1 tablespoon fish sauce

METHOD

Steam the mussels and clams separately in about 5 mm (¼ inch) water until they just open. Strain the liquid and leave to cool. Discard any mussels that remain stubbornly closed. Remove the mussels and clams from their shells, discarding the shells.

Put the oysters, their juices, and the lime juice in a bowl, mix together and leave for 2 minutes to 'cook' the oysters, then strain.

To make the dressing, mix together the chilli, sea salt, caster sugar, lime juice and fish sauce and stir until the sugar dissolves, then add the cooled steaming liquid from the mussels and clams.

Gently toss together the mussels, clams, oysters, Chinese celery, lemongrass, shallots, mint, coriander and the dressing. Serve immediately, sprinkled with deep-fried shallots.

GRILLED LOBSTER WITH TAMARIND

This will impress friends and family with its wonderful sweet and sour flavour. I love the fruitiness that the tamarind brings to this dish. The sauce is also good with other seafood such as crabs and prawns.

1 x 700–800 g (1 lb 9–12 oz) live lobster
2½ tablespoons tamarind water (page 32)
2 coriander (cilantro) roots, scraped and finely chopped
3 cloves garlic, finely sliced
2 red shallots, finely sliced
3 tablespoons vegetable oil
2½ tablespoons grated palm sugar (jaggery)
1½ tablespoons fish sauce
a pinch of chilli powder

METHOD

Kill the lobster humanely (see page 139 for instructions), halve lengthways and clean well.

Pound the coriander roots, garlic and shallots in a mortar with a pestle to form a fine paste. Heat 2 tablespoons of the oil in a wok until just smoking and stir-fry the paste until fragrant, then add the palm sugar, fish sauce, tamarind water, chilli powder and 4 tablespoons water. Bring to the boil, then taste and adjust the seasoning if necessary.

Heat a grill or barbecue to hot. Brush the lobsters with the remaining oil and place them, cut-side-down, on the grill. Cook for 3–4 minutes, then turn and cook until just cooked through. Leave to rest for 5 minutes in a warm place.

Chop each lobster half into three pieces and arrange on a plate. Drizzle the sauce over the top to serve.

SHANGHAI-STYLE STEAMED FISH

This is a slightly more robust dish than the ginger and spring onion version on page 110. Don't be afraid of the pork and fish mix; it's a classic because it's so good and yet so very easy to prepare.

1 x 500–600 g (1 lb 2–5 oz) whole snapper, scaled and
    cleaned
60 g (2¼ oz) minced (ground) pork
1 small knob of ginger, peeled and cut into julienne
1 tablespoon light soy sauce
½ teaspoon sesame oil
zest from half an orange, cut into julienne
¼ teaspoon sea salt
2 dried shiitake mushrooms, soaked in warm water for
    30 minutes, stalks removed, finely sliced
1 spring onion (scallion), cut into julienne
3 tablespoons peanut oil

SAUCE
125 ml (4 fl oz/½ cup) fresh chicken stock (page 58)
2 tablespoons light soy sauce
1 teaspoon sesame oil
a pinch of white pepper

METHOD

Pat the fish dry with paper towel and put it on a chopping board. Make three diagonal cuts into the thickest part of the fish, then repeat in the opposite direction to make a diamond pattern — this will help the fish cook more evenly. Turn the fish over and do the same on the other side, then lay the fish in a heatproof bowl that will fit into your steamer basket.

Mix together the pork, ginger, soy sauce, sesame oil, orange zest and salt and press evenly over the top of the fish. Sprinkle the mushrooms over the top. Put the bowl in a large bamboo steamer over a pot or a wok of rapidly boiling water, cover with the lid and steam for 10 minutes. The fish should be just setting on the bone — be careful not to overcook it.

Scatter spring onion over the fish, then heat the peanut oil until just smoking and douse the fish with the hot oil. Bring the sauce ingredients to the boil in a small pot, then pour over the fish to serve.

STEAMED BLUE EYE WITH PROSCIUTTO & BAMBOO

This is very simple — you just put the whole thing together and steam. It comes over as very exotic for your guests, so it's a good one for showing off. I love these self-saucing steamed dishes as they really work well for large shared tables.

350 g (12 oz) blue eye fillets
4 thin slices of prosciutto
80 g (2¾ oz) tinned bamboo shoots
1 tablespoon peanut oil
4 dried shiitake mushrooms, soaked in warm water for
    30 minutes, stalks removed, cut in half on the
    diagonal through the middle
2 spring onions (scallions), cut into julienne
a pinch of freshly ground white pepper

SEASONING
2 tablespoons light soy sauce
3 tablespoons fresh chicken stock (page 58)
½ teaspoon sugar
1 tablespoon peanut oil
¼ teaspoon sesame oil
½ teaspoon sea salt

METHOD

Cut the blue eye fillets into eight equal portions. Cut the bamboo shoots into eight slices, roughly the same size as the fish pieces, and halve each piece of prosciutto.

Brush the peanut oil over two round plates, each large enough to hold four pieces of fish. Put the fish on the plates, allowing a little space between each piece, and layer the prosciutto, bamboo shoots and mushrooms over the top of each piece of fish. Mix the seasoning ingredients together and drizzle over and around the fish pieces.

Put the plates in a steamer (you will have to do this in two batches if you don't have a double-decker steamer) over a pot or a wok of rapidly boiling water, cover with the lid and steam for 6 minutes, or until the fish is just cooked through. Carefully remove the plates from the steamer and sprinkle with spring onions and white pepper to serve.

STEAMED MURRAY COD WITH BLACK BEANS

The black beans and chilli sauce punch a little more flavour into this steamed dish. I really like the bacon flavour here, and will often mix a spoonful of hot bean paste through at the end to turn it into a nice spicy fish dish.

350 g (12 oz) Murray cod, thickly sliced
2 tablespoons fermented black beans
½ teaspoon sea salt
½ small carrot, cut into julienne
1 knob of ginger, peeled and cut into julienne
1 slice of bacon, finely sliced
4 cloves garlic, finely chopped
1 long red chilli, deseeded and cut into julienne
2 spring onions (scallions), cut into 2 cm (¾ inch) lengths
fresh chilli sauce (page 44), to serve

MARINADE
1 tablespoon oyster sauce
2 tablespoons shaoxing
1 tablespoon sesame oil
2 teaspoons yellow bean soy sauce
1 teaspoon caster (superfine) sugar

METHOD

Season the fish pieces with salt. To make the marinade, mix together the oyster sauce, shaoxing, sesame oil, soy sauce and sugar and pour over the top, then leave for 10 minutes.

Scatter the carrot and ginger julienne over a deep round plate. Put the fish pieces on top in a single layer, then pour over the marinade and sprinkle with the black beans, bacon, garlic, chilli and spring onions.

Put the plate in a large bamboo steamer over a pot or a wok of rapidly boiling water, cover with the lid and steam the fish for 10 minutes, or until just cooked through. Remove from the steamer and serve with chilli sauce.

STIR-FRIED BLUE EYE WITH ASPARAGUS

You can use any fish you like here and replace the asparagus with your favourite vegetable for this simple stir-fry — perfect for a quick meal after work. This dish also works well with the light flavours of chicken.

350 g (12 oz) blue eye fillet, cut into 1.5 cm (⅝ inch) strips
6 thick green asparagus spears, cut into 4 cm (1½ inch)
    lengths on the diagonal
4 tablespoons vegetable oil
1 knob of ginger, peeled and cut into julienne
2 cloves garlic, finely chopped
3 spring onions (scallions), cut into 4 cm (1½ inch)
    lengths
3 tablespoons shaoxing
8 fresh shiitake mushrooms, stalks removed, sliced
1 teaspoon sea salt
1 tablespoon light soy sauce
1 teaspoon crushed yellow rock sugar
3 tablespoons fresh chicken stock (page 58)

METHOD

Heat a wok until just smoking. Add half the vegetable oil and, when hot, gently stir-fry the blue eye in batches until just cooked, then remove. Heat the rest of the oil in the wok and stir-fry the ginger, garlic and spring onions until fragrant, then deglaze the wok with shaoxing. Add the asparagus and stir-fry until bright green, then add the blue eye, shiitake mushrooms, salt, soy sauce, sugar and stock and cook for 1 minute to allow the flavours to mingle.

Using a slotted spoon, pile all the ingredients onto a large plate. Increase the heat under the wok and reduce the sauce until it thickens slightly, then pour the sauce over the fish and vegetables to serve.

STIR-FRIED MURRAY COD

Again, this simple stir-fry works well with any firm-textured fish, and is really all about the wonderful fresh taste of the ingredients.

350 g (12 oz) Murray cod, skin removed, thickly sliced
1 egg white
2 teaspoons cornflour (cornstarch)
1 teaspoon sea salt
2 tablespoons vegetable oil
1 small carrot, finely sliced on the diagonal
3 spring onions (scallions), cut into 4 cm (1½ inch) lengths
6 slices of peeled ginger
6 cloves garlic, finely sliced
2 tablespoons shaoxing
120 g (4¼ oz) snow peas (mangetout), trimmed
125 ml (4 fl oz/½ cup) fresh chicken stock (page 58)
1 teaspoon sesame oil
¼ teaspoon freshly ground white pepper

METHOD

Mix together the egg white, cornflour, half the sea salt and the cod, and leave for 10 minutes.

Heat a wok until almost smoking. Add the vegetable oil and, when hot, remove the fish from the marinade and stir-fry in batches until golden brown, then remove from the wok. Reheat the wok and stir-fry the carrot, spring onions, ginger and garlic until fragrant. Deglaze the wok with shaoxing, then add the snow peas, stock, sesame oil, remaining sea salt and white pepper and stir-fry for 1 minute more. Return the cod to the wok and toss together before serving.

SINGAPORE-STYLE SQUID

This is a combination stir-fry and braise dish. The squid becomes more tender the longer you braise it. Make sure you don't burn the garlic as it can get quite bitter — I know I usually like to do it the other way round, but this dish is cooked in one go, so we add the garlic with the ginger and squid.

350 g (12 oz) squid, cleaned
2 tablespoons peanut oil
1 knob of ginger, peeled and cut into julienne
8 cloves garlic, finely sliced
1 teaspoon shrimp paste
2 small wild green chillies, finely chopped
1 small Spanish onion, finely sliced
1 red capsicum (pepper), thickly sliced

SAUCE
1 tablespoon kecap manis
2 teaspoons light soy sauce
1 teaspoon Chinkiang vinegar
½ teaspoon sea salt
½ teaspoon sugar

METHOD

To prepare the squid, cut off the tentacles and cut down the centre of the squid so it will open out flat. Score the inside with a crisscross pattern, then cut the squid into large squares. Cut the tentacles into 4 cm (1½ inch) lengths.

To make the sauce, mix together the kecap manis, soy sauce, Chinkiang, sea salt and sugar in a small bowl.

Heat a wok until almost smoking. Add the peanut oil and, when hot, add the ginger and garlic and stir-fry for 10 seconds, then add the shrimp paste, chillies, onion and capsicum and stir-fry for 20 seconds. Add the squid and stir-fry for 1–2 minutes, or until it just begins to curl, then add the sauce and bring to the boil. Cover the wok, reduce the heat to low and braise the squid for about 10 minutes, or until tender. Use a slotted spoon to transfer the squid and vegetables to a serving plate. Increase the heat under the wok and reduce the sauce until it thickens slightly. Spoon the sauce over the squid to serve.

STIR-FRIED KINGFISH WITH BLACK BEANS & CUCUMBER

This nice simple stir-fry has a great texture from the cucumber and a little kick from the black beans. The combination of ingredients here is all about enhancing the natural flavours of the fish.

350 g (12 oz) kingfish fillet, cut into bite-sized pieces
1 tablespoon fermented black beans
1 Lebanese (short) cucumber, halved lengthways and
    sliced on the diagonal
2 teaspoons light soy sauce
½ teaspoon sugar
1 teaspoon sesame oil
1 teaspoon sea salt
2 tablespoons vegetable oil
4 cloves garlic, finely sliced
1 red capsicum (pepper), thickly sliced
2 teaspoons shaoxing
3 tablespoons fresh chicken stock (page 58)

METHOD

Mix together the kingfish, soy sauce, sugar, sesame oil and sea salt and leave to marinate for 30 minutes. Use a slotted spoon to remove the kingfish.

Heat a wok until just smoking. Add the oil and, when hot, stir-fry the kingfish in batches until golden, then remove. Add the black beans, garlic and capsicum to the wok and stir-fry until fragrant. Deglaze the wok with shaoxing and then return the kingfish to the wok along with the cucumber and stock. Toss together to serve.

SHAOXING-MARINATED KING PRAWNS

This involves stir-frying, boiling and steaming; all the elements are at work. You need to cook the prawns with the shell on so you can pick them up with your fingers and suck on them. This really simple dish works well for a shared table as it takes no time at all.

500 g (1 lb 2 oz) green king prawns (shrimp)
250 ml (9 fl oz/1 cup) shaoxing
2 tablespoons peanut oil

DIPPING SAUCE
2 tablespoons yellow bean soy sauce
3 small wild green chillies, finely chopped
2 tablespoons Chinese rice vinegar
2 teaspoons sesame oil
1 teaspoon caster (superfine) sugar
1 spring onion (scallion), cut into julienne
½ knob of ginger, peeled and cut into julienne

METHOD

Mix together the dipping sauce ingredients and 1 tablespoon water.

Remove the legs from the prawns and then use a small sharp knife or a pair of scissors to make a shallow incision along the length of the belly of each prawn, but don't peel or remove the heads. Marinate the prawns in the shaoxing for 10 minutes.

Heat a wok until just smoking. Add the peanut oil and, when hot, remove the prawns from the marinade and add to the wok. Stir-fry for 1 minute, then pour in the marinade and simmer until the wine evaporates and the prawns are cooked. Pile the prawns onto a plate and serve with the dipping sauce.

STIR-FRIED SEA SCALLOPS WITH ASPARAGUS

Sea scallops from Queensland are sweet and firm textured, but you could use whatever variety is available where you happen to be cooking. This dish is one of three scallop stir-fries in this section. In this one, the sauce plays a supporting role to the natural flavour of the scallops and asparagus.

10 large sea scallops
6 thick green asparagus spears, cut into 4 cm (1½ inch)
    lengths on the diagonal
4 tablespoons vegetable oil
4 fresh shiitake mushrooms, stalks removed, cut in half
    on the diagonal through the middle
1 knob of ginger, peeled and cut into julienne
2 cloves garlic, finely chopped
3 spring onions (scallions), cut into 4 cm (1½ inch)
    lengths
1 tablespoon shaoxing
1 tablespoon yellow bean soy sauce
1 tablespoon hoisin sauce
1 teaspoon crushed yellow rock sugar
2 tablespoons fresh chicken stock (page 58)

METHOD

Heat half the oil in a wok until just smoking, stir-fry the scallops until almost cooked through and remove. Add the asparagus and mushrooms to the wok and stir-fry for 2 minutes, then remove.

Heat the rest of the oil in the wok and stir-fry the ginger, garlic and spring onions until fragrant. Deglaze the wok with shaoxing, then return the scallops, asparagus and mushrooms to the wok with the soy sauce, hoisin, sugar and stock and cook briefly to allow the flavours to mingle.

Use a slotted spoon to pile the scallops and vegetables onto a large plate. Boil the sauce over high heat until it has reduced and thickened slightly and then pour over the scallops and vegetables to serve.

KING PRAWN SAMBAL

This is a really tasty, simple dish, and once you've made the paste, it's so easy from there. If you want to cut down on cooking time, you could use peeled prawns. For me, though, half the fun of this dish is sucking the prawn shells.

500 g (1 lb 2 oz) green king prawns (shrimp)
125 ml (4 fl oz/½ cup) vegetable oil
2 tablespoons grated palm sugar (jaggery)
1 teaspoon sea salt
4 tablespoons coconut cream
3 tablespoons tamarind water (page 32)
juice of 2 limes

SPICE PASTE
4 long red chillies
4 wild green chillies
4 red shallots
6 cloves garlic
1 tablespoon chopped galangal
1 tablespoon chopped lemongrass
1 tablespoon belachan
3 candlenuts

METHOD

Pound all the spice paste ingredients in a mortar with a pestle. Or use a blender to process the ingredients, adding a little water if necessary.

Heat the oil in a wok and, when hot but not smoking, add the spice paste. Cook over medium heat for about 10 minutes, or until fragrant. Add the prawns and cook for a minute, then add the palm sugar, sea salt, coconut cream and tamarind water and simmer for a further 1–2 minutes, or until the prawns are cooked. Squeeze the lime juice into the wok, transfer the prawns to a plate and pour the sauce over to serve.

NOTE Candlenuts can be toxic if consumed raw, so make sure the paste is cooked thoroughly.

STIR-FRIED KING PRAWNS WITH BLACK BEANS

A classic black bean and seafood stir-fry, this is quick to cook and tastes great. You can substitute any shellfish or fish fillet you like and it will still work wonderfully.

500 g (1 lb 2 oz) green king prawns (shrimp), peeled, deveined and butterflied
1 tablespoon fermented black beans
4 tablespoons peanut oil
2 cloves garlic, finely chopped
1 knob of ginger, peeled and cut into julienne
½ small red capsicum (pepper), diced
½ small green capsicum (pepper), diced
4 spring onions (scallions), cut into 4 cm (1½ inch) lengths
2 tablespoons shaoxing
3 tablespoons light soy sauce
3 tablespoons oyster sauce
1 teaspoon sugar
2 tablespoons fresh chicken stock (page 58)
1 small handful of coriander (cilantro) leaves

METHOD

Heat a wok until just smoking. Add the oil and, when hot, stir-fry the prawns until they are golden, then remove. Stir-fry the black beans, garlic, ginger, capsicum and spring onions until fragrant, then deglaze the wok with shaoxing. Return the prawns to the wok with the soy sauce, oyster sauce, sugar and stock, cook for 1 minute, then transfer the prawns and vegetables to a plate with a slotted spoon. Allow the sauce to boil until it reduces and thickens slightly, then pour over the prawns and vegetables and sprinkle with the coriander leaves to serve.

Banquet Menu Seven

FIVE-SPICE BEEF SHIN ✦ PAGE 224

STEAMED FRIED CHICKEN ✦ PAGE 250

STIR-FRIED GARLIC SPINACH ✦ PAGE 349

SHANGHAI-STYLE STEAMED FISH ✦ PAGE 293

RECIPES ARE PICTURED ON FOLLOWING PAGES CLOCKWISE FROM TOP LEFT

STIR-FRIED PIPIS IN BEAN SAUCE WITH CHILLIES

I really love the taste of fermented bean curd; it adds complexity of flavour here. This works well with mussels as well as pipis, and a combination of the two would be great with some noodles tossed in at the end — a sort of Asian spaghetti vongole.

500 g (1 lb 2 oz) pipis or clams (vongole)
2 teaspoons fermented red bean curd
1 tablespoon yellow bean soy sauce
3 tablespoons fresh chicken stock (page 58)
½ teaspoon sugar
2 tablespoons vegetable oil
4 cloves garlic, finely chopped
3 small wild green chillies, finely sliced
2 tablespoons shaoxing
1 small red capsicum (pepper), diced

METHOD

Wash the pipis in cold water, discarding any that are open.

Mash the fermented red bean curd with a fork then stir in the yellow bean soy sauce, stock and sugar.

Heat a wok until just smoking. Add the vegetable oil and, when hot, add the garlic and chillies and stir-fry until fragrant. Deglaze the wok with shaoxing, add the pipis and stir-fry for 2–3 minutes. Add the capsicum and bean sauce mixture to the wok and toss together. Cover the wok with a lid and cook for 2–3 minutes, shaking the wok occasionally, until the shells just begin to open up, then use a slotted spoon to transfer the pipis into a bowl. Return the wok to the heat and simmer the sauce, uncovered, until it reduces and thickens slightly. Pour the sauce over the pipis to serve.

STIR-FRIED SEA SCALLOPS WITH BLACK BEAN SAUCE

The black beans add zing and the oyster sauce adds a silkiness to the texture of this dish. You can also add some freshly chopped red or wild green chillies to really lift the intensity of the sauce and make it a classic black bean and chilli.

10 large sea scallops
2 tablespoons fermented black beans
2 cloves garlic, crushed
6 slices of peeled ginger
2 teaspoons sugar
2 teaspoons light soy sauce
2 tablespoons oyster sauce
2 tablespoons vegetable oil
3 spring onions (scallions), cut into 2 cm (¾ inch) lengths
3 tablespoons fresh chicken stock (page 58)

METHOD

Mix together the black beans, garlic, ginger, sugar, soy sauce and oyster sauce in a bowl.

Heat a wok until just smoking. Add the vegetable oil and, when hot, stir-fry the scallops for 30 seconds, then add the spring onions, continuing to stir-fry until the scallops are just cooked through. Remove from the wok.

Reheat the wok and stir-fry the black bean mixture until fragrant. Add the stock and bring to the boil, then return the scallops and spring onions to the wok and toss together.

STIR-FRIED SEA SCALLOPS WITH HOT BEAN PASTE

The flavours are spicy, but the taste of the shellfish still comes through. This makes a great Sunday lunch for two with some rice and a good glass of Riesling. You can add any vegetables you like, and even though the black beans make this similar to the last dish, the chilli paste, black vinegar and yellow bean soy sauce add another dimension.

10 large sea scallops
4 tablespoons peanut oil
100 g (3½ oz) snow peas (mangetout), trimmed
1 small knob of ginger, peeled and finely chopped
8 cloves garlic, finely chopped
3 tablespoons hot bean paste
1 tablespoon shaoxing
1 tablespoon yellow bean soy sauce
1 tablespoon Chinkiang vinegar
1 teaspoon sugar
3 tablespoons fresh chicken stock (page 58)
freshly ground white pepper
2 spring onions (scallions), finely chopped
1 small handful of coriander (cilantro) leaves

METHOD

Heat a wok until smoking. Add half the peanut oil and, when hot, stir-fry the scallops in batches until almost cooked through; remove and wipe the wok clean. Reheat the wok with another tablespoon of oil and stir-fry the snow peas until just tender, then remove from the wok. Reheat the last tablespoon of oil in the wok and stir-fry the ginger, garlic and hot bean paste until fragrant. Deglaze the wok with the shaoxing, then add the soy sauce, vinegar, sugar and stock and simmer for 2 minutes. Return the scallops and snow peas to the wok and toss together.

Spoon into a bowl, give it a good grind of white pepper and sprinkle with spring onions and coriander to serve.

STIR-FRIED OYSTERS WITH BLACK BEANS

I love this combination; you'll see me using black beans a lot with seafood because they have a wonderful affinity, the black beans lifting the flavour of the seafood beautifully. It's a strong flavour, but it shouldn't overpower. For the oysters to have the right texture and the sauce the right clarity, you must blanch the oysters in boiling water first — don't skip that step.

24 Pacific oysters, freshly shucked
1 tablespoon fermented black beans
2 tablespoons peanut oil
4 cloves garlic, finely chopped
2 teaspoons finely chopped ginger
1 long red chilli, finely sliced
½ red capsicum (pepper), finely chopped
8 spring onions (scallions), cut into 4 cm (1½ inch)
    lengths
2½ tablespoons light soy sauce
2 teaspoons sesame oil
1 tablespoon chopped coriander (cilantro) leaves

METHOD

Blanch the oysters in boiling water for 1 minute, then remove and drain on paper towel.

Heat a wok until just smoking. Add the peanut oil and, when hot, stir-fry the black beans, garlic, ginger, chilli and capsicum until fragrant. Add the spring onions, soy sauce and sesame oil and stir-fry for another minute, then add the oysters and toss to heat through. Sprinkle with coriander to serve.

BLUE EYE WITH TOFU & PORK

This is one of my favourite dishes as the crisp texture of the fish and tofu are great with the pancetta and the complex sauce. I'll occasionally swap the sweet bean paste for hot bean paste in this dish.

250 g (9 oz) blue eye, thickly sliced
150 g (5½ oz) firm tofu, cut into 1 cm (½ inch) strips
100 g (3½ oz) piece of pancetta, cut into lardons
vegetable oil, for deep-frying
3 spring onions (scallions), cut into 4 cm (1½ inch) lengths
2 red shallots, finely sliced
4 cloves garlic, finely sliced
4 dried shiitake mushrooms, soaked in warm water for 30 minutes, stalks removed, finely sliced
1 teaspoon sweet bean paste
1 tablespoon light soy sauce
2 teaspoons oyster sauce
2 teaspoons sugar
¼ teaspoon sea salt
250 ml (9 fl oz/1 cup) fresh chicken stock (page 58)
1 spring onion (scallion), cut into julienne
1 handful of coriander (cilantro) leaves, finely chopped

METHOD

Heat the oil in a wok or deep-fryer until smoking (180°C/350°F), and deep-fry the tofu until golden, then remove and drain on paper towel. Next deep-fry the blue eye until golden, then remove and drain. Drain the oil from the wok and wipe clean.

Reheat the wok with 2 tablespoons of vegetable oil and stir-fry the pancetta, spring onions, red shallots, garlic and mushrooms until fragrant. Add the sweet bean paste, soy sauce, oyster sauce, sugar, sea salt and stock, and simmer until the sauce reduces and thickens a little. Add the fish and tofu to heat through, spoon onto a plate, and sprinkle with julienned spring onion and coriander to serve.

DEEP-FRIED LEATHERJACKET WITH THREE-FLAVOURED SAUCE

The reason I like leatherjacket for this classic dish is that it has a really simple bone structure so it's easy to eat. You could use sole, ocean perch, snapper, or in fact any fish you like. I also like to deep-fry the fish fillets in a light batter and drizzle this sauce over the top.

3 small leatherjackets, scaled and cleaned
vegetable oil
90 g (3¼ oz/½ cup) grated palm sugar (jaggery)
2 tablespoons tamarind water (page 32)
2 tablespoons fish sauce
2 long red chillies, deep-fried until black and crisp
1 handful of Thai basil leaves, deep-fried until crisp

PASTE
4 coriander (cilantro) roots, scraped and chopped
a pinch of sea salt
3 long red or green chillies, deseeded and chopped
4 cloves garlic
3 red shallots, chopped

METHOD

To make the paste, pound the coriander roots, sea salt, chillies, garlic and shallots in a mortar with a pestle until you have a fine paste. Or use a blender to process the ingredients, adding a little water if necessary.

Heat a wok until almost smoking. Add 2 tablespoons of the vegetable oil and, when hot, add the paste and stir-fry until fragrant. Add the palm sugar and 2–3 tablespoons water and continue to stir-fry until caramelised. Season with tamarind water and half the fish sauce, then check for balance; the sauce should be sweet, sour, hot and salty.

Toss the leatherjackets with the remaining fish sauce and leave for 10 minutes. Heat the oil in a wok or deep-fryer until just smoking (180°C/350°F), and deep-fry the fish in batches until golden brown and cooked through, then drain on paper towel.

Arrange the fish on a platter and drizzle with the sauce. Crumble the chillies and the basil and sprinkle them over the fish to serve.

SWEET & SOUR BLUE EYE

Very simple to make — you just deep-fry the fish, make the sauce and toss it all together.

I was never a big fan of sweet and sour fish at restaurants, but there is something nice about it when the fish is spanking fresh and the pineapple isn't tinned.

300 g (10½ oz) blue eye, skin removed and thickly sliced
1½ tablespoons shaoxing
½ teaspoon sea salt
2 eggs, lightly beaten
30 g (1 oz/¼ cup) plain (all-purpose) flour
vegetable oil, for deep-frying
½ knob of ginger, peeled and finely chopped
3 spring onions (scallions), cut into 4 cm (1½ inch)
    lengths
½ red capsicum (pepper), cut into large dice
½ green capsicum (pepper), cut into large dice
125 ml (4 fl oz/½ cup) fresh chicken stock (page 58)
2 tablespoons light soy sauce
4 tablespoons sugar
4 tablespoons Chinese red vinegar
2 tablespoons tomato sauce (ketchup)
80 g (2¾ oz/½ cup) roughly chopped fresh pineapple
½ teaspoon sesame oil
1 small handful of coriander (cilantro) leaves

METHOD

Mix together the blue eye, ½ tablespoon of shaoxing and the sea salt in a bowl and leave to marinate for 30 minutes. Beat the egg and flour with about 2 tablespoons water until you have a light batter.

Heat the oil in a wok or deep-fryer until just smoking (180°C/350°F). Dip the fish in the batter and carefully drop into the wok in batches, deep-frying until golden, then remove and drain on paper towel. Pour the oil from the wok and wipe clean.

Reheat the wok with 2 tablespoons of vegetable oil until just smoking and stir-fry the ginger, spring onions and capsicums until fragrant. Deglaze with the remaining shaoxing, and then add the stock, soy sauce, sugar, vinegar and tomato sauce. Bring to the boil, reduce the heat and simmer until thickened slightly. Add the pineapple and fish pieces and cook for 30 seconds more. Spoon onto a plate and sprinkle with the sesame oil and coriander leaves to serve.

CRISP SNAPPER WITH HOT BEAN PASTE
If you really want to avoid bones in the fish you can make this with fillets, battered and then deep-fried.

1 x 500–600 g (1 lb 2–5 oz) whole snapper, cleaned and
   scaled
1 tablespoon hot bean paste
2 tablespoons shaoxing
2 teaspoons sea salt
vegetable oil, for deep-frying
4 spring onions (scallions), sliced
½ knob of ginger, peeled and finely chopped
3 cloves garlic, finely chopped
185 ml (6 fl oz/¾ cup) fresh chicken stock (page 58)
1 tablespoon sugar
1 tablespoon sesame oil

METHOD

Make a few deep cuts in the thickest part of the fish, then turn over and repeat on the other side. Combine half the shaoxing and half the sea salt, rub all over the fish and then leave to marinate for 10 minutes.

Heat the oil in a wok or deep-fryer until just smoking (180°C/350°F), and deep-fry the fish until golden brown and crisp, then remove and drain on paper towel. Pour the oil from the wok and wipe clean.

Reheat the wok with 2 tablespoons of vegetable oil until just smoking. Stir-fry the spring onions, ginger, garlic and hot bean paste until fragrant. Deglaze the wok with the remaining shaoxing, then add the sugar, sesame oil, remaining salt, and stock. Bring to the boil, then reduce the heat and simmer until the sauce thickens. Put the fish onto a serving plate and pour over the sauce to serve.

CRUMBED WHITING FILLETS WITH SWEET & SOUR SAUCE

This is another way to make sweet and sour sauce — perfect with really crispy fish. I love all the sweet and sour bites from the pickles.

350 g (12 oz) whiting fillets, with skin
1 tablespoon peanut oil
4 spring onions (scallions), cut into julienne
5 long red chillies, deseeded and cut into julienne
70 g (2½ oz) pickled ginger, finely sliced
100 g (3½ oz) pickled cucumber in syrup, drained and finely sliced
plain (all-purpose) flour, for dusting
1–2 eggs, lightly beaten
90 g (3¼ oz/1½ cups) Japanese breadcrumbs (panko)
vegetable oil, for deep-frying

SAUCE
350 ml (12 fl oz) fresh chicken stock (page 58)
4 tablespoons tomato sauce (ketchup)
100 ml (3½ fl oz) rice vinegar
100 g (3½ oz) sugar
1 teaspoon sea salt
1 tablespoon light soy sauce

METHOD

To make the sauce, mix together the chicken stock, tomato sauce, rice vinegar, sugar, sea salt and soy sauce in a bowl.

Heat a wok until just smoking. Add the peanut oil and, when hot, stir-fry the spring onions and chillies until fragrant. Add the ginger, cucumber and the sauce, bring to the boil, then reduce the heat and simmer until the sauce has reduced and thickened.

Meanwhile, crumb the whiting fillets by first dusting them with flour, then dipping them in the egg wash, and finally pressing them in the breadcrumbs.

Remove the sauce from the wok and keep warm. Wash and dry the wok and heat the oil until almost smoking (180°C/350°F). Deep-fry the fish in batches until golden brown, then drain on paper towel. Put the fish on a serving plate and pour over the warm sauce to serve.

CHILLI SALT SQUID

This is a dish I've been cooking for about 20 years and I never tire of it. With a little squeeze of lemon it goes from good to great. I usually have it as a little starter, or pass it around as a canapé.

300 g (10½ oz) squid
vegetable oil, for deep-frying
40 g (1½ oz/⅓ cup) plain (all-purpose) flour
2 tablespoons sea salt
1 tablespoon freshly ground white pepper
2 tablespoons chilli powder
1 handful of coriander (cilantro) leaves, plus extra to
    serve
half a lemon, cut into 3 wedges

METHOD

Put one squid at a time on a chopping board and pull out the tentacles. Pull off the side flaps and cut the squid down the centre so that it will open flat. With a small knife open the squid and remove the ink sack and discard. Scrape the skin off the body and flaps (it will peel off easily) and cut off and discard the hard beak. Cut the squid into strips about 1 cm (½ inch) wide.

Heat the oil in a wok or deep-fryer until just smoking (180°C/350°F). Mix together the flour, sea salt, white pepper and chilli powder, then toss the squid in the mixture, making sure it's coated well. Shake off any excess flour and put half of the squid into the wok. Deep-fry for 2 minutes, or until crispy, remove with a slotted spoon and drain on crumpled paper towel. Repeat with the remaining squid. Add the coriander to the oil and deep-fry for 1 minute, or until crisp — this has a tendency to spit, so be careful. With a slotted spoon, transfer the coriander to the paper towel.

Put the squid and deep-fried coriander in the centre of a large plate, with lemon wedges on the side, and top with fresh coriander to serve.

PRAWN ROLLS WITH TOFU SKIN

A little variation on a spring roll, these use tofu skin instead of spring roll wrappers (you can use them as wonton wrappers also). They're really fun to make and you can use any filling you like. Make sure you don't try to deep-fry them in oil that is too hot — at 180°C (350°F) they will blow apart.

500 g (1 lb 2 oz) green king prawns (shrimp), peeled,
    deveined and roughly chopped
2 tofu sheets
2 tablespoons shaoxing
2 tablespoons hot bean paste
1 clove garlic, finely chopped
1 tablespoon finely chopped ginger
½ teaspoon sea salt
1 tablespoon cornflour (cornstarch)
vegetable oil, for deep-frying
lemon wedges, to serve
chilli sauce (page 42), to serve

METHOD

Put the prawns, shaoxing, hot bean paste, garlic, ginger and sea salt in a food processor and pulse a few times until the mixture has combined and you have a rough paste. Be careful not to overwork the mixture.

Make a paste by combining the cornflour and 2 teaspoons water. Cut each tofu sheet into six triangles. Place some prawn mixture along a straight edge of each tofu sheet and roll them up to enclose the filling, folding in the sides as you go. Seal the openings with the cornflour paste.

Heat the oil in a wok or deep-fryer (160°C/315°F), and deep-fry the prawn rolls until they are golden and cooked through, then drain on paper towel. Serve the rolls with wedges of lemon and chilli sauce.

NOTE To soften the tofu sheets, soak them in a little lukewarm water, drain immediately and gently squeeze out any excess water.

SOUR ORANGE CURRY OF SALMON

Classic Gang Som Thai curry has a wonderful shrimpiness and sour bite from the tamarind. Use the curry for any type of seafood you like; it's distinct and delicious. In fact, one of my all-time favourite mussel dishes is made with this curry sauce, boiled, with mussels opened up in it.

300 g (10½ oz) salmon fillet, skin removed, cut into
　　bite-sized pieces
375 ml (13 fl oz/1½ cups) fresh chicken stock (page 58)
4 tablespoons tamarind water (page 32)
1 teaspoon sugar
2 tablespoons fish sauce
8 cherry tomatoes, halved
120 g (4¼ oz) snake or green beans, cut into 4 cm
　　(1½ inch) lengths
1 small handful of baby spinach leaves
1 small handful of Thai basil leaves

CURRY PASTE
5 dried long red chillies, deseeded, soaked in warm water
　　for 30 minutes
a large pinch of sea salt
1 tablespoon chopped galangal
5 red shallots, chopped
1 teaspoon Thai shrimp paste, wrapped in foil and
　　roasted until fragrant

METHOD

Pound all the paste ingredients in a mortar with a pestle until you have a fine paste. Or process in a blender, adding a little water if necessary.

Bring the stock to the boil in a small pot and add the curry paste, tamarind water, sugar and fish sauce, then simmer for 5 minutes. Add the tomatoes and snake beans and simmer for another 2 minutes, then add the salmon and cook for a further minute. Stir through the spinach and basil leaves to serve.

CRISP PRAWNS WITH CASHEW & CHILLI SAUCE

This works well on two fronts: everyone loves crisp prawns, and the sauce can be made in advance and reheated. It's perfect for a shared table.

6 green king prawns (shrimp), peeled and deveined with
    tails left intact
vegetable oil, for deep-frying

BATTER
85 g (3 oz/⅔ cup) plain (all-purpose) flour
3 teaspoons cornflour (cornstarch)
a pinch of sea salt
125 ml (4 fl oz/½ cup) iced water

CASHEW & CHILLI SAUCE
2 tablespoons vegetable oil
½ small red capsicum (pepper), diced
½ small Spanish onion, diced
1 tablespoon shaoxing
3 tablespoons chilli sauce (page 42)
2 tablespoons sugar
1 teaspoon sea salt
1 teaspoon ground white pepper
1 tablespoon rice vinegar
2 teaspoons sesame oil
3 tablespoons fresh chicken stock (page 58)
80 g (2¾ oz/½ cup) cashews, roasted
2 dried long red chillies, deseeded, deep-fried until black
    and crisp and broken into small pieces

METHOD

To make the cashew and chilli sauce, heat the oil in a wok until just smoking. Add the capsicum and onion and stir-fry until fragrant, then deglaze the wok with the shaoxing. Add the chilli sauce, sugar, sea salt, white pepper, vinegar, sesame oil and chicken stock to the wok, bring to the boil, then reduce the heat and simmer until the sauce has reduced by about a quarter. Stir in the cashews and chillies and remove from the heat.

To make the batter, mix together the flour, cornflour, sea salt and water until smooth. Dip the prawns into the batter and allow any excess to drip away. Heat the oil in a wok until smoking (180°C/350°F) and deep-fry the prawns until golden, then drain on paper towel. Spoon the sauce onto a plate and top with the fried prawns to serve.

DRY LOBSTER CURRY

This dish is delicious and, once you get used to dispatching lobsters, it isn't too difficult. You can add some coconut milk to make it a little saucier but don't overdo it; it's great dry with the paste just coating the lobster. You can use this dry curry with pretty much anything that can be stir-fried.

1 x 1 kg (2 lb 4 oz) live lobster
vegetable oil, for deep-frying
3 tablespoons grated palm sugar (jaggery)
1 tablespoon fish sauce
125 ml (4 fl oz/½ cup) fresh chicken stock (page 58)
5 kaffir lime leaves, cut into julienne
1 handful of coriander (cilantro) leaves

PASTE
½ teaspoon white peppercorns, roasted and ground
½ teaspoon cumin seeds, roasted and ground
10 dried long red chillies, deseeded, soaked in warm
    water for 30 minutes and chopped
a large pinch of sea salt
1½ tablespoons chopped galangal
2 lemongrass stalks, tough outer leaves removed,
    chopped
finely grated zest of 1 kaffir lime
4 coriander (cilantro) roots, scraped and chopped
½ small Spanish onion, chopped
4 cloves garlic, chopped
2 teaspoons Thai shrimp paste, wrapped in foil and
    roasted until fragrant

METHOD
Pound the paste ingredients in a mortar with a pestle until you have a fine paste. Or process with a blender, using a little water if necessary.

Kill the lobster humanely (see page 139 for instructions), then cut it in half lengthways and clean the insides. Cut each half crossways into thirds.

Heat the oil in a wok or deep-fryer until just smoking (180°C/350°F), and deep-fry the lobster in batches until golden brown, then remove and drain on paper towel. Discard all but 2 tablespoons of oil from the wok.

Add the paste to the wok and stir-fry over medium heat until fragrant. Add the sugar, fish sauce and stock, bring to the boil, add the cooked lobster and toss together. Sprinkle with the lime and coriander leaves.

BLUE SWIMMER CRAB WITH ROASTED CHILLI PASTE

This chilli paste is just wonderful with crabs — split the shells open and let them absorb the flavours. You could of course use mud crab or spanner crab, but the paste is great with any kind of seafood. It's also wonderful if you deep-fry the prawns in crispy batter and spoon chilli paste all over them. Then you just need rice and you'll be in heaven.

3 x 1 kg (2 lb 4 oz) blue swimmer crabs, cleaned and
    chopped into quarters
300 g (10½ oz/1 cup) chilli paste (page 48)
vegetable oil, for deep-frying
3 tablespoons coconut cream
4 kaffir lime leaves, crushed
4 tablespoons fish sauce
60 g (2¼ oz/⅓ cup) grated palm sugar (jaggery)
1 small handful of Thai basil leaves

METHOD

Heat the oil in a wok until just smoking (180°C/350°F), and deep-fry the crab in batches until bright red and cooked through, then drain on paper towel.

Pour all but 3 tablespoons of oil from the wok, and reheat the wok until just below smoking point. Add the coconut cream and stir-fry until it 'splits', then add the lime leaves and chilli paste, stir-fry for 2 minutes more, then finally add the fish sauce and palm sugar, and cook for another minute for the flavours to mingle. Add the crab to the wok and toss together. Stir in the basil and spoon onto a large plate to serve.

STIR-FRIED PRAWNS WITH CHINESE CHIVES & CHILLI

This is simple and delicious; the chives and garlic add a wonderful flavour, and the complexity of the vinegar, chilli and sesame really makes this divine. It is worth chasing down the yellow Chinese chives if you can — they're more subtle and sweet than the green and thus add an extra dimension. If you can't, don't panic. The yellow chives are actually blanched, like white asparagus, which means that they've been covered and don't photosynthesise with sunlight, so they don't turn green. If Chinese chives aren't available, rinse and chop half a bunch of English spinach; it makes a worthy substitute.

500 g (1 lb 2 oz) green king prawns (shrimp), peeled and deveined
100 ml (3½ fl oz) peanut oil
2 cloves garlic, finely sliced
1 tablespoon julienned ginger
1 spring onion (scallion), minced
1 teaspoon dried chilli flakes
15 g (½ oz/½ bunch) yellow Chinese chives, cut into 2 cm (¾ inch) lengths
15 g (½ oz/½ bunch) green Chinese chives, cut into 2 cm (¾ inch) lengths
1 long red chilli, deseeded and finely sliced
2 tablespoons shaoxing
1 tablespoon light soy sauce
1 teaspoon Chinkiang vinegar
a pinch of sea salt
1 teaspoon sesame oil

METHOD

Heat the wok until just smoking. Add 3 tablespoons of peanut oil and, when hot, add the prawns in two batches and stir-fry until half cooked. Remove from the wok — make sure you don't overcook the prawns at this stage.

Add the remaining 2 tablespoons of oil to the wok and return to the heat. Stir-fry the garlic, ginger, spring onion and chilli flakes until fragrant. Add the chives and fresh chilli and then return the prawns to the wok.

Deglaze with the shaoxing and add the soy sauce, vinegar and a pinch of sea salt. At this point the chives should be softened and the prawns heated through. Spoon the prawns and chives onto a plate and drizzle with sesame oil to serve.

Banquet Menu Eight

THAI-STYLE BEEF WITH CHILLIES & SNOW PEAS ⚘ page 233

STIR-FRIED MUD CRAB WITH CURRY POWDER ⚘ page 140

SILKEN TOFU WITH XO SAUCE ⚘ page 184

CHICKEN CURRY ⚘ page 278

RECIPES ARE PICTURED ON FOLLOWING PAGES CLOCKWISE FROM TOP LEFT

Vegetables

The vegetables in this chapter are written as side dishes to go with your choice of protein, but they're all really great with a bowl of rice as well. As they all have great flavour, you can simply stir-fry some pork, beef, seafood or poultry and add it to any of these dishes to turn them into a substantial meal.

Feel free to swap vegetables in and out of these recipes depending on what you love — just because I have a recipe for Chinese broccoli and oyster sauce, it doesn't mean you can't use whatever vegetable or combination you like in the same recipe.

Look for exotic vegetables and try them; every supermarket seems to have gai larn (Chinese broccoli), Chinese cabbage (wombok), bok choy (pak choy) and choy sum. They seem to have taken their place alongside the traditional Mediterranean vegetables we are so familiar with. Don't forget that something as simple as a plate of stir-fried snow peas with a touch of garlic can be a wonderful thing. Buy fresh and the final result will taste so much better.

WARM MUSHROOM & ROAST RICE SALAD

This is a lovely little stir-fry with Nam Jim added at the end to give it a hot and sour taste. Make sure you remove the wok from the heat before you mix in the Nam Jim because if the dressing boils fiercely it will lose its freshness. You can use this dressing on any vegetables you like to create a fiery addition to a shared table. Just don't then serve a Thai-style salad with similar flavours.

300 g (10½ oz) assorted mushrooms such as enoki, shiitake, shimeji and oyster
1 teaspoon ground roast rice (page 27)
2 tablespoons peanut oil
1 Spanish onion, halved and finely sliced
1 handful of combined mint and coriander (cilantro) leaves
1 spring onion (scallion), cut into julienne
2 red shallots, finely sliced and deep-fried until golden

DRESSING
1 clove garlic
3 coriander (cilantro) roots, scraped and chopped
2 small wild green chillies
a pinch of sea salt
a pinch of caster (superfine) sugar
3 tablespoons lime juice
2 tablespoons fish sauce

METHOD

To make the dressing, pound the garlic, coriander roots, chillies, sea salt and sugar in a mortar with a pestle to form a paste. Add the lime juice and fish sauce and taste for balance, adjusting if necessary.

Tear the mushrooms into even-sized pieces. Heat a wok until just smoking. Add the peanut oil and, when hot, stir-fry the mushrooms and onion for only 30 seconds to 1 minute, until just starting to soften. Remove from the heat, add the dressing, herbs and spring onion and toss together. Sprinkle the salad with ground roast rice and fried shallots to serve.

COLD SPINACH & SESAME SALAD

Great for a lunch with a couple of other dishes, the earthiness of the spinach
with the aroma of sesame is wonderful — this is the taste of Asia.
For a hot dish, stir-fry the spinach and then add the dressing.

2 bunches English spinach, trimmed and rinsed
1 teaspoon sesame seeds, roasted

DRESSING
1 tablespoon shaoxing
1 tablespoon light soy sauce
1 tablespoon sesame oil
3 tablespoons cold fresh chicken stock (page 58)

METHOD

In salted boiling water, blanch the spinach for 30 seconds, then refresh in
iced water. Drain the spinach and squeeze out excess moisture.

To make the dressing, mix together the shaoxing, soy sauce, sesame oil
and the chicken stock in a small bowl.

Put the spinach on a serving plate, drizzle with the dressing and sprinkle
with the roasted sesame seeds to serve.

BRAISED BITTER MELON

This was one of my father's favourite dishes, along with black bean and chilli stir-fried bitter melon. It took me a long time to appreciate the bitter flavour but, once I got the hang of it, I was a true convert. Blanching the melon and removing the membrane before braising makes the bitterness a little more moderate.

2 x 600 g (1 lb 5 oz) bitter melons, rinsed
2 tablespoons vegetable oil
2 tablespoons light soy sauce
2 tablespoons sugar
2 teaspoons chilli oil
1 teaspoon sesame oil

METHOD

Halve the melons lengthways, scoop out the seeds and soft inner membrane with a spoon, and then cut the melon into bite-sized pieces. Cook the pieces in boiling water for 7 minutes, then drain and refresh under cold water.

Heat a wok until just smoking. Add the oil and, when hot, stir-fry the melon until starting to colour. Add the soy sauce, sugar, 250 ml (9 fl oz/1 cup) water and chilli oil and simmer over medium heat until the sauce has reduced and become syrupy. Transfer the melon and sauce to a bowl and drizzle with sesame oil to serve.

BRAISED CHINESE CABBAGE WITH CHESTNUTS

I'm very keen on this recipe as it uses two of my favourite ingredients. I love cabbage and dried chestnuts, with their crunchy texture and slight smoky nuttiness. They're both good to add to any stir-fry.

½ Chinese cabbage (wombok), washed and cut into large
   chunks
120 g (4¼ oz) dried chestnuts
vegetable oil, for deep-frying
½ knob of ginger, peeled and finely chopped
1 spring onion (scallion), finely chopped
1 tablespoon shaoxing
1 teaspoon sea salt
1½ teaspoons sugar
1½ tablespoons light soy sauce
1 teaspoon dark soy sauce
375 ml (13 fl oz/1½ cups) fresh chicken stock (page 58)

METHOD

Cook the chestnuts in simmering water for about 45 minutes, or until tender, then drain. Blanch the cabbage in boiling water for 2 minutes, then refresh in iced water and drain on paper towel.

Heat the oil in a wok or deep-fryer until just smoking (180°C/350°F), and deep-fry the cabbage in two batches until golden. Remove with a slotted spoon and drain on paper towel. Deep-fry the chestnuts in the same oil for 2–3 minutes, then drain on paper towel. Discard all but 1 tablespoon of oil from the wok.

Return the wok to the heat and reheat until smoking. Stir-fry the ginger and spring onion until fragrant. Deglaze the wok with the shaoxing, and then add the salt, sugar, both soy sauces and chicken stock. Return the cabbage and chestnuts to the wok and stir-fry over high heat until the sauce boils and reduces by about half. Transfer to a bowl to serve.

CHINESE BROCCOLI WITH OYSTER SAUCE

This is a classic and works well as a side dish for any shared table. It's extremely versatile — use any vegetable or combination of vegetables you like — you may need to adjust their cooking times accordingly.

1 bunch Chinese broccoli (gai larn)
2 tablespoons oyster sauce
2 tablespoons vegetable oil
4 tablespoons fresh chicken stock (page 58)
1 tablespoon light soy sauce
1 tablespoon sugar
¼ teaspoon sea salt

METHOD

Rinse and drain the Chinese broccoli. Bring 1.25 litres (44 fl oz/5 cups) water to the boil with 1 tablespoon of the oil and blanch the broccoli for 2 minutes, then remove and drain and arrange in a shallow bowl.

Heat a wok with the remaining oil, stir-fry the oyster sauce briefly, then add the stock, soy sauce, sugar and salt. Bring to the boil and pour over the broccoli to serve.

STIR-FRIED CABBAGE WITH CHINKIANG VINEGAR

I love Chinese cabbage with anything, but the Chinkiang vinegar gives this dish a distinct sweet and sour taste. I often just stir-fry cabbage with garlic and extra virgin olive oil for a great result.

½ Chinese cabbage (wombok), cut into large chunks
2 tablespoons Chinkiang vinegar
125 ml (4 fl oz/½ cup) peanut oil
1 teaspoon finely chopped ginger
1 clove garlic, finely chopped
1 tablespoon shaoxing
1 teaspoon white vinegar
2 tablespoons grated palm sugar (jaggery)
2 tablespoons oyster sauce

METHOD

Heat a wok until just smoking. Add half the oil and, when hot, stir-fry the ginger and garlic until fragrant. Add the cabbage, stir-fry for 1 minute, then deglaze the wok with the shaoxing. Add the Chinkiang and white vinegars, palm sugar and oyster sauce and cook for another minute, then spoon the cabbage onto a serving plate. Heat the remaining oil until just smoking and carefully douse the cabbage with the hot oil before serving.

STIR-FRIED BEAN SPROUTS & YELLOW CHIVES

This stir-fry highlights the wonderful texture and natural flavour of sprouts and chives. Be careful not to burn the ginger and garlic.

420 g (15 oz/4 cups) bean sprouts, trimmed
100 g (3½ oz) Chinese yellow chives
2 tablespoons vegetable oil
½ knob of ginger, peeled and cut into julienne
2 cloves garlic, finely chopped
1½ tablespoons light soy sauce
½ teaspoon sea salt
¼ teaspoon sugar
3 tablespoons fresh chicken stock (page 58)
1 small handful of coriander (cilantro) leaves

METHOD

Rinse the bean sprouts and chives and drain well. Heat a wok until just smoking. Add the vegetable oil and, when hot, stir-fry the ginger and garlic until fragrant, about 30 seconds. Add the bean sprouts and chives and stir-fry until just limp, then add the soy sauce, sea salt, sugar and stock and cook for another minute. Stir in the coriander leaves to serve.

Banquet Menu Nine

STIR-FRIED CABBAGE WITH CHINKIANG VINEGAR ✤ PAGE 343

GRILLED LOBSTER WITH TAMARIND ✤ PAGE 292

LEMON CHICKEN ✤ PAGE 266

RED-BRAISED PORK HOCK WITH SHIITAKE MUSHROOMS ✤ PAGE 88

RECIPES ARE PICTURED ON FOLLOWING PAGES CLOCKWISE FROM TOP LEFT

SICHUAN-STYLE SNAKE BEANS

This classic dish works with green beans as well. The pork gives the sauce a great texture and, by all means, add more chilli if you like. I personally like this dish quite fiery.

300 g (10½ oz) snake beans, cut into 10 cm (4 inch)
   lengths
4 tablespoons vegetable oil
1 teaspoon chilli oil
100 g (3½ oz) minced (ground) pork belly
½ knob of ginger, peeled and finely chopped
1 tablespoon shaoxing
3 tablespoons fresh chicken stock (page 58)
1 teaspoon sugar
1 teaspoon sea salt
1 tablespoon Chinkiang vinegar
1 teaspoon sesame oil
2 spring onions (scallions), finely chopped

METHOD

Heat a wok until just smoking. Add 2 tablespoons of the vegetable oil and, when hot, reduce the heat to medium and stir-fry half the beans for 3–4 minutes, or until they begin to wrinkle. Remove the beans with a slotted spoon, then reheat the wok with another tablespoon of vegetable oil and repeat the process with the remaining beans. Wipe the wok clean.

Heat the remaining vegetable oil and chilli oil in the wok until just smoking and stir-fry the pork, breaking it up with a spoon, until it starts to colour. Add the ginger and stir-fry until fragrant, then deglaze the wok with the shaoxing. Return the beans to the wok and add the stock, sugar, salt and vinegar. Cook until the liquid has almost completely evaporated, then turn off the heat and add the sesame oil. Transfer to a serving plate and sprinkle with the spring onions to serve.

STIR-FRIED GARLIC SPINACH

I love this very Cantonese way of dealing with spinach. Equally gorgeous would be to add ginger and crumbled dried chilli to the oil, and some sesame and chilli oil at the end — it would make it very Sichuan.

2 bunches English spinach, trimmed and rinsed
3 cloves garlic, finely chopped
2 tablespoons vegetable oil
2 tablespoons shaoxing
1 teaspoon sea salt
1 teaspoon sugar

METHOD

Heat a wok until it just starts smoking. Add the vegetable oil and, when hot, stir-fry the garlic until fragrant. Add the spinach and stir-fry for 30 seconds, then deglaze the wok with the shaoxing. Add the sea salt and sugar and stir-fry for 1–2 minutes, or until the spinach is tender but still bright green.

STIR-FRIED BOK CHOY

The natural flavour of bok choy is highlighted in this simple stir-fry. Feel free to use any vegetable you like here; I'm very fond of asparagus cooked this way as well.

1 bunch baby bok choy (pak choy), quartered lengthways
    and rinsed
1 tablespoon vegetable oil
3 slices of peeled ginger
1 tablespoon shaoxing
3 tablespoons fresh chicken stock (page 58)
½ teaspoon sugar
¾ teaspoon sea salt
1 teaspoon sesame oil

METHOD

Heat a wok until just smoking. Add the vegetable oil and, when hot, stir-fry the ginger until fragrant. Add the bok choy and cook for 1–2 minutes, or until the leaves are just limp, then deglaze the wok with the shaoxing and add the stock, sugar and salt. Stir-fry for another minute, or until the bok choy is just cooked. Transfer to a serving plate, spoon over the juices and drizzle with sesame oil to serve.

SICHUAN-STYLE EGGPLANT

In my restaurants I'll quite often serve this as a garnish to barbecued quail, chicken or seafood. I love anything with hot bean paste in it, but the combination of the mellow sweetness of yellow rock sugar, the sourness of vinegar and the spicy hot numbing flavour of Sichuan pepper is really great here. You can sauté the eggplant rather than deep-frying, then stir-fry it in the sauce — you'll get the same result.

500 g (1 lb 2 oz) Japanese eggplants (aubergines),
   trimmed
500 ml (17 fl oz/2 cups) vegetable oil
2 cloves garlic, finely chopped
½ knob of ginger, peeled and finely chopped
3 spring onions (scallions), sliced into rounds
3 tablespoons shaoxing
3 tablespoons hot bean paste
2½ tablespoons yellow bean soy sauce
100 ml (3½ fl oz) rice vinegar
65 g (2½ oz/⅓ cup) crushed yellow rock sugar
½ teaspoon ground Sichuan pepper

METHOD

Cut the eggplants in half lengthways. Heat the oil in a wok or deep-fryer until just smoking (180°C/350°F), and deep-fry the eggplant in batches until golden brown. Drain on paper towel.

Return the wok to the heat with 2 tablespoons of oil and when the oil is just smoking, add the garlic, ginger and spring onions and stir-fry until fragrant. Deglaze the wok with the shaoxing, then add the bean paste, soy sauce, vinegar and sugar and boil for 2 minutes. Return the eggplant to the wok and cook for 2 minutes, mashing slightly so that the eggplant absorbs the flavour of the sauce. Spoon onto a large platter and sprinkle with Sichuan pepper.

CHOY SUM WITH PROSCIUTTO

Obviously this would traditionally be made with Chinese ham, but prosciutto is a good, and easily available, substitute, which adds another layer of flavour to this dish.

You can have the choy sum blanched and ready in advance; just give it a quick stir-fry when you're ready to serve.

1 bunch choy sum, trimmed and cut into 4 cm (1½ inch)
   lengths
60 g (2¼ oz) piece of prosciutto, cut into small batons
1 knob of ginger, peeled and finely sliced
3 tablespoons sea salt
2 teaspoons peanut oil

METHOD

Put the ginger, salt and 4 litres (16 cups) cold water in a large pot and bring to the boil. Add the choy sum to the boiling water and blanch for 3 minutes, then refresh in iced water and drain.

Heat a wok until just smoking. Add the peanut oil and, when hot, stir-fry the prosciutto for about 15 seconds, then add the drained choy sum and stir-fry for a further 30 seconds. Spoon into a bowl to serve.

STIR-FRIED MUSHROOMS WITH WHITE ASPARAGUS & CORIANDER

There are quite a few ingredients in this dish, but it's well worth the shopping effort, and the stir-frying happens quite quickly. You can, of course, use green asparagus instead of the white, and beans will also work well. Do try to use a mixture of mushrooms as they add great texture and taste variations.

300 g (10½ oz) mixed mushrooms such as shiitake, oyster, shimeji and enoki
4 white asparagus spears, trimmed and sliced on the diagonal into thirds
1 small handful of coriander (cilantro) leaves
2 tablespoons vegetable oil
2 cloves garlic, finely chopped
1 teaspoon finely chopped ginger
1 tablespoon shaoxing
2 teaspoons sugar
1 tablespoon mushroom soy sauce
a few drops of sesame oil
3 tablespoons fresh chicken stock (page 58)
75 g (2⅔ oz) bean sprouts, trimmed
a pinch of freshly ground white pepper

METHOD

Trim the mushrooms if necessary and tear any large ones in half. Heat a wok until just smoking. Add the vegetable oil and, when hot, stir-fry the asparagus for 1 minute. Add the mushrooms (except the enoki if using), garlic and ginger and stir-fry until fragrant. Deglaze the wok with the shaoxing, then add the sugar, soy sauce, sesame oil and chicken stock and allow the sauce to reduce slightly. Add the enoki, toss together and check for balance. Remove from the heat, fold in the bean sprouts and coriander and sprinkle with white pepper to serve.

STIR-FRIED COS LETTUCE

I adore the crunchy texture of quickly cooked lettuce. I particularly like iceberg lettuce stir-fried with oyster sauce. It's a really amazing dish, but I suspect it's a Neil Perry special, as every time I ask for it at my favourite Chinese restaurant, they look at me as if I have two heads.

1 baby cos (romaine) lettuce, cut into large chunks
    and rinsed
2 tablespoons vegetable oil
5 cloves garlic, smashed
1 tablespoon shaoxing
1 tablespoon light soy sauce
¾ teaspoon sugar
a pinch of sea salt
1 teaspoon sesame oil

METHOD

Heat a wok until just smoking. Add the vegetable oil and, when hot, add the garlic and stir-fry until fragrant. Add the lettuce and stir-fry for 1–2 minutes, or until it becomes limp. Deglaze the wok with the shaoxing, then add the soy sauce, sugar and salt and continue to cook until the lettuce is tender. Remove from the heat and toss with sesame oil to serve.

Banquet Menu Ten

STIR-FRIED RICE WITH SHRIMP PASTE ⚜ PAGE 376

SPICY BARBECUED CHICKEN WINGS ⚜ PAGE 244

SOUR ORANGE CURRY OF SALMON ⚜ PAGE 323

STIR-FRIED BEEF FILLET WITH LEEK & SPANISH ONION ⚜ PAGE 226

RECIPES ARE PICTURED ON FOLLOWING PAGES CLOCKWISE FROM TOP LEFT

Noodles and Rice

I love noodles as much as I love pasta and rice (so if I ever have to go on a no-carbs diet, just shoot me!). I adore fresh noodles, but even a packet of dried noodles in the pantry can be the base of a really great, quick meal.

Just the other day I stir-fried cabbage and carrot, flavoured the oil with ginger and garlic, added the cabbage and carrot back to the wok and splashed in some shaoxing, soy sauce, a pinch of sugar, water, sesame oil and a good hit of chilli oil. I poured the whole lot over egg noodles that I'd blanched for two minutes and presto — a great satisfying quick dinner. What a happy way to spend Sunday night in front of the TV.

You'll probably use these noodles most in your cooking:

Egg noodles. Made from wheat flour and egg, these come in various thicknesses — from thin spaghetti-like noodles, to thicker, flatter tagliatelle-like ones. They're really filling and are best fresh, quickly blanched and then stir-fried or served in soups.

Shanghai noodles. These wonderful thick, creamy-white noodles have a similar texture to dumplings. Perfect for slurping, they're available fresh in Chinatown and are still made by hand.

Glass noodles. Sometimes called cellophane or bean thread noodles, these translucent noodles are made from mung bean starch and water. They should be well soaked before use and should retain a wonderfully crunchy texture.

Fresh rice noodles. Made from rice flour and water, these beautiful pearly-white noodles have a silky texture and are marvellous in stir-fries and soups. They're available in Asian food stores in various widths, and are best used on the day of purchase, although they can be refrigerated for a couple of days.

Dried rice noodles. Also called rice sticks, these are very narrow like rice vermicelli pasta or wider and flatter like tagliatelle. They're rehydrated in hot water and then used in stir-fries and soups. They have a much chewier texture than fresh rice noodles, which makes them work well in some stir-fried dishes.

Hokkien noodles. These round, medium-thick noodles originated in Malaysia, where they're a key ingredient in Hokkien Chinese and Nyonya cooking. Many of the hawker-style dishes are based on these noodles, which are made from wheat flour and have a distinctive golden-yellow colour.

For more information on cooking rice, go to page 38.

WONTONS IN CHILLI OIL

This is a really simple wonton recipe. If you like, these can be prawn alone, pork and prawn, or just straight pork wontons. You could also just place a sea scallop between the wonton sheets to create a sumptuous dumpling. This dressing is a killer and, once you've made it, you'll find yourself using it with lots of other things. Try dressing master-stock chicken with it, or using it as a salad dressing.

square wonton skins or round dumpling skins
flour

PORK WONTON FILLING
200 g (7 oz) minced (ground) pork belly
½ carrot, finely diced
2 coriander (cilantro) roots, scraped and finely chopped
2 braised shiitake mushrooms (page 87), finely chopped
½ knob of ginger, peeled and finely chopped
2 spring onions (scallions), finely sliced
½ teaspoon caster (superfine) sugar
1 teaspoon yellow bean soy sauce
1 teaspoon oyster sauce
a few drops of sesame oil

DRESSING
2 teaspoons kecap manis
1 tablespoon chilli oil
4 cloves garlic, finely chopped
1 spring onion (scallion), finely chopped
1 teaspoon Chinkiang vinegar
a pinch of freshly ground black pepper

METHOD

To make the dressing, mix together the kecap manis, chilli oil, garlic, spring onion, Chinkiang and black pepper.

To make the wonton filling, mix together all of the ingredients in a bowl.

Make a paste by combining a little flour with just enough water to make a medium thick paste. Use 1 teaspoon of wonton filling for each wonton skin. Fold it into a triangle, then fold the bottom up towards the end; finally fold the left side towards the right side and seal with the flour and water paste. Round dumpling skins simply need to be filled, folded in half and sealed with the flour and water paste.

Cook the wontons in rapidly boiling water for 3 minutes. Remove from the water, drain and drizzle with the dressing.

BEEF, CHILLI & TAMARIND NOODLES

A great street food dish, these noodles are quite addictive. Remember to simmer the beef gently so that it doesn't dry out too much.

250 g (9 oz) beef brisket
150 g (5½ oz) fresh hokkien noodles
5 red shallots, roughly chopped
1 clove garlic
½ teaspoon Thai shrimp paste
6 small wild green chillies, roughly chopped
3 teaspoons grated palm sugar (jaggery)
2 tablespoons vegetable oil
3 teaspoons kecap manis
1.25 litres (44 fl oz/5 cups) fresh chicken stock (page 58)
125 ml (4 fl oz/½ cup) tamarind water (page 32)
2 teaspoons sea salt
1 long red chilli, deseeded and cut into julienne
1 spring onion (scallion), cut into julienne

METHOD

Blanch the beef in boiling water for 1 minute, then drain, rinse and cut into 3 cm (1¼ inch) wide pieces. Put the beef into a small pot and cover with fresh water. Bring to the boil and simmer gently for 1½ hours, skimming any impurities from the surface during the first 15 minutes. With a slotted spoon, remove the beef and drain.

Pound the red shallots, garlic, shrimp paste, chillies and palm sugar in a mortar with a pestle until you have a fine paste. Or use a blender to process the ingredients, adding a little water if necessary.

Heat a wok until just smoking. Add the vegetable oil and, when hot, stir-fry the paste until fragrant. Add the beef and kecap manis and stir-fry for 2 minutes, then add the chicken stock, tamarind water and sea salt, and simmer gently for about 1 hour until the beef is tender. Blanch the noodles for 3 minutes in boiling water, then drain.

To serve, transfer the noodles to a large serving bowl or plate. Spoon in the beef and pour on the hot broth, then scatter with chilli and spring onion.

STEWED TOMATO & BEEF NOODLES

This is a very warming and simple stew. I love the flavour of the tomatoes, which loom large — it's not a common taste in Chinese cooking, but it works well here.

300 g (10½ oz) beef brisket, cut into bite-sized pieces
5 tomatoes, roughly chopped
150 g (5½ oz) shanghai noodles
2 tablespoons peanut oil
3 cloves garlic, finely sliced
1 large knob of ginger, peeled and finely sliced
3 spring onions (scallions), cut into 4 cm (1½ inch)
   lengths
250 ml (9 fl oz/1 cup) shaoxing
1 teaspoon sea salt
3 tablespoons light soy sauce
2 litres (8 cups) fresh chicken stock (page 58)

METHOD

Put the beef in a large pot, cover with cold water and bring to the boil. Drain the beef as soon as the water comes to the boil and rinse off any scum.

Heat a wok until just smoking. Add the peanut oil and, when hot, stir-fry the beef in batches until golden in colour. Return all the beef to the wok, add the garlic, ginger and spring onions and stir-fry until fragrant. Add the tomatoes and let them cook down for about 5 minutes, then add the shaoxing and simmer for 2 minutes.

Tip the wok ingredients into a large pot. Add the salt, soy sauce and stock to the pot, and bring to the boil over medium heat, skimming off any impurities. Reduce the heat and gently simmer, uncovered, for 2¼ hours.

Cook the noodles in a large pot of salted boiling water until just tender, then drain. Ladle the beef soup over the noodles to serve.

SESAME NOODLES

This dish couldn't be any simpler. It's great for summer entertaining and is an easy dish to throw into the middle of a shared table. Add a braise, a salad and a stir-fry and you will look very well organised.

300 g (10½ oz) fresh hokkien noodles, blanched and
    refreshed
2 tablespoons finely sliced pickled mustard greens
1 tablespoon Chinese sesame seed paste
1 teaspoon sesame oil
1 teaspoon sea salt
1 spring onion (scallion), finely sliced
1 tablespoon yellow bean soy sauce
1 tablespoon peanuts, roasted and crushed
1 small handful of coriander (cilantro) leaves, chopped
1 Lebanese (short) cucumber, deseeded and cut into
    julienne
½ long red chilli, deseeded and cut into julienne

METHOD

Mix together the mustard greens, sesame paste, sesame oil, sea salt, spring onion, soy sauce, peanuts and 2–3 tablespoons water in a bowl.

Cook the noodles in a large pot of salted boiling water until just tender, then drain and add to the bowl with the dressing. Add the coriander leaves and mix well before piling it all into a serving bowl. Top with cucumber and chilli julienne to serve.

STIR-FRIED SPICY SHANGHAI NOODLES

I'm very fond of the thick luscious shanghai noodles in this dish; they're made with semolina flour in Australia and have a wonderful bite to them. You could add pork or chicken, leave the seafood, remove it, or change the type of noodle if you wish.

250 g (9 oz) fresh shanghai noodles, blanched and
    refreshed in iced water
2 tablespoons vegetable oil
6 cloves garlic, finely chopped
2 long red chillies, finely sliced
6 baby corn, halved lengthways
1 small carrot, finely sliced on the diagonal
25 g (1 oz/½ cup) finely sliced Chinese cabbage
40 g (1½ oz/¼ cup) green peas
4 green king prawns (shrimp), peeled and deveined with
    tails left intact
8 small clams, steamed open
1 small handful of Thai basil leaves, fried until crisp and
    well drained

SAUCE
2 tablespoons oyster sauce
1 tablespoon kecap manis
1 tablespoon light soy sauce
2 tablespoons roasted chilli paste
2 tablespoons sugar

METHOD

To make the sauce, mix together the oyster sauce, kecap manis, soy sauce, chilli paste and sugar.

Heat a wok until just smoking. Add half the vegetable oil and, when hot, stir-fry the prawns until coloured on both sides, then remove.

Heat the remaining oil in the wok and stir-fry the garlic and chillies until fragrant. Add the corn, carrot, cabbage and peas, and stir-fry for 1 minute, then add the noodles, prawns, clams and sauce and toss to heat through. Pile onto a large plate and top with fried basil leaves to serve.

STIR-FRIED HOKKIEN NOODLES

The pork mince adds a nice texture to this simple, street-food inspired dish.
Any sort of noodles would work well here.

350 g (12 oz) fresh hokkien noodles, blanched and
   refreshed
50 g (1¾ oz) Chinese cabbage, coarsely chopped
3 tablespoons vegetable oil
90 g (3¼ oz) minced (ground) pork
1 teaspoon sugar
1 tablespoon dark soy sauce
2 tablespoons light soy sauce
½ teaspoon sesame oil
a pinch of Sichuan pepper

METHOD

In boiling salted water, blanch the cabbage for 30 seconds, then refresh
in iced water.

Heat a wok until just smoking. Add the oil and, when hot, add the pork
mince and cook, stirring, until the meat is coloured. Add the cabbage and cook
for a further minute, then add the sugar, soy sauces and sesame oil and cook
until combined. Add the noodles and toss to heat through. Transfer to a serving
plate and sprinkle with the Sichuan pepper.

SPICY PRAWN & TOFU NOODLES

There are a few ingredients in this simple dish, reminiscent of the street-side noodle dishes you can get in Malaysia or southern Thailand.

6 large cooked king prawns (shrimp), peeled
1 block firm tofu, cut into 6 pieces and deep-fried
    until golden brown
300 g (10½ oz) rice vermicelli, soaked in boiling water for
    1 minute and drained
750 ml (26 fl oz/3 cups) coconut milk
125 ml (4 fl oz/½ cup) tamarind water (page 32)
100 g (3½ oz) bean sprouts
125 g (4½ oz) garlic chives, cut into 3 cm (1¼ inch)
    lengths
2 hard-boiled eggs, peeled and quartered
2 limes, quartered

SPICE PASTE

10 dried red chillies, soaked in warm water for 30 minutes
12 red shallots, finely chopped
1 lemongrass stalk, tough outer leaves removed, finely
    chopped
1 teaspoon Thai shrimp paste, wrapped in foil and
    roasted until fragrant
3 tablespoons peanut oil
2 heaped tablespoons salted soy beans, lightly crushed
1 teaspoon salt
1 tablespoon sugar

METHOD

To make the spice paste, pound the chillies, shallots, lemongrass and shrimp paste in a mortar with a pestle until fine. Heat the oil in a heavy-based pot and gently stir-fry the paste for 3–4 minutes. Add the soy beans and cook for 1 minute, stirring all the time. Sprinkle in the salt and sugar and stir-fry for another minute. Remove and reserve half of the paste, and leave the rest in the pot.

To make the sauce, put the reserved spice paste into a clean pot with the coconut milk. Bring to the boil, stirring all the time, then add the tamarind water. Continue to stir and simmer for 2–3 minutes.

Reheat the spice paste, add the bean sprouts and cook over high heat for 1 minute. Add the prawns and chives and cook for 30 seconds, stirring in the vermicelli a little at a time. When heated through, put into a serving dish with the eggs and tofu on top, then pour over the sauce and squeeze the limes on top.

STIR-FRIED RICE NOODLES WITH CHICKEN

I love the sweet, sour and hot nature of these noodles. I use chicken thighs as I find breasts dry out too much. You can use fresh noodles and king prawns or sea scallops. Or, I like to simmer pork belly for about 1½ hours, then cut it into thin strips and stir-fry that instead of the chicken thighs.

250 g (9 oz) dried flat rice noodles, soaked in boiling
    water until tender
200 g (7 oz) free-range or organic chicken thigh fillets,
    finely sliced across the grain
5 dried long red chillies, deseeded, soaked in warm water
    for 30 minutes and chopped
4 red shallots, chopped
8 cloves garlic, chopped
a pinch of sea salt
4 tablespoons vegetable oil
45 g (1⅔ oz/¼ cup) grated palm sugar (jaggery)
3 tablespoons fish sauce
3 tablespoons tamarind water (page 32)
45 g (1⅔ oz/½ cup) bean sprouts, trimmed
50 g (1¾ oz/½ bunch) garlic chives, trimmed, chopped
    into 5 cm (2 inch) lengths
2 limes, cut into wedges

METHOD

Pound the chillies, shallots, garlic and sea salt in a mortar with a pestle until you have a fine paste. Or use a blender to process the ingredients, adding a little water if necessary.

Heat a wok until just smoking. Add the oil and, when hot, stir-fry the chicken in batches until golden, then remove. Add the paste to the wok and stir-fry until fragrant, then add the palm sugar, fish sauce and tamarind water. Add the noodles and chicken and toss to heat through, then mix in half the bean sprouts and the chives. Spoon onto a serving plate and serve with the remaining bean sprouts and wedges of lime on the side.

SPICY SICHUAN NOODLES

This is without a doubt one of my favourite noodle dishes — Chinese Spaghetti Bolognaise! It's great to sit down with a cold beer and dig into a big bowl of these noodles; you really don't bother talking until it's all gone. The fresh shanghai noodles have a wonderful silkiness and the minced pork looks like a good bolognaise sauce. The cucumbers give it a really great crunch and coolness, and the Sichuan pepper brings that wonderful hot numbing sensation. All up, it's a cracking dish.

300 g (10½ oz) minced (ground) pork
350 g (12 oz) fresh shanghai noodles
100 ml (3½ fl oz) dark soy sauce
2 teaspoons salt
125 ml (4 fl oz/½ cup) peanut oil
2 cloves garlic, finely chopped
1 tablespoon chopped ginger
2 spring onions (scallions), minced
3 tablespoons Chinese sesame seed paste
2 tablespoons chilli oil
2 tablespoons light soy sauce
500 ml (17 fl oz/2 cups) fresh chicken stock (page 58)
½ teaspoon Sichuan pepper
1 small Lebanese (short) cucumber, peeled, deseeded
    and cut into julienne

METHOD

Marinate the pork in the dark soy sauce and 1 teaspoon of the salt for 10 minutes. Heat a wok until smoking. Add the peanut oil and, when hot, add the pork mix and stir continuously until browned, about 3 minutes. Remove with a slotted spoon and drain on paper towel.

Reheat the wok and stir-fry the garlic, ginger and spring onions until fragrant. Add the sesame paste, chilli oil, soy sauce, remaining salt and chicken stock and simmer for 5 minutes, then return the pork to the wok. Cook the noodles in a large pot of boiling water for 2 minutes and drain well.

Put the hot noodles in a large bowl, ladle the sauce over the top and sprinkle with the Sichuan pepper. Top with the cucumber to serve.

CHICKEN & PRESERVED DUCK EGG CONGEE

Congee is total comfort food and makes a really good lunch. My children started eating plain congee when they were very young. You basically simmer the soaked rice until it makes a starchy soup, season it and then add anything you like: barbecued pork, duck, blanched vegetables, salted duck eggs, boiled hen's eggs, seafood or whatever else will add great flavour and texture. Plus, I love to stir in a big dollop of chilli. You should really try this. Most Westerners steer clear, but once you have had a good congee or 'jook' for breakfast or lunch, you will never look back; it's especially good for hangovers!

100 g (3½ oz/½ cup) long-grain rice
2 teaspoons salt
½ teaspoon vegetable oil
1.25 litres (44 fl oz/5 cups) fresh chicken stock (page 58)
55 g (2 oz/¼ cup) Sichuan preserved vegetables
200 g (7 oz) white-cut chicken (page 84), sliced
2 preserved duck eggs, peeled and quartered
1 small handful of coriander (cilantro) leaves
3 spring onions (scallions), sliced

METHOD

Wash the rice in several changes of cold water. Put the rice, 750 ml (26 fl oz/ 3 cups) cold water, salt and vegetable oil in a pot and soak overnight at room temperature. The next day, add the chicken stock and bring to the boil over high heat. Reduce the heat to a low simmer, cover and cook for 2 hours, stirring from time to time, until the congee is almost smooth and very creamy.

Wash the preserved vegetables in cold water to remove the coating, and chop finely. Add the vegetables, chicken and duck eggs to the congee, stir and cook for 3 minutes until heated through.

Pour into a large bowl and top with the coriander and spring onions.

CHINESE SAUSAGE STEAMED IN RICE

I love the earthiness that the mushrooms, sausage and shrimp lend to this simple and satisfying dish.

2 Chinese sausages, sliced into rounds
400 g (14 oz/2 cups) cooked rice (page 38)
4 tablespoons vegetable oil
1 knob of ginger, peeled and finely chopped
10 cloves garlic, finely chopped
2 tablespoons dried shrimp, soaked in warm water for
    20 minutes
3 dried shiitake mushrooms, soaked in warm water for
    30 minutes, stalks removed, finely sliced
40 g (1½ oz/¼ cup) peanuts, roasted
2 tablespoons oyster sauce
2 tablespoons light soy sauce
750 ml (26 fl oz/3 cups) fresh chicken stock (page 58)

METHOD

Heat a wok until just smoking. Add the oil and, when hot, stir-fry the ginger and garlic until fragrant. Add the sausage and stir-fry for another minute, then add the shrimp, mushrooms and peanuts and toss together. Add the rice and oyster and soy sauces, and work the mixture together thoroughly with a spoon, then transfer to a clay pot.

Add the stock to the rice and stir. Cover the pot and cook over low heat for 25 minutes. Turn off the heat and let the dish stand for a further 10 minutes, or until the rice is tender.

STIR-FRIED RICE WITH SHRIMP PASTE

This Thai-inspired rice dish is a wonderful meal with left-over rice. The shrimp paste gives it a beautiful sweet fragrance that makes it irresistible.

555 g (1 lb 4 oz/3 cups) cooked rice (page 38)
1 teaspoon Thai shrimp paste
2 tablespoons vegetable oil
4 cloves garlic, finely chopped
1 tablespoon grated palm sugar (jaggery)
1 tablespoon fish sauce
3 spring onions (scallions), finely sliced
2 eggs, lightly beaten
3 tablespoons dried shrimp, deep-fried until golden
1 large handful of coriander (cilantro) leaves, roughly
    chopped
1 long red chilli, finely sliced
2 Lebanese (short) cucumbers, finely sliced
2 limes, cut into wedges

SWEET PORK
250 g (9 oz) pork neck, finely sliced
2 tablespoons vegetable oil
4 cloves garlic, finely chopped
2 tablespoons grated palm sugar (jaggery)
1 tablespoon fish sauce
2 tablespoons dark soy sauce

METHOD

For the sweet pork, heat a wok until smoking, add the oil and, when hot, stir-fry the pork until golden brown. Add the garlic and stir-fry until fragrant, then add the palm sugar and cook for about a minute to allow it to caramelise. Add the fish sauce, soy sauce and 3 tablespoons water, and simmer until the liquid has reduced to a dark, sticky glaze, then remove. Clean and dry the wok.

For the rice, heat a wok until smoking. Add half the oil and, when hot, stir-fry the garlic until fragrant. Mix in the shrimp paste, sugar and fish sauce and reduce the heat. Add the rice and stir-fry until hot, then add the spring onions, mix thoroughly, and remove from the wok.

Heat the remaining oil in the wok, swirl it around and then pour in the egg, spreading it into a thin layer. When set, remove from the wok, roll the egg up and finely slice. Spoon the rice onto plates, top with the egg, sweet pork and fried shrimp, then sprinkle on the coriander and chilli and serve with cucumber slices and wedges of lime.

Banquet Menu Eleven

LOBSTER WITH XO SAUCE ⚜ page 138

STIR-FRIED ZUCCHINI ⚜ page 127

CHICKEN WITH SNOW PEAS & SICHUAN PEPPER ⚜ page 261

SWEET & SOUR PORK ⚜ page 132

ABALONE, CHICKEN, HAM & MUSHROOM SOUP ⚜ page 287

RECIPES ARE PICTURED ON FOLLOWING PAGES CLOCKWISE FROM TOP LEFT

FRUIT AND SWEET THINGS

I think the perfect end to a beautiful shared Asian meal is as simple as fresh fruit.

You can slice fruit and make a platter if you wish, but I think the nicest way to serve it is to place a bowl of fruit in the middle of the table, give your guests a plate and a small sharp knife and invite them to help themselves. If a brilliant fruit is available, depending on the season, it's quite nice to offer just one type — a bowl of cherries, lychees, mango or peaches would be nice. Smaller fruits are particularly nice served on ice.

As a matter of fact, one of the most generous acts I've seen came from a friend of mine, Melina Young. She is a fantastic hostess and brilliant cook. I was lucky enough to be invited to her house and, not only was the wine beautiful (her husband NK is one of Singapore's foremost wine collectors), but Melina's laksa and chilli crab are to die for. However, in addition to all that great food, wine and company, the thing I really remember about that day was that she stood and offered to peel mangosteens for each of her guests. She would cut around their equator and remove the skin, giving each guest the chance to suck out these wonderfully exotic fruits. She peeled half a dozen for each of us and then tended to her own needs. Now, if that isn't hospitality, I'm not sure what is. So, thank you Melina.

Buy beautifully ripe fruit in season if you want to do something as wonderful as Melina did; it's perfect to eat on the day and you can finish your meal in style.

Dessert in Asia doesn't play the same role as it would in a Western meal. Most Asian sweet things would usually be eaten as snacks between meals, so in this selection, I've just given you a few simple classic desserts.

PINEAPPLE, LIME & GINGER GRANITA

Granitas are so easy and simple. Just about any fruit juice can be seasoned with sugar and frozen in a tray, then raked with a fork to create a refreshing ice dessert.

The other thing about granitas is that they go well with sliced raw or poached fruit. Serve them in a nice glass for a stunning presentation.

1 large pineapple, juiced (about 400 ml/14 fl oz)
1 lime, juiced
1 small knob of ginger, peeled and juiced
2–3 tablespoons caster (superfine) sugar

METHOD

Whisk together the pineapple, lime and ginger juice with the sugar until the sugar has completely dissolved. Pour the mixture into a shallow metal tray and freeze until firm. Remove the tray from the freezer and break up the ice with a fork to form the granita. Serve immediately, or freeze until ready to serve.

WHITE STICKY RICE

This, like the black sticky rice that follows, is a classic. I love the sticky texture and earthy taste of the rice with the sweetness of mangoes. You really can't fail with this one, but don't make the portion too big as it's very filling.

500 g (1 lb 2 oz) white sticky rice
750 ml (26 fl oz/3 cups) coconut cream, plus extra,
    to serve
350 g (12 oz) caster (superfine) sugar
a pinch of sea salt
1 pandanus leaf, tied in a knot
fresh mango or other tropical fruit, to serve

METHOD

Soak the rice in a bowl of cold water for several hours or overnight. Drain and rinse well. Spread it into a muslin-lined steamer, cover with the lid and steam over a pot or a wok of boiling water for about 20 minutes, or until tender.

Meanwhile, whisk together the coconut cream, sugar and sea salt until the sugar has completely dissolved, then add the pandanus leaf. Add the steamed rice and stir, then cover the bowl and set aside in a warm place for several hours, or until the rice absorbs most of the cream.

Spoon the rice into bowls, top with fresh mango slices and drizzle with extra coconut cream to serve.

BLACK STICKY RICE WITH COCONUT CREAM

This has such a rich taste and great, chewy texture. You'll become addicted to this, I promise.

500 g (1 lb 2 oz) black sticky rice
1 pandanus leaf, tied in a knot
180 g (6½ oz/1 cup) crushed dark Indonesian palm
    sugar (jaggery)
500 ml (17 fl oz/2 cups) coconut milk
fresh banana and mango slices, to serve

METHOD

Rinse the rice under cold running water and place in a pot with the pandanus leaf and 1 litre (35 fl oz/4 cups) water. Bring to the boil, then reduce the heat and simmer gently for about 10 minutes, or until all the water has been absorbed. Remove from the heat and cover the pot with foil or a lid. Set aside and allow the rice to steam through until it's tender. Remove the pandanus leaf.

Meanwhile, put the palm sugar in a small pot with 375 ml (13 fl oz/ 1½ cups) water and stir over low heat until the sugar has dissolved. Bring to the boil, and then remove from the heat.

Return the pot of rice to low heat. Gradually stir through 435 ml (15¼ fl oz/1¾ cups) of the coconut milk and most of the palm sugar syrup, stirring until heated through.

Divide the sticky rice between serving bowls and top with fresh fruit. Drizzle with the remaining coconut milk and syrup to serve.

TOASTED COCONUT ICE CREAM

This ice cream has a delicious coconut flavour. Although some recipes use coconut milk as the base, I prefer not to make mine like this.

100 g (3½ oz) shredded coconut
600 ml (21 fl oz) milk
10 egg yolks
200 g (7 oz) caster (superfine) sugar
300 ml (10½ fl oz) cream

METHOD

Preheat the oven to 150°C (300°F/Gas 2). Spread the coconut evenly over a baking tray, then place in the oven to toast. Shake the tray occasionally, until the coconut is an even golden brown colour, about 5–10 minutes.

Heat the milk until hot, add the toasted coconut and set aside to infuse for 2–3 hours. Strain the milk through a fine sieve, pressing out as much liquid from the coconut as possible, then discard the coconut.

Whisk the egg yolks and sugar with an electric mixer until thick and pale. Reheat the milk until hot, and gently pour it into the egg mixture, whisking the whole time. Pour the milk and egg mixture into a saucepan and stir constantly over low heat until the mixture thickens enough to coat the back of a spoon — do not allow the mixture to boil, as it will curdle. Strain the mixture through a fine sieve and cool over an ice bath.

Once cool, add the cream and churn in an ice-cream machine according to the manufacturer's instructions. Transfer to a tub and store in the freezer.

NOTE   This recipe makes about a litre of coconut ice cream.

COCONUT SAGO WITH DARK PALM SUGAR SYRUP

Again, this one is all about the texture. The sago carries the flavour of the sugar and coconut cream beautifully.

375 g (13 oz) sago, rinsed well
200 ml (7 fl oz) coconut cream
a pinch of sea salt
200 g (7 oz) crushed dark Indonesian palm
    sugar (jaggery)

METHOD

Bring a large pot of water to the boil. Add the sago and cook, whisking frequently, for 12–15 minutes, or until the granules are completely transparent. Drain and then rinse under cold running water to remove any excess starch. Combine the sago with 3 tablespoons of the coconut cream and a pinch of salt.

Put the palm sugar in a small pot with 125 ml (4 fl oz/½ cup) water. Stir over low heat until the sugar has completely dissolved, then increase the heat and simmer for about 1 minute.

Spoon the sago into bowls, drizzle with syrup and spoon over a little of the remaining coconut cream to serve.

NOTE If the syrup is left to stand, it may solidify. If so, simply place over low heat until it melts again.

INDEX

ACKNOWLEDGMENTS

Once again I have lots of people to thank for being able to put my name on such a beautiful book.

First off, to China and South-East Asia — thank you for the generations of wonderful food that have made my life richer and more delicious.

To all the cooks who have worked with me and all the cooks around the world who have inspired me, I owe a great debt. You have all helped open my eyes to the wonderful world of cooking.

Specifically, to my wonderful chefs — Khan Danis, Catherine Adams, Michael McEnearney, Paul Eason, Dave Young, Angel Fernandez, Andy Evans and Ben Pollard; you make all my restaurants great places to eat in.

Thanks to my business partner, Trish Richards, and new partner, Dave Doyle, for investing in my dreams.

A huge thanks to Sarah Swan for being so organised and making these book projects fun rather than torture... well, a bit of torture maybe. And to Jess Sly for her wonderful help with recipe testing.

Major thanks, of course, to all the crew at Murdoch Books. You are such a team of perfectionists, always ready to respond to my ever-changing books as they start as one thing and end up another. Thank you Kay Scarlett — you're the best publisher ever. And to Sarah Odgers and Jo Byrne — it's an awesome design. Of course, thanks to Jane Price and Elizabeth Anglin — great editing... it almost sounds as if I can communicate in English. And thanks to Vivien, too. You Murdoch girls are something else.

Of course, an enormous thanks to Sue Fairlie-Cuninghame and Earl Carter. Without you two there wouldn't be the Three Musketeers and this book wouldn't feel, look and taste half as good as it does.

Thanks to my three wonderful daughters — Josephine, Macy and Indy. They shower me with devoted love that makes my life richer, and will hopefully look after me when I'm old.

The biggest thanks of all goes to my amazing wife, Sam, who keeps our life together. I'm sure she would love to see me more, but then again, she knew what she was getting herself in to. Thanks for all the love and patience, my darling.

Published in 2008 by Murdoch Books Pty Limited

Murdoch Books Australia
Pier 8/9
23 Hickson Road
Millers Point NSW 2000
Phone: +61 (0) 2 8220 2000
Fax: +61 (0) 2 8220 2558
www.murdochbooks.com.au

Murdoch Books UK Limited
Erico House
6th Floor North
93–99 Upper Richmond Road
Putney, London SW15 2TG
Phone: +44 (0) 20 8785 5995
Fax: +44 (0) 20 8785 5985
www.murdochbooks.co.uk

Chief Executive: Juliet Rogers
Publishing Director: Kay Scarlett

Project manager: Jane Price
Editor: Elizabeth Anglin
Design concept: Sarah Odgers
Cover concept: Joanna Byrne
Designer: Joanna Byrne
Photographer: Earl Carter
Stylist and art director: Sue Fairlie-Cuninghame
Production: Tiffany Johnson and Nikla Martin
Assistants to Neil Perry and food preparation: Sarah Swan, Jessica Sly
Text copyright © Neil Perry 2008, Photography copyright © Earl Carter 2008
Design copyright © Murdoch Books Pty Limited 2008

National Library of Australia Cataloguing-in-Publication entry
Perry, Neil, 1957-
Title: Balance and harmony : Asian food / Neil Perry.
ISBN: 978 1 74045 908 2 (hbk.)
Notes: Includes index.
Subjects: Cookery, Asian.
Dewey Number: 641.595

Colour reproduction by Colour Chiefs, Brisbane, Australia.
Printed by Imago in 2008. PRINTED IN CHINA.
The Publisher and Neil Perry would like to thank the following for the use of their merchandise in the photography of this book: David Prior for merchandising assistance; All Hand Made, 252–4 Bronte Road, Waverley, NSW, Australia; Anthony Puharich, Vic's Meat, 10 Merchant Street, Mascot, NSW, Australia; Planet on Crown, 419 Crown Street, Surry Hills, NSW, Australia; Porter's Paints, 895 Bourke Street, Waterloo NSW, Australia.

IMPORTANT: Those who might be at risk from the effects of salmonella poisoning (the elderly, pregnant women, young children and those suffering from immune deficiency diseases) should consult their doctor with any concerns about eating raw eggs.